IMAGES
of America

Oklahoma City's African American Education

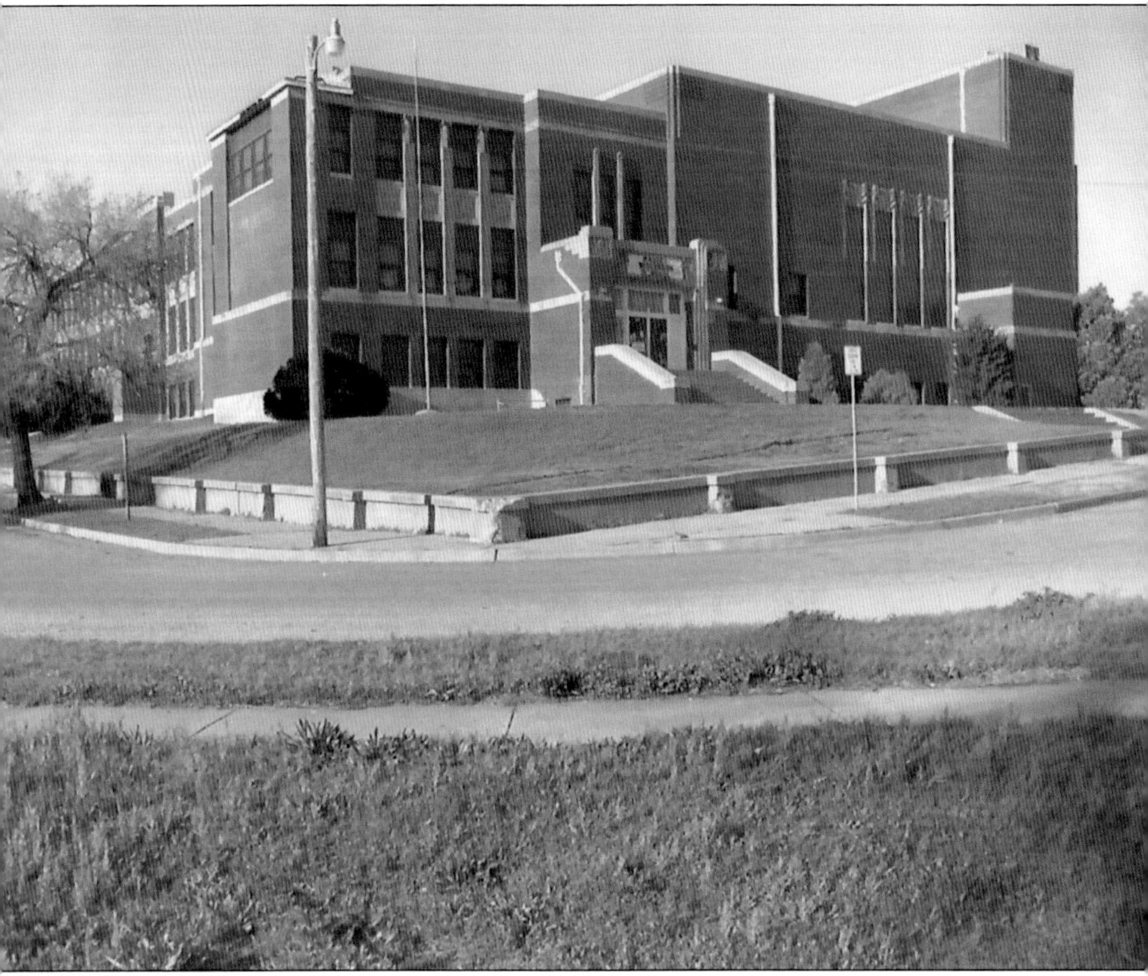

This 1936 photograph shows Frederick A. Douglass Junior/Senior High School located at 600 North High Street in Oklahoma City. This school building was the center of creativity in Oklahoma City from 1934 until 1955. The auditorium featured operettas, stage shows, band concerts, graduations, and concerts by national artists. (Courtesy of Robert C. Watson.)

On the Cover: This 1952 photograph shows the Douglass Junior High School Band on the south portal of Frederick A. Douglass High School. Douglass was known for its many award-winning bands. This band was under the direction of W.E. Perry. (Courtesy of Marvelle Newsome Holmes.)

IMAGES
of America

OKLAHOMA CITY'S AFRICAN AMERICAN EDUCATION

Anita G. Arnold
Foreword by James R. Johnson

ARCADIA
PUBLISHING

ISBN 978-1-4671-2740-0

Published by Arcadia Publishing
Charleston, South Carolina

Printed in the United States of America

Library of Congress Control Number: 2017938445

For all general information, please contact Arcadia Publishing:
Telephone 843-853-2070
Fax 843-853-0044
E-mail sales@arcadiapublishing.com
For customer service and orders:
Toll-Free 1-888-313-2665

Visit us on the Internet at www.arcadiapublishing.com

This book is dedicated to Frederick A. Douglass High School Trojans, students and teachers, who have gone on before us. Remember, Hope is Alive!

Contents

Foreword

Organized school education in Oklahoma City began a scant three decades after the end of slavery. The year 1891 was the start of the "colored" school that became Frederick A. Douglass High School. There is no better way to chronicle the first 100 years of this august institution than with a person who was born in the very middle of this century of education. That story is to be found in the pages that follow.

Anita Arnold is an accomplished author of several books in addition to her distinguished career as a telecommunications industry executive. More recently, she has shaped the vision and programmatic offerings of Black Liberated Arts Center Inc. She has spent countless hours in both discussions and research in compiling this book.

If you are interested to know about the oldest high school in Oklahoma and what made it become the "Pride of the Eastside" in Oklahoma City, you will want to read this volume. What is found is not only capability and aptitude demanded of the students in "the three R's" of reading, writing, and arithmetic, but also the discipline required in the fine arts and vocational education.

From a one-room classroom that had previously been a horse stable, Douglass has grown to a grand complex covering 30 square blocks of city acreage. Douglass High School has prospered with the ebb and flow of Oklahoma City's growth, development, decline, and now renaissance.

Anita Arnold treats a continuing thread about how more was done with less. How teaching in this system was a high call to order, and it attracted the best in class to train future generations. The expectations were great for the students, and the models of success were present in their eyes. In the beginning, while limited opportunities existed for some, it did not preclude breaking down barriers for many.

From a West Point cadet to a man who had previously served as a president of two universities to the longest-serving principal in history, you will be reminded of the caliber and quality of leadership found in this 126-year-old school.

—James Johnson

ACKNOWLEDGMENTS

Oklahoma City's African American Education would have been impossible without the encouragement of many members of the National Oklahoma City Frederick A. Douglass Alumni Association. In the beginning, Deola Harris and Lucy Livingston provided wonderful pictures from their Douglass High School memoirs. Marvella Newsome Holmes and her husband, Carl Holmes, provided insights into the monumental body of work that Carl did to institutionalize executive training for firefighters all over the United States, Africa, and beyond.

James Johnson contributed invaluable research in finding rare facts and photographs of Trojans who deserved to be recognized for their outstanding efforts at making a real difference in the lives of others. He came through at crucial times when it seemed all hope was gone in telling a remarkable story of brilliant contributors who would surely be forgotten without this book. With a dogged determination coupled with excellent skills, Johnson brought forth those unknown life-changing contributions of giants no longer with us. Thanks, James.

Eula Pitts almost made me cry when she recalled her too-few moments with husband, Riley Leroy Pitts, who made the ultimate sacrifice for our country. Even though landmarks are named in his honor in the United States, Germany, and other places in the world and though it happened so long ago, it was a painful recollection for her. He was her young Trojan. Thank you, Eula.

Brenda Johnson and Leonardo DeBose provided "missing" photographs that were essential to the truth of these many stories. Actually, Brenda's father, Walter Seward, took tens of thousands of photographs recording the history for decades. My gratitude is extended to Bill Welge, of the Oklahoma History Center, who helped immeasurably in getting photographs of important education leaders from the "glory days."

Thanks to those who gave their time and efforts doing the work of editing, listening, and following through without question. They include Dr. Rosemary K. Harkins, Charles "Ceedy" Morgan, Dr. Donna Cox, Dr. Melvin Todd, and John Temple, who overcame his "private" persona and shared historical photographs. Many thanks to Suzanne Walker for computer expertise in a crisis.

Praise God for an understanding, supportive family who brought comfort and peace throughout this process. I am thankful to Liz Gurley and Arcadia Publishing for bearing with me through traumatic times with the sudden death of my beloved sister, Donna Davis Edwards, and even through my busiest and most stressful times. Thank you!

INTRODUCTION

The purpose of this book is to recapture and reflect on the golden era of African American education in Oklahoma City, which inspired generations throughout the city, state, and nation. The hope is that this generation and future generations are encouraged and inspired to begin, again, to meet the challenges of new heights of knowledge and understanding that opens doors of wisdom that launch dreams and visions of possibilities yet unspoken.

There is no better way to introduce a great history than by providing context that puts people and places at significant points in time. Highlights of African American education experiences in Oklahoma City are captured by starting with the oldest high school in the city and state, then moving through the establishment of other schools in Oklahoma City and nearby communities.

Education for African Americans in Oklahoma City began in a two-room unnamed schoolhouse simply called the Colored School. It was January 5, 1891, when the Oklahoma City School Board met to establish the public schools of Oklahoma City, which included the Colored School. In February, the school opened with Jefferson Davis Randolph as principal.

It was 1898 when Principal J.W. Sharpe asked the students to name their school. They selected the name Frederick Douglass. The first graduates received their diplomas on May 26, 1903. There were six graduates, five young women and one young man. Prof. George F. Porter was the principal of the school. During those early days, the school moved twice. Growth of the student body caused the first move, but the second move was the result of a fire that consumed the building. James Henry A. Brazelton was principal at the time. The school relocated to 221 East California Street, currently the location of the Chickasaw Bricktown Ballpark. Brazelton served 12 years.

The school began to stabilize around 1918 when Zelia N. Page Breaux, daughter of Langston University president Inman E. Page, was added to the staff in music. Breaux would become a legend, and Douglass High School would be widely known for its music and fine arts programs. Music was one of the foundational cornerstones put in place that produced legends, icons, and more.

On September 1, 1921, Inman E. Page was elected principal of Douglass High School. Under his leadership, two years later, daughter Zelia established the first Douglass High School Band with 24 members. Page served 14 years, but his daughter remained until her retirement in 1948.

In 1925, Emma Lee Jones Freeman won the annual queen contest and was featured in the first annual, *The Tellus*, published by Douglass High School students. The physical education teacher filed a civil rights suit challenging unequal pay against the board of education and won.

On November, 20, 1934, the first Douglass Alumni Association was organized. Also, Clifford Williams wrote the lyrics to the Trojan song, and Zelia Breaux added the music in 1939. In September 1937, Nellie Douglas, trumpet; Dorothy Jean Swop, saxophone; and twirlers Ratha Mae Duckett and Mildred Bunn broke a 14-year male tradition to become the first females in the Douglass band. In 1938, Douglass High School was accepted and accredited by the North Central Association.

By September 1927, the Douglass High School Band was featured at the opening of the Oklahoma State Fair. Breaux developed outstanding musicians who became famous locally and nationally. Among them were Charlie Christian, Ralph Ellison, and Jimmy Rushing. Rushing and Christian became legendary in music, but Ellison moved from music to literature to become one of the most well-known writers of the 20th century with his book *The Invisible Man*. Ellison remembered his hometown of Oklahoma City in his book *Shadow and Act*.

Breaux took her Douglass High School Band to the world's fair in Chicago in 1935, drawing national attention to the music and her drum majors, W.A. McCauley and Alonzo D. Williams, while collecting awards. Bandleader Duke Ellington was there and was fascinated and impressed with the music. Breaux and Ellington remained friends until her death. Ellington attended her services in Oklahoma City.

From the mid-1920s, there were informal partnerships between white community organizations and Frederick A. Douglass Junior/Senior High School. Among the first were the YMCA, YWCA, and Girl Scouts. Others such as the Kiwanis Club and the Oklahoma City Symphony added to the partnerships, though Douglass was a separate segregated school. It would be nearly 20 years before the next colored high school, Dunjee, was established in 1940, the same year F.D. Moon became principal of Douglass High School. Moon is credited with many advances in education for African Americans. He envisioned a school that would prepare every student to earn a good living after graduation. Moon started the work on his model in Crescent, Oklahoma, many years before arriving at Douglass. He was ready for the task. His model worked very well, and his reputation preceded his leadership in Oklahoma City.

Dunjee High School was the next colored school, established in 1940. Previously the two-room building was named Dunbar School and was located on Northeast Thirty-Sixth Street. Dunbar teachers taught grades one through eight. Later, the school moved across the street and was named after civil rights icon Roscoe Dunjee. The school expanded to a high school with its first graduation ceremony in 1941. Maycola Jones was the only graduate. The school employed 10 teachers and patterned itself after F.D. Moon's model of education. Other elementary schools established on the eastside in the 1940s included Dunbar, Edison, Orchard Park, Carver, Wheatley, Choctaw, Inman Page, and Edwards.

From 1945 until 1970, Douglass was a force to be reckoned with. The school grew in stature in almost any kind of city, state, and national competition. The school's reputation spread far and wide, beginning with the principal. F.D. Moon was described by many as being a brilliant strategist who knew how to work the politics for the good of the community. He wasted no time in establishing himself with the community and the Oklahoma City School Board. Five years after he assumed the leadership of the school, he was faced with a growing student population that was bursting at the seams at Northeast Sixth and High Streets. Moon added several temporary buildings to house many of the subjects that were being added to the curriculum. But that was not enough. Success was contagious at the new school. Students wanted to go to school. Parents and other members of the community were engaged. Churches worked with the school. In short, Douglass was the center of a developing community.

In 1945, Moon rallied the community and other communities to successfully get two bond issues passed to fund a new Douglass High School, to be located at 900 North Eastern Avenue, which would accommodate student growth for many years. The work had just begun. The project required close coordination with many city leaders because the 30-acre plot was occupied by the Oklahoma State Fair. It took time. At his retirement in 1961, Moon had accomplished his dream and was now Dr. Moon. He was not satisfied being the longest-serving principal at Douglass. Dr. Moon ran, successfully, to become the first African American to serve on the Oklahoma City Public Schools board. He resigned as president of the school board some years later due to failing health. He was known as "the Dean of Negro Education."

While Dr. Moon worked to get the school built with the best equipment, facilities, and more, the teachers were creating new partnerships and entering their students in competitions. Douglass was reigning in sports. The basketball and football teams were winning titles, both in and out of state. The coaching team was strengthened with the addition of Moses "PiYi" Miller and Jake Diggs. Douglass teams also competed in track, baseball, wrestling, and swimming. Monroe Huel won the Mr. Oklahoma trophy in the lifting competition. Lawrence Cudjo was named basketball coach.

Jessie Mae Thomas won the City-Wide Science Fair competition and participated in the National Science Fair in Oak Ridge, Tennessee. Henry Curtis, Walter Dillard, Frank Wilson, George Counts, and Jack McDonald attended the first interracial Hi-Y and Tri Hi-Y officers training camp at Camp Parthenia in 1951. That year, Earl Scarborough won the I Speak for Democracy contest sponsored by the Oklahoma City Chamber of Commerce, and Ronald Lee was the first African American student to give an address in the Oklahoma State Senate chambers.

Teacher Consuelo V. Tompkins and Cenoria M. McGown Johnson, with the Urban League, sponsored the first statewide speech tournament at Douglass Junior/Senior High School. In 1961, Dr. F.D. Moon received recognition as one of 13 excellent principals in America in the first National Principal of the Year Award, established by Ben Brodinsky, editor-in-chief of Croft Publications. Brodinsky was well known in education circles, serving Presidents Herbert Hover and Franklin D. Roosevelt as secretary of education. Gallup Polls, at the request of Brodinsky, performed the national survey. Ben Brodinsky came from New York to present the citation of recognition to Moon for being one of the nation's top principals. He was the only black principal among the finalists and the only principal from Oklahoma among the finalists.

Frederick A. Douglass High School continued to excel throughout the 1950s until the late 1970s. The Moon Model drew people and many celebrities from across the United States to see the school, speak, perform at the school, copy the model, or support the school. This celebrated education model taught life lessons for all. Why? Because everyone was fully engaged and supported the idea of a great education for all.

One

Starting from Scratch

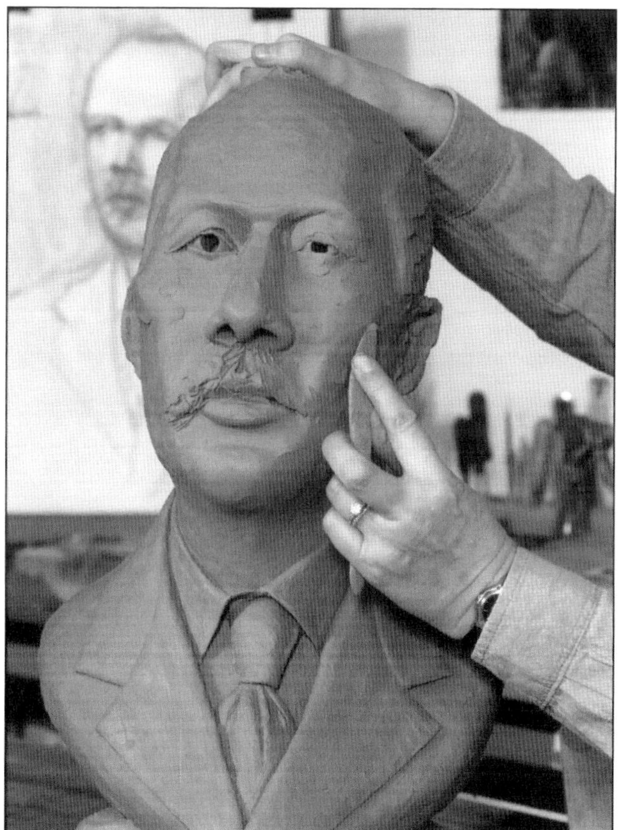

Pictured is a bust of Inman Page sculpted for Langston University. Page was the first president of the university before becoming a principal at Frederick A. Douglass High School. He is credited with establishing a curriculum of sports and fine arts as cornerstones that would remain important to African American education in Oklahoma City. Page was supervising principal of the Oklahoma City Separate Schools. (Courtesy of Oklahoma Historical Society.)

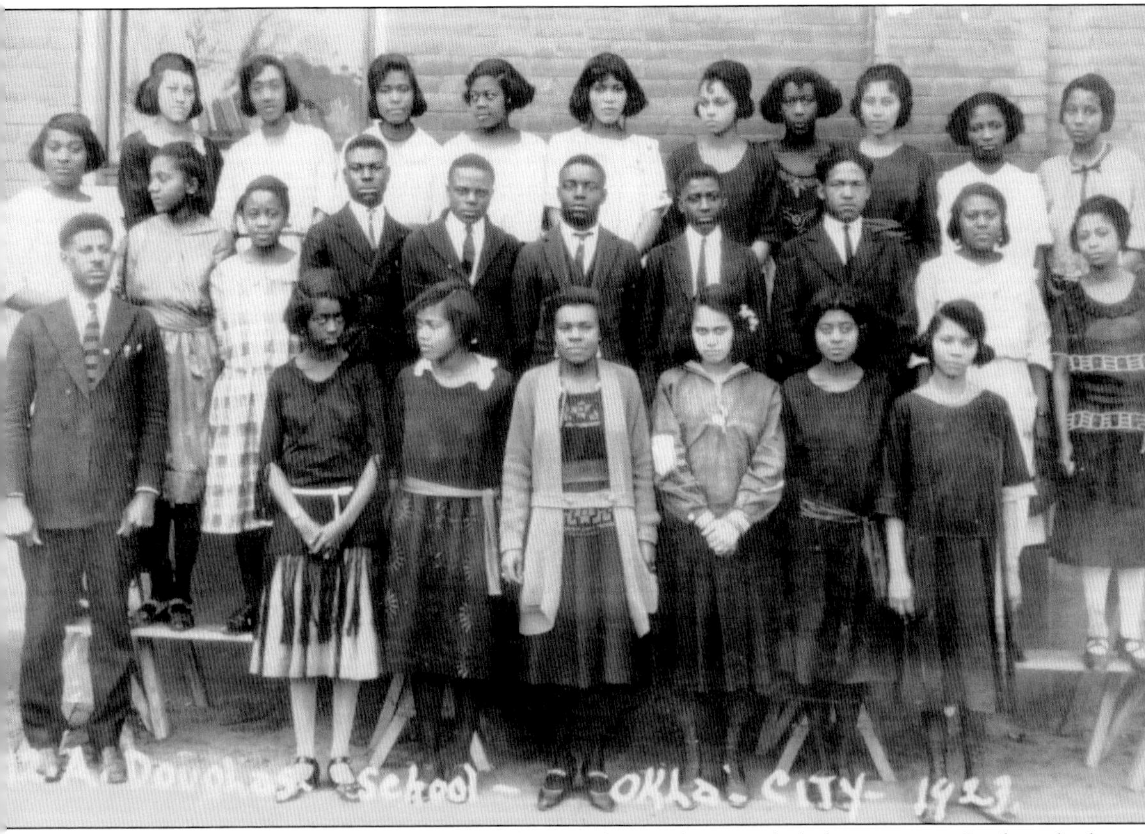

By 1923, graduation classes had increased in numbers and now included young men. Students had named their school Frederick A. Douglass High School. New organizations and departments were created as a means to increase opportunity and spark new inspiration and greater efficiency in the life of the student body. The class motto was "Genius is Hard Work." The senior class of 1925 created the first annual, known as *The Tellus*, named by the junior class. It told the Douglass story through pictures and narrative. The book, shared with school patrons, was an overview of what students and staff were accomplishing. The first competition for a school queen was established and the junior class's Emily Jones was the winner of what would become a long-standing tradition. (Courtesy of Kenneth Arinwine and Charles Morgan.)

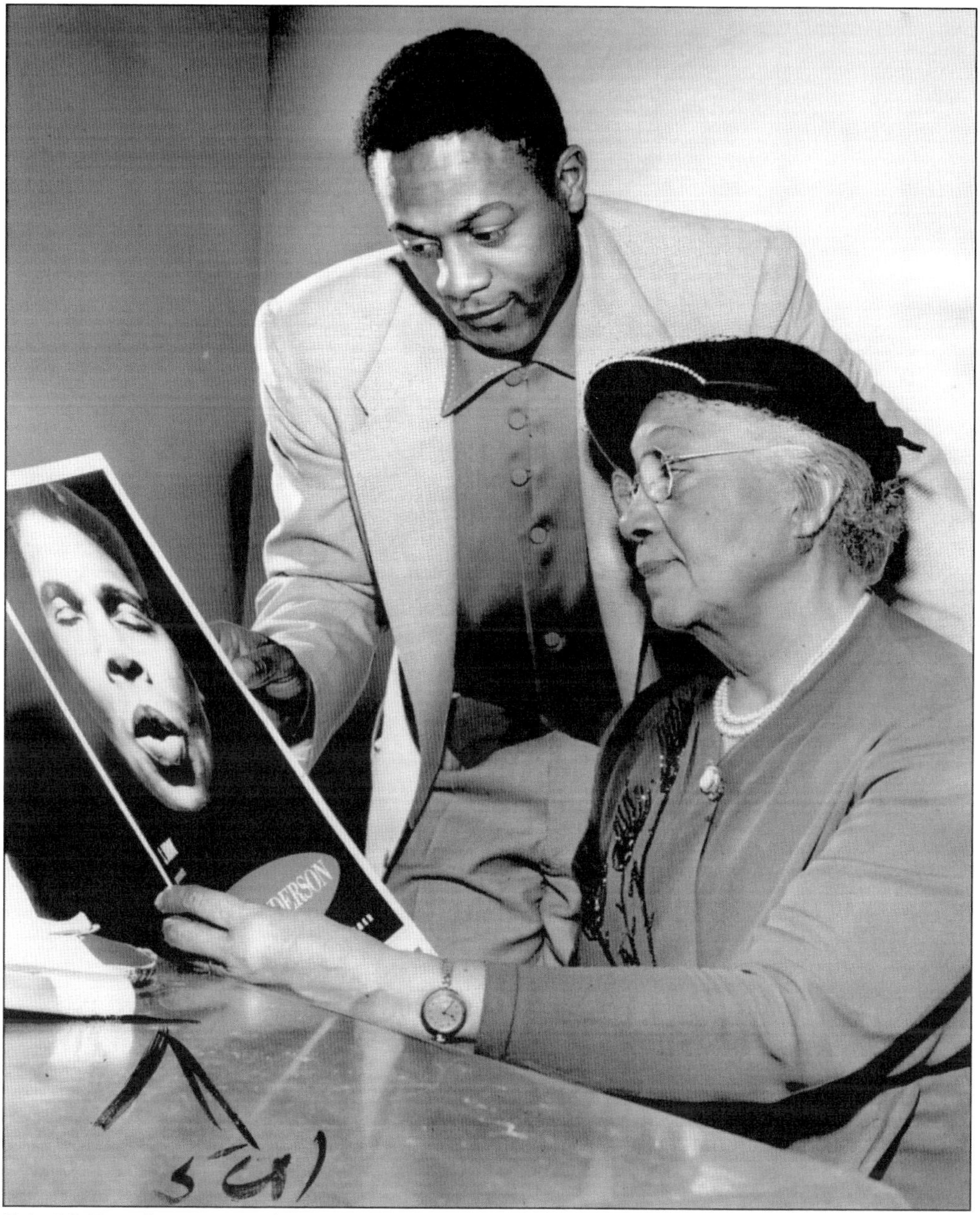

Zelia N. Page Breaux was the music instructor at Douglass High School and supervisor of music for Oklahoma City Separate Schools in 1923. The rest of the 14-member faculty included her father, Inman Edward Page, principal, and her mother, Zelia Ball Page, matron. This was a family of highly qualified educators who were teachers with master's degrees in education from prestigious universities. Zelia had received her bachelor's degree at the age of 18. During her career of more than 26 years in Oklahoma City Public Schools, she organized music programs for all of the black schools and established school bands, orchestras, community bands, show bands, music programs that included operettas, and much more. She is shown with an unidentified student admiring a photograph of nationally renowned contralto Marian Anderson, who appeared at Douglass High School. (Courtesy of Oklahoma Historical Society.)

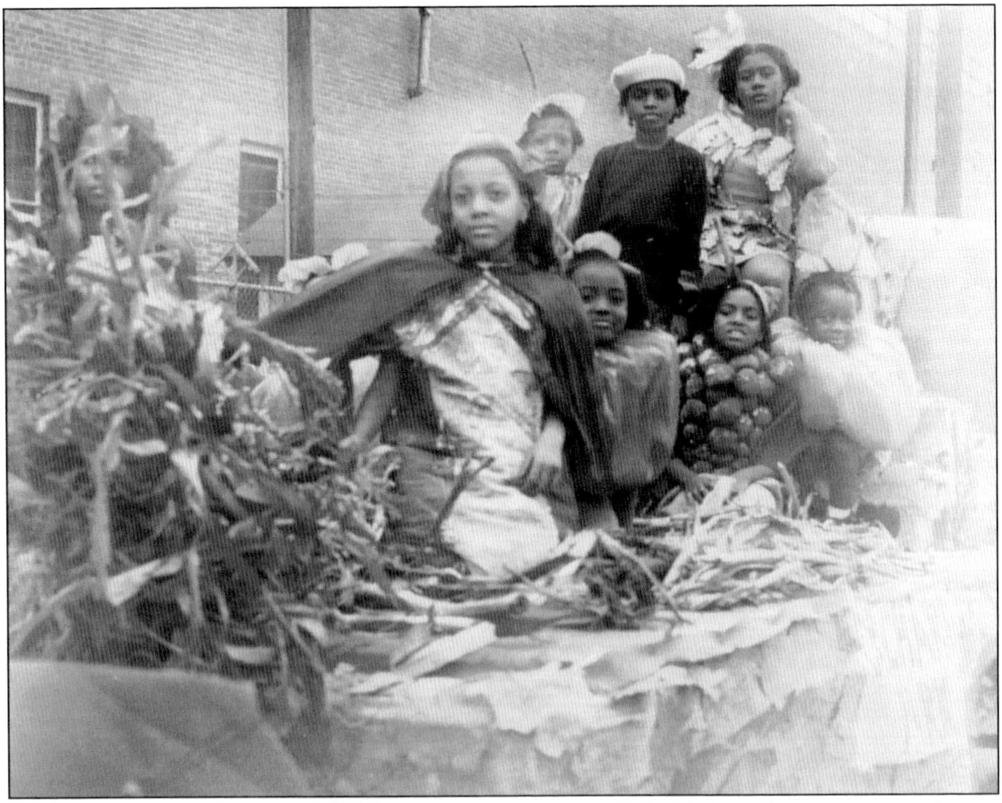

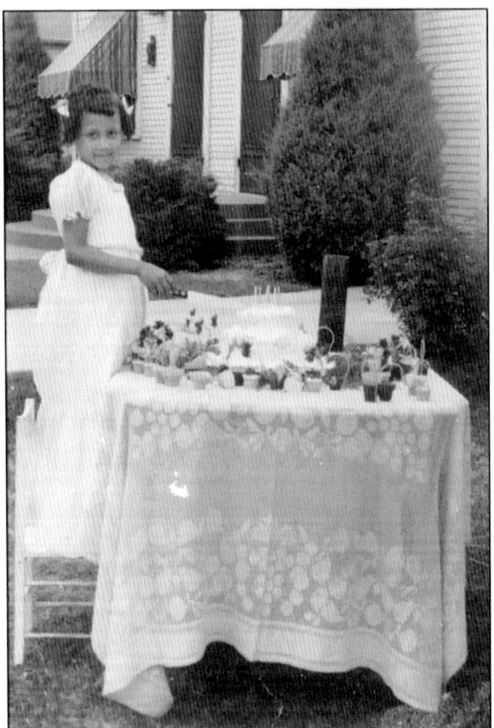

In 1932, Zelia N. Page Breaux organized and founded the May Day celebrations for Oklahoma City Public Schools. The celebrations were similar at many of the schools. Some schools were fortunate to have the Douglass band playing while the students wrapped the maypoles. Schools later participated in a May Day parade with floats that featured students who participated in competitions to become the May Day queen. Above is the queen and her royal court outfitted in full regalia. Marvenne Jenkins is shown at left cutting her birthday cake at the May Day festival. Lots of flowers and other reminders of spring were customary. (Both, courtesy of Leonardo DeBose, from the Freddie Stephens Collection.)

At right, Mary Elaine Williams, an Orchard Park Elementary student, performs a dance number during the May Day program. Special performances were commonly integrated into these popular programs. Many times, bands participated in May Day festival parades. Although girls were most often featured, boys participated and many times did most of the cleanup. The photograph below shows young men in their cowboy hats and boots. This event shows the genius of Zelia N. Page Breaux's integration of ancient European culture with American education and culture. (Both, courtesy of Leonardo DeBose, from the Freddie Stephens Collection.)

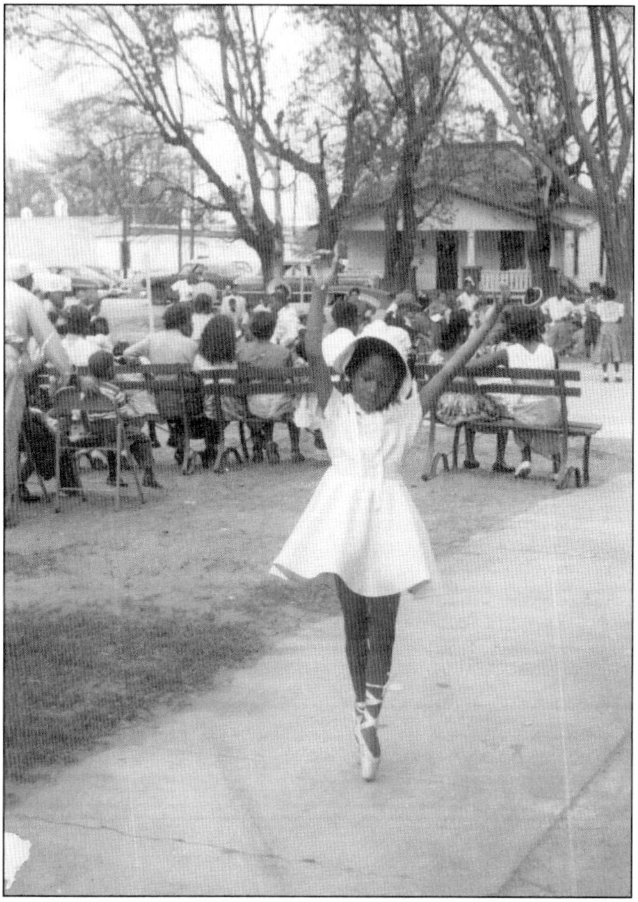

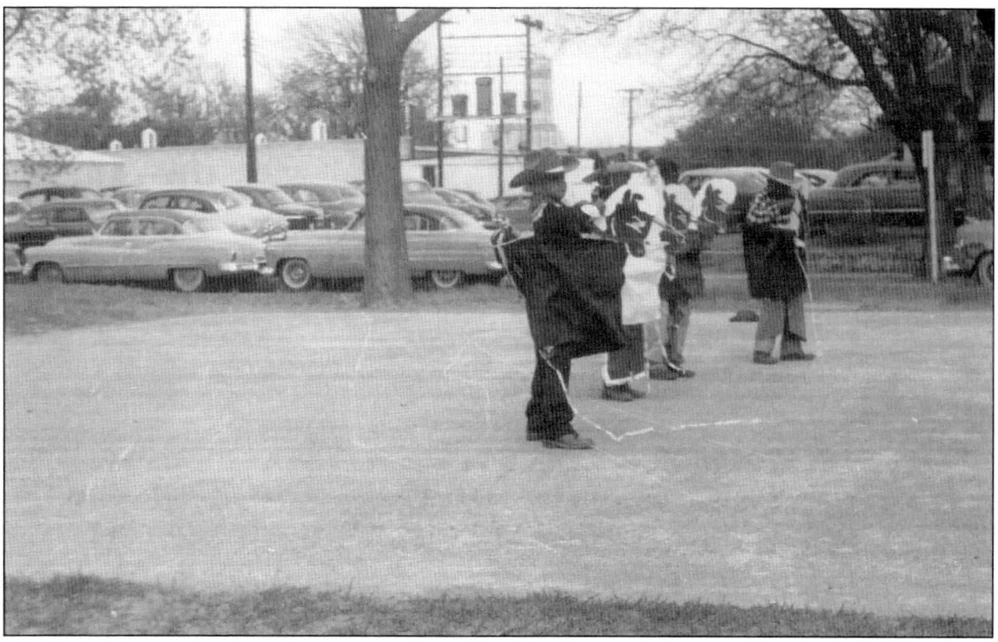

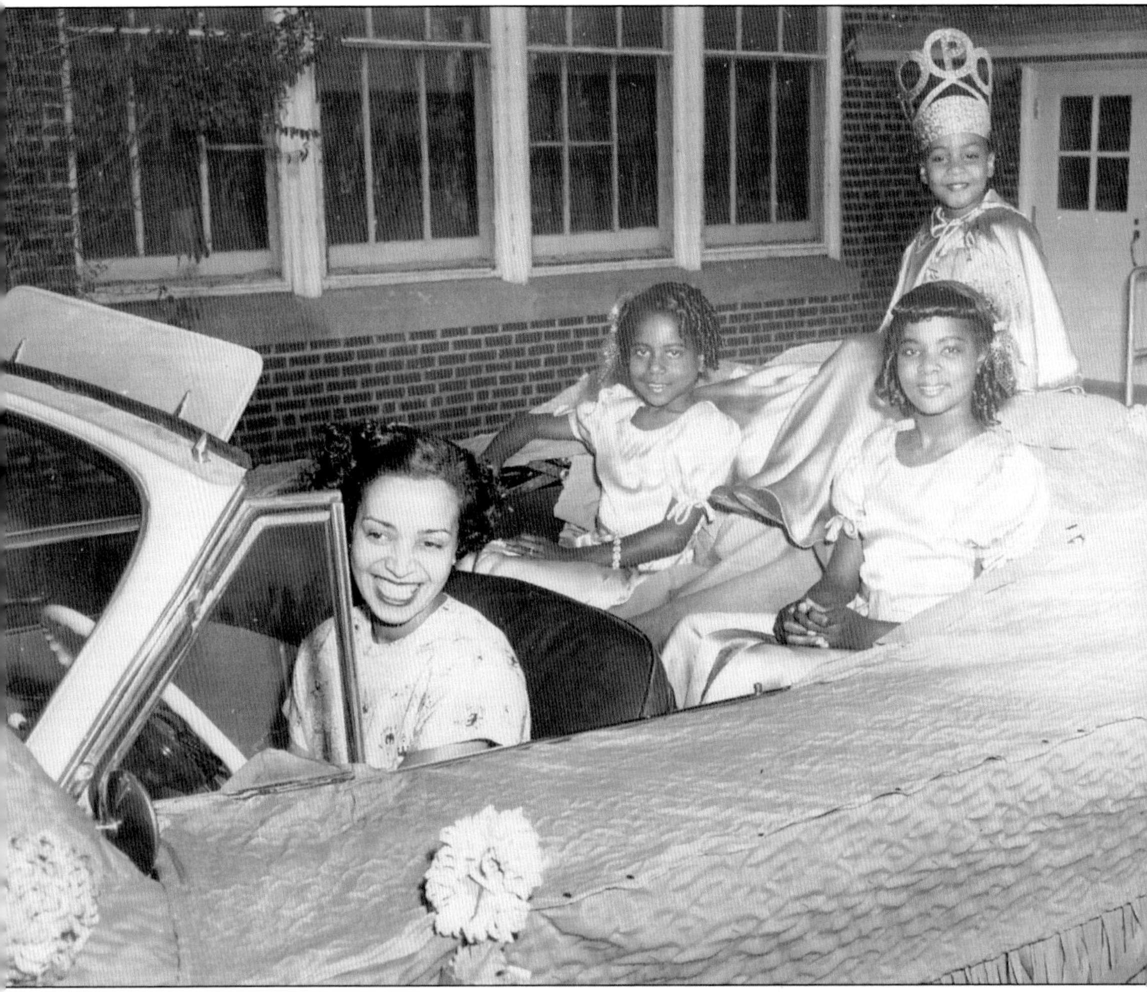

As Frederick A. Douglass High School and its several elementary schools were evolving into an impressive model of excellence, the May Day celebrations continued to draw parents, teachers, students, and community together in a powerful collaborative force that everyone enjoyed. The May Day parade was one of Zelia Breaux's ideas of having a more expansive celebration in which all schools could participate and the Douglass High School Band could really showcase its flexibility. Inman Page Elementary School showed off its queen in this 1949 photograph at the May Day parade. Teacher Maedella Cox provided the elaborately decorated convertible in which the queen and her attendants rode. The unidentified queen is accompanied by Lucy Thurmond, first attendant, seated on the left, and Joyce Richardson, second attendant, on the right. The traditional celebration of flowers is included on the float designed by teachers, students, and parents. (Courtesy of Lucy Thurmond Livingston.)

Two

Education First

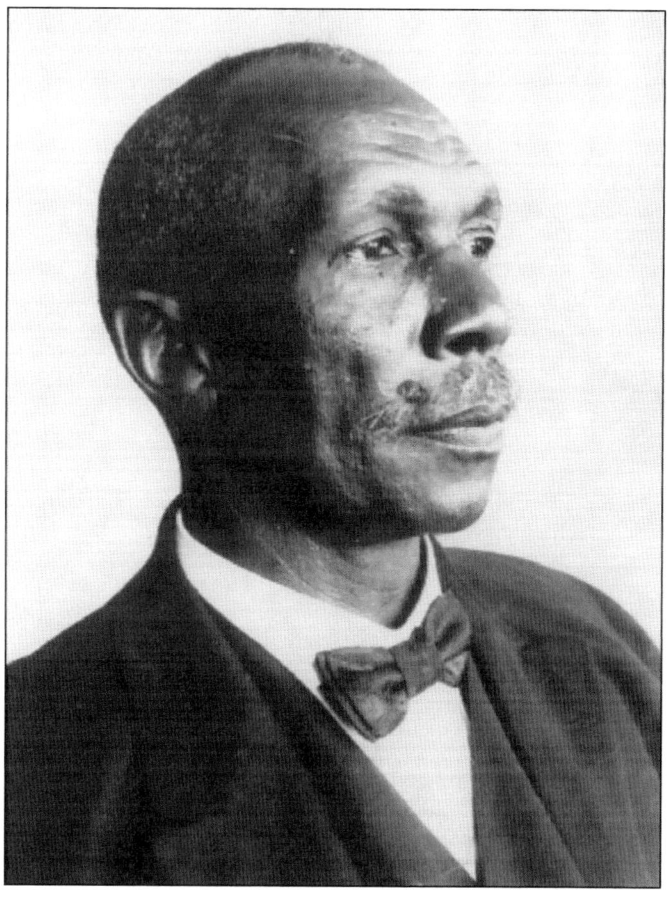

Before becoming principal at Douglass High School in Oklahoma City, Inman Edward Page was a college president at two universities, Lincoln University in Jefferson City, Missouri, and Langston University in Langston, Oklahoma. He received a master's degree from Brown University and was honored with honorary degrees from Wilberforce and Howard Universities. (Courtesy of Oklahoma Historical Society.)

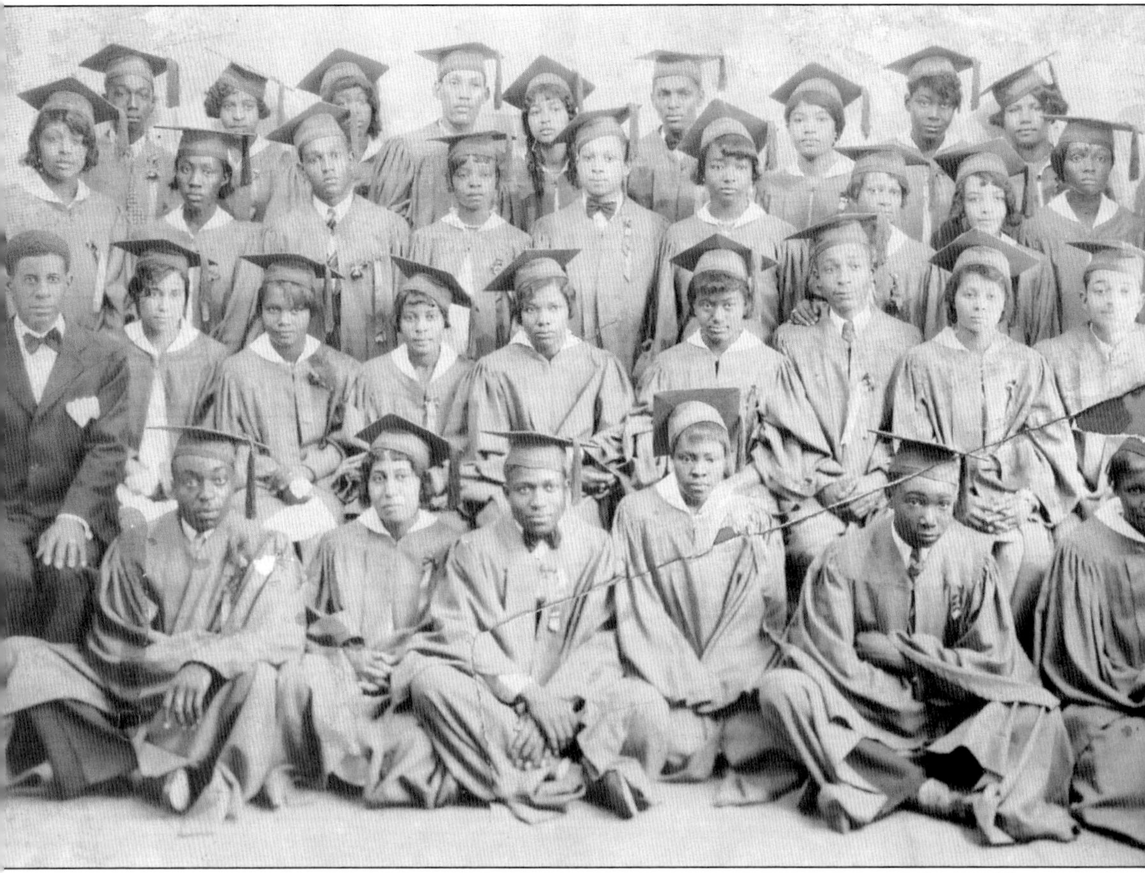

The Frederick A. Douglass class of 1929 included 32 graduates. From left to right are (first row, seated) Haywood Jackson, Minnie Lee Horton, Marie Jones, Willie Jones, and Mattie Williams; (second row) Prof. Henry A. Berry, Eleanor Jones, Edna Duncan, Hazel Cooper, Katherine Chatman, Addie Moran, Floyd Alexander, Leona Kennedy, and Foster Thompson; (third row) Elva Sherman, Daihlia Anderson, Allen Bethel, Priscilla Anglin, Carl Thomasson, Marina Fowler, Mattie Morgan, Lennie Brewer, and Oretha Lounds; (fourth row) Peter Milton, Erycina Berry, Terrie Lee Robinson, Dick Herne, Bernita Skinner, Lemuel Harkey, Edna Dennis, Gertrude Galbreath, and Andrew Evans. Some of these graduates continued their education to become teachers or principals at schools in Oklahoma. Floyd Alexander became principal at Truman Elementary, Culbertson Elementary, Moon Junior High, and Kennedy Junior High Schools. Mattie Williams, an accomplished musician, appeared in operettas at Zelia Breaux's Aldridge Theater and became a teacher at Choctaw Elementary School. (Courtesy of Leonardo DeBose, from the Freddie Stephens Collection.)

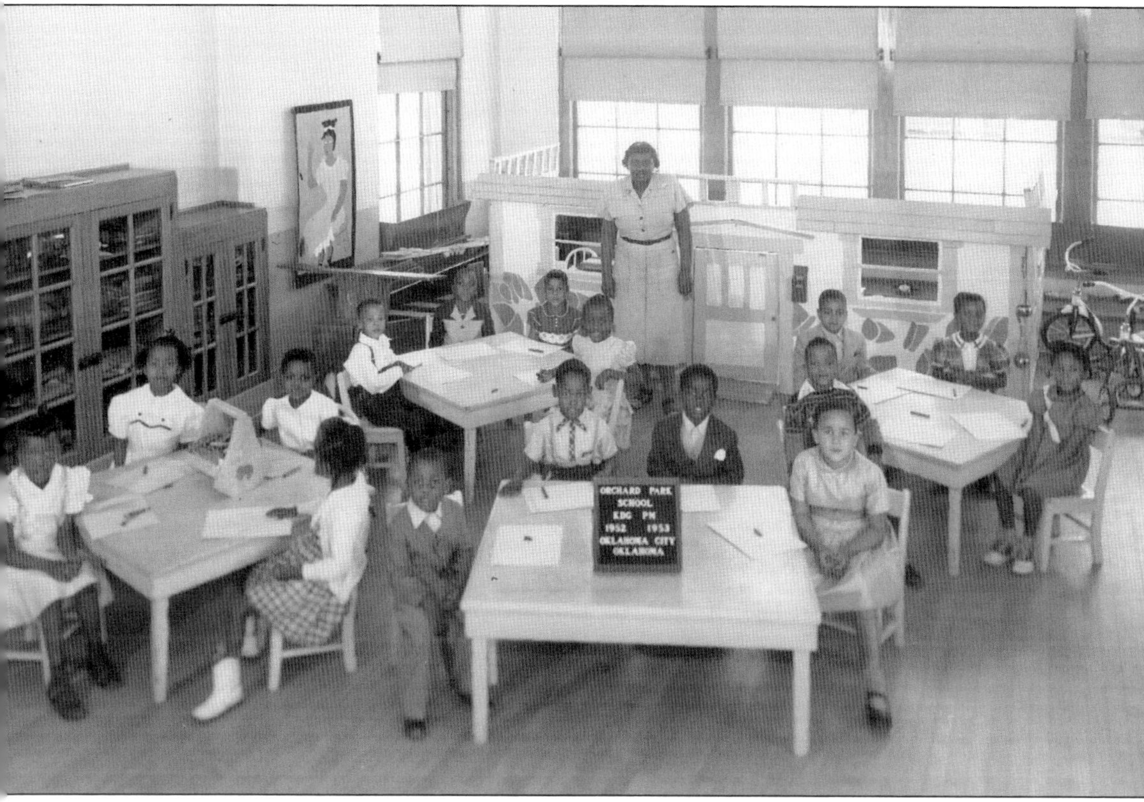

Freddie Stephens is pictured with her kindergarten class at Orchard Park Elementary School in 1952. Class sizes at Orchard Park, and all the Oklahoma City Separate Schools, had increased since World War II. Stephens saw an opportunity to provide happiness among students in her classroom around the Christmas holidays. She knew mothers could not afford to buy toys for their children. Recognizing that families were struggling because husbands and older sons were away fighting for America, she asked five-and-dime stores in downtown Oklahoma City for toys that were damaged and in need of repair. Merchants gladly responded and supplied her with toys, but it was not enough for each child to have one. She then started a Toy Library for the children. Stephens repaired the toys and allowed the children to check them out of the Toy Library, so that each child had a chance to play with a toy during the holidays. (Courtesy of Leonardo DeBose, from the Freddie Stephens Collection.)

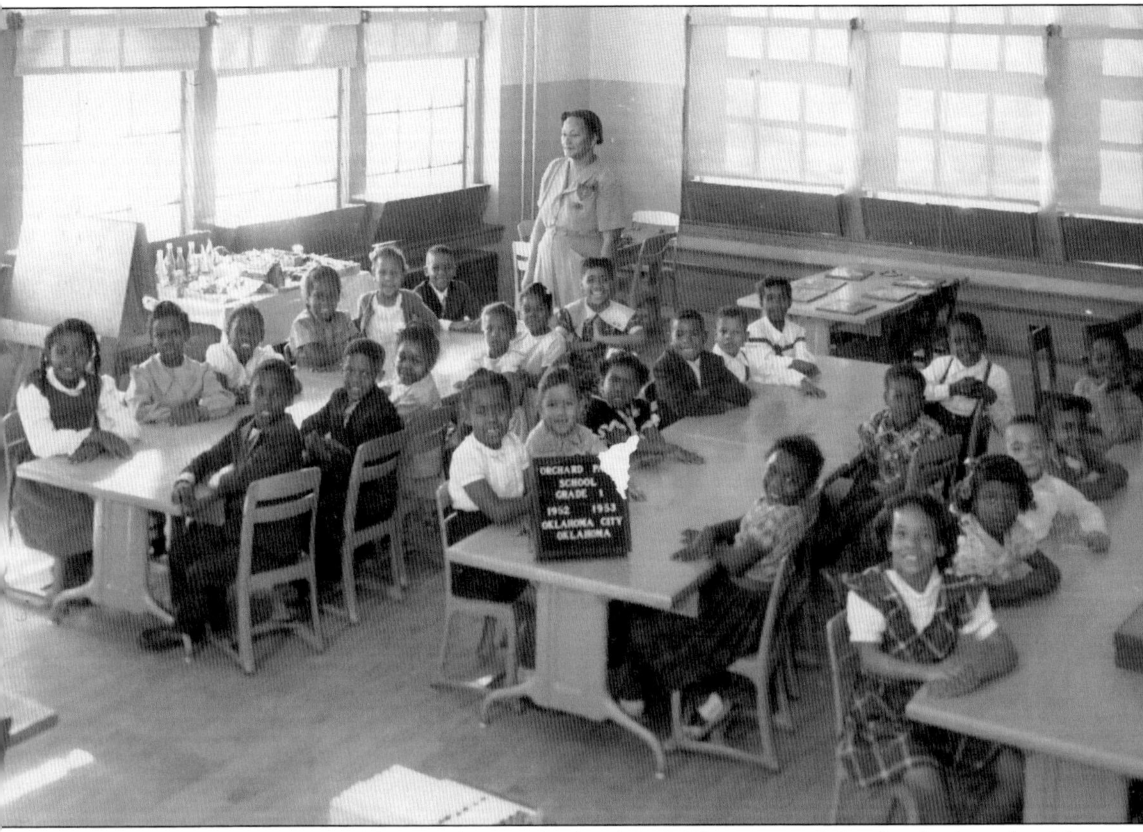

June Franklin was one of five teachers at Orchard Park Elementary School, a feeder school for Frederick A. Douglass High School, until the early 1960s. Enrollment at the school increased after World War II and continued to grow until the mid-1950s. In fact, Orchard Park Elementary School had a total enrollment of 67 students near the time of its closing. Music was a requirement for all Oklahoma City Separate Schools under Zelia N. Page Breaux's leadership. During the 1920s, Douglass High School had only three departments—athletics, music, and health. There was great concern about students being healthy and fit. Tuberculosis and other infectious diseases were common during those days. Many schools employed a staff nurse who made house calls to assist with students who were ill and a doctor who performed general exams. (Courtesy of Leonardo DeBose, from the Freddie Stephens Collection.)

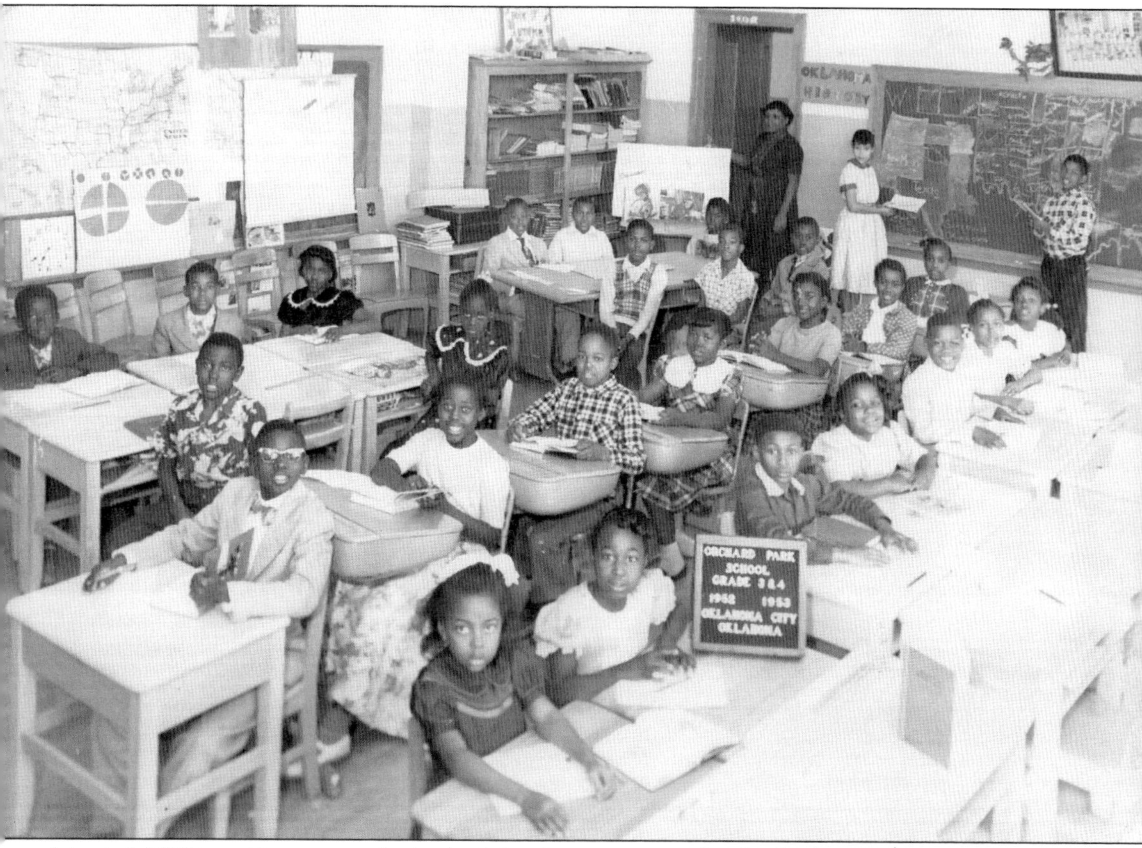

Mattie J. Williams Counter, at the back of the classroom near the display board, was an example of the well-qualified teachers who could be found in the classrooms of Oklahoma City Separate Schools. Counter had received a bachelor of arts degree from Langston University and a master of education degree from the University of Oklahoma. She was an accomplished musician who had studied under Zelia N. Page Breaux and had performed professionally in the community, appearing in operettas and performances at the Aldridge Theater. In the Oklahoma City Separate Schools, teachers had to be flexible to provide students with a well-rounded education. Counter taught both third and fourth grade classes in the same classroom, a common practice in the elementary schools of that era. Before retiring, she was recognized for meritorious service and genuine interest in the youth of the Oklahoma City Public Schools by the Association of Classroom Teachers of Oklahoma City. She also received a Distinguished Meritorious Award from the Oklahoma City Langston alumni chapter. (Courtesy of Leonardo DeBose, from the Freddie Stephens Collection.)

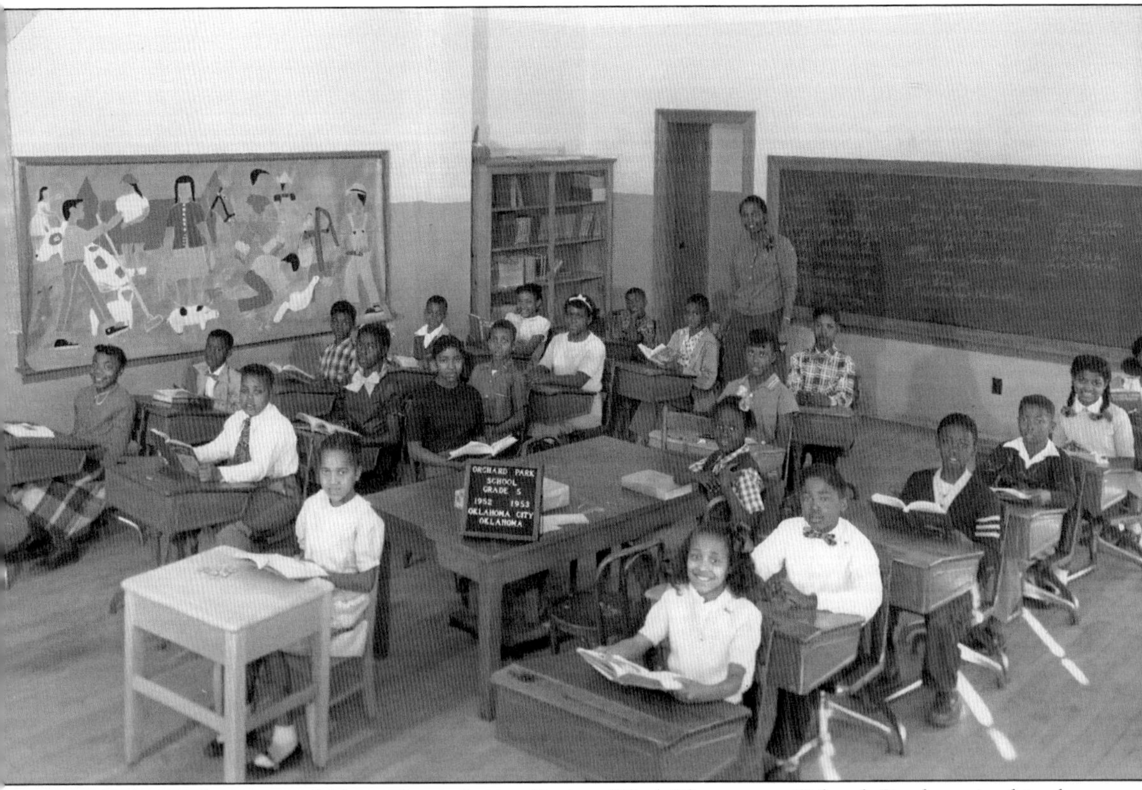

Rubye Dabney was a fifth grade teacher at Orchard Park Elementary School. Students in this class were clearly exposed to art. They were also taught how to dress appropriately and in good taste. Students were taught high moral values and were encouraged to participate in church and school activities that displayed their talents. Students were careful to follow teachers' instructions and held them in high esteem. Life skills were taught at an early age, and students looked forward to going as far as possible in school so that they could earn a good living. Most Oklahoma City Public Schools teachers were from Oklahoma after the early 1900s. Rubye's sister Margaret Dabney was a career educator who taught art in the Oklahoma City Public Schools. Prior to that time, black teachers came from other states with the hope of establishing an all-black state in Oklahoma. (Courtesy of Leonardo DeBose, from the Freddie Stephens Collection.)

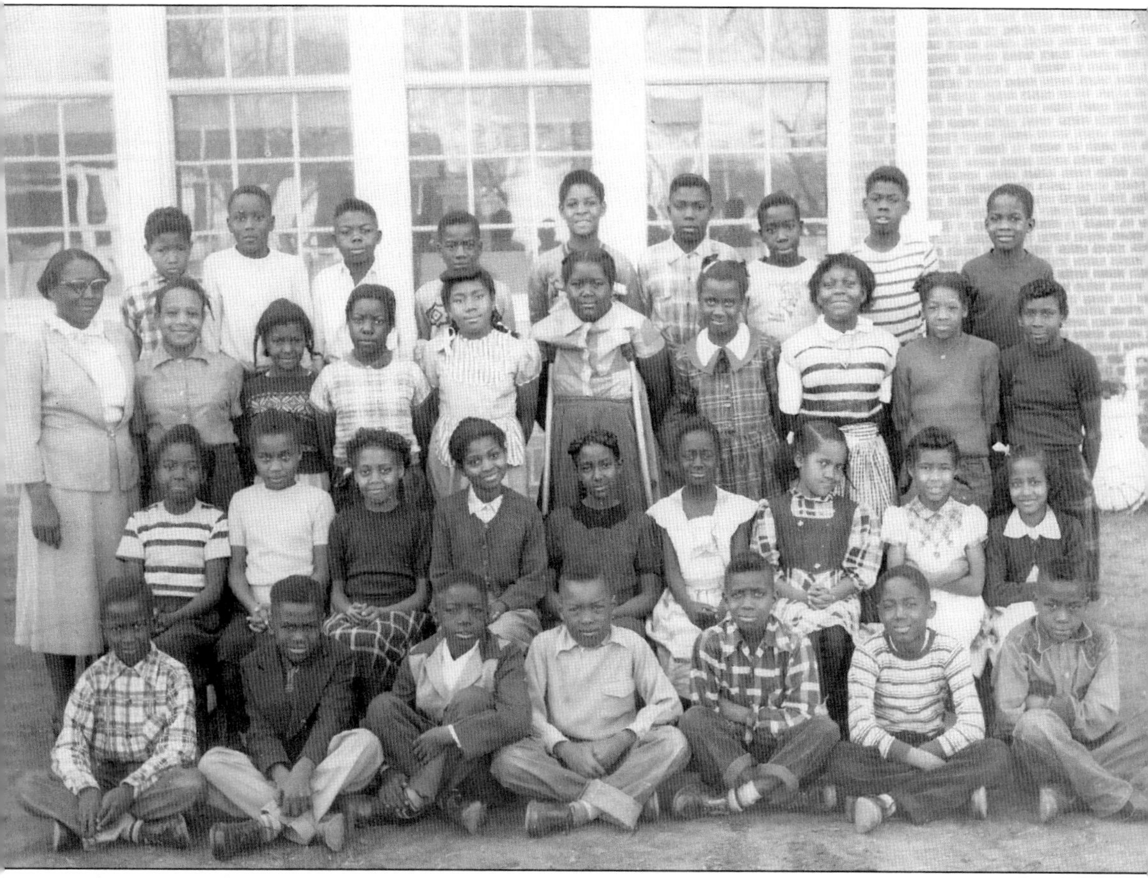

In the 1950s, Oklahoma City Separate Schools had their own education system, created by principals, teachers, and parents, until the fall of 1955, when they came under the auspices of the Oklahoma City Public Schools. Prior to that, Douglass High School principals were supervisors of all the Oklahoma City Separate Schools. Frederick Douglass Moon was the supervisor of Orchard Park Elementary School, where Edna Hobbs was principal. She stands at left between rows three and four. Hobbs, a career educator, taught sixth grade in addition to providing leadership at Orchard Park. Like other teachers and principals, she was committed to progressive education for black students in Oklahoma City. Also, as a parent, she was passionate in her role of "passing the baton" by enrolling her daughter Joleen in one of the Oklahoma City Separate Schools in pursuit of excellence. Joleen Hobbs was a graduate of Frederick A. Douglass High School in 1957. (Courtesy of Leonardo Debose, from the Freddie Stephens Collection.)

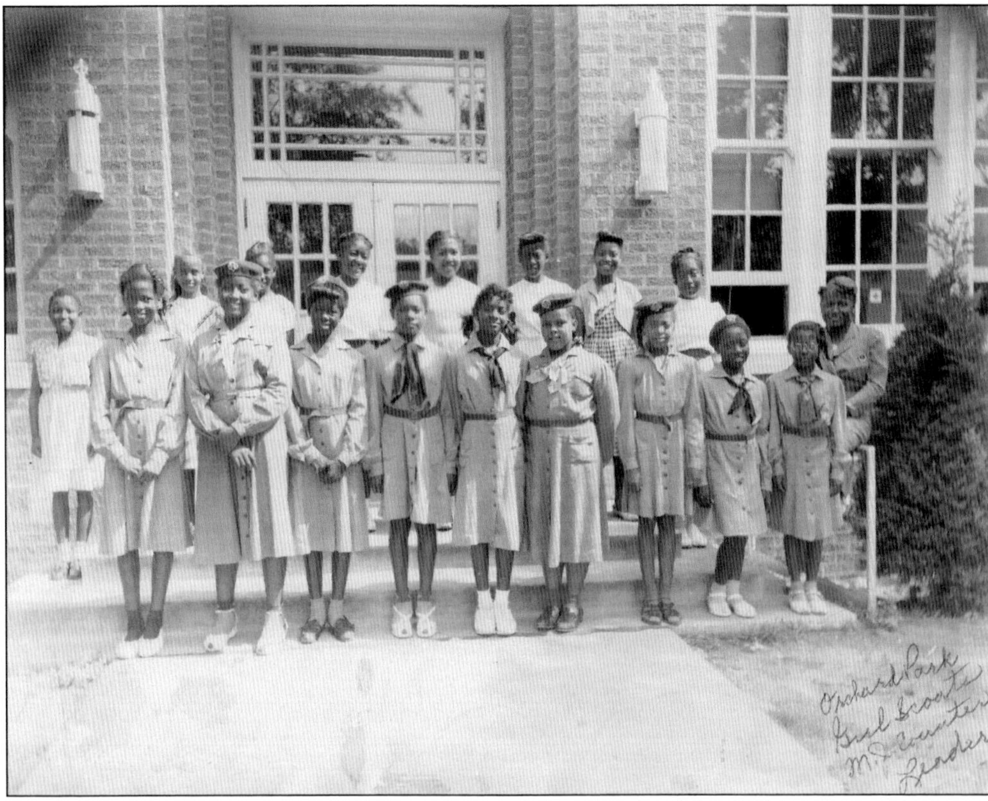

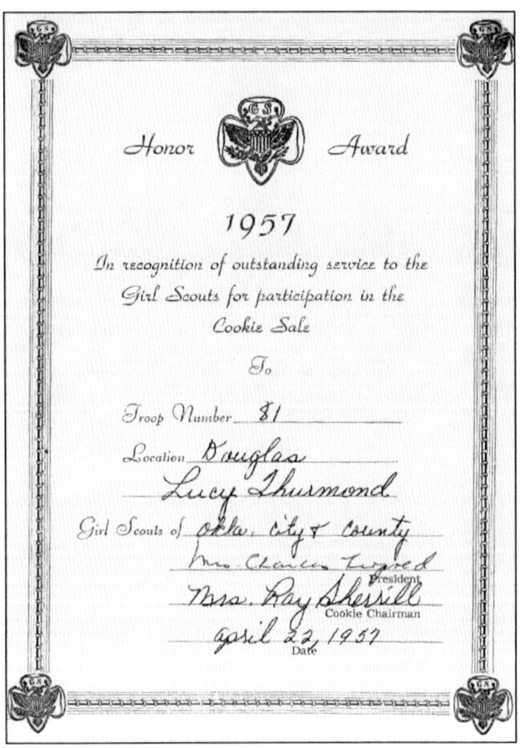

Honor Award

1957

In recognition of outstanding service to the Girl Scouts for participation in the Cookie Sale

To

Troop Number 81

Location Douglas

Lucy Thurmond

Girl Scouts of Okla. City & County

Mrs. Charles Tugred
President

Mrs. Ray Sherrill
Cookie Chairman

April 22, 1957
Date

Principals of the Oklahoma City Separate Schools had collaborations with the wider community. In spite of segregation in Oklahoma, these leaders upheld and were committed to the idea of the greater good of mankind. Principals followed the developing model of education by requiring teachers to sponsor activities, organizations, and programs that included collaborations. From the early days, organizations and institutions that were patriotic, developed character, valued integrity, and embraced development of the whole person had great appeal to the evolving school system. The Girl Scouts, YMCA, YWCA, and the Kiwanis Club participated. Mattie Williams Counter, the third and fourth grade teacher, was sponsor and leader of the Orchard Park Girl Scouts. At left is a certificate of recognition from the Girl Scouts. (Above, courtesy of Leonardo DeBose, from the Freddie Stephens Collection; left, courtesy of Lucy Thurmond Livingston.)

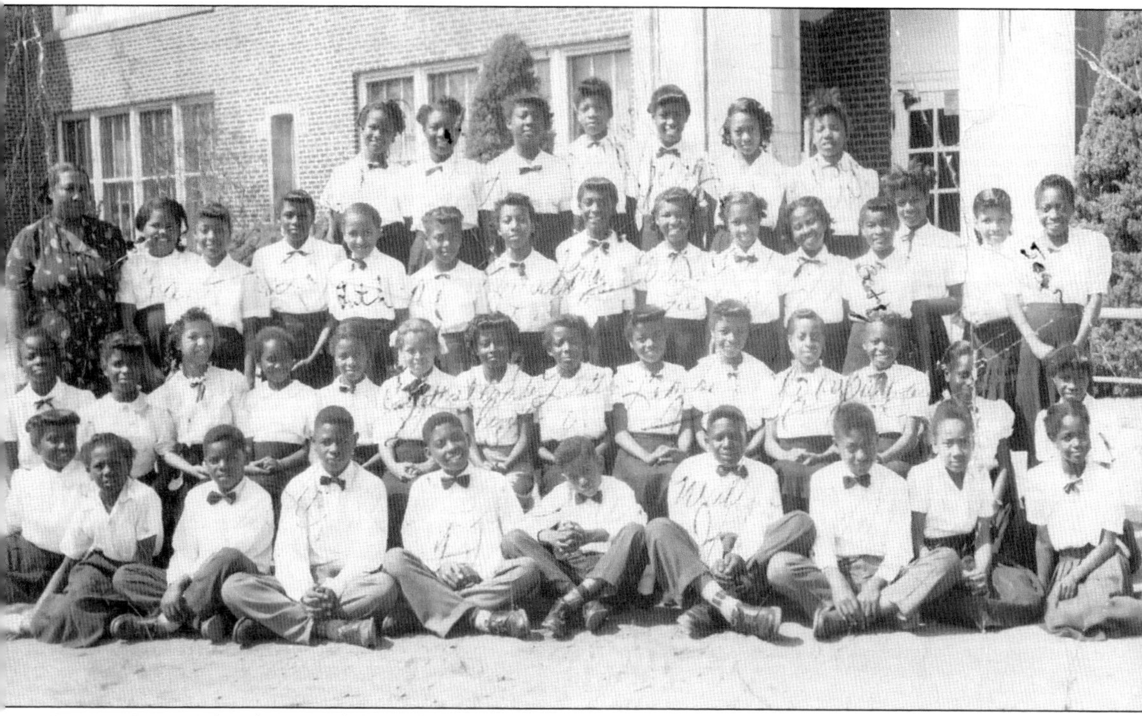

Inman Page School, named for Zelia N. Page Breaux's father, Inman Page, was established in 1926 prior to Page's retirement as principal of Douglass High School in June 1935 and his death in December 1935. The school was located at Northeast Third and Byers Streets until it was torn down in 1974. Several buildings bear his name, including Lincoln University Library in Jefferson City, Missouri, and Page Hall at Langston University in Langston, Oklahoma, where he is buried. Page was the principal who moved Frederick A. Douglass High School to 600 North High Street. He brought discipline to the school and instilled a high spirit of achievement with his daily chapels and demeanor, according to Henry Hawkins, a 1958 graduate who wrote a comprehensive history of Douglass High School. Zelia Breaux was supervisor of music for the Oklahoma City Separate Schools. This photograph shows the choir at Inman Page School around 1949, a year after Zelia Breaux retired. (Courtesy of Lucy Thurmond Livingston.)

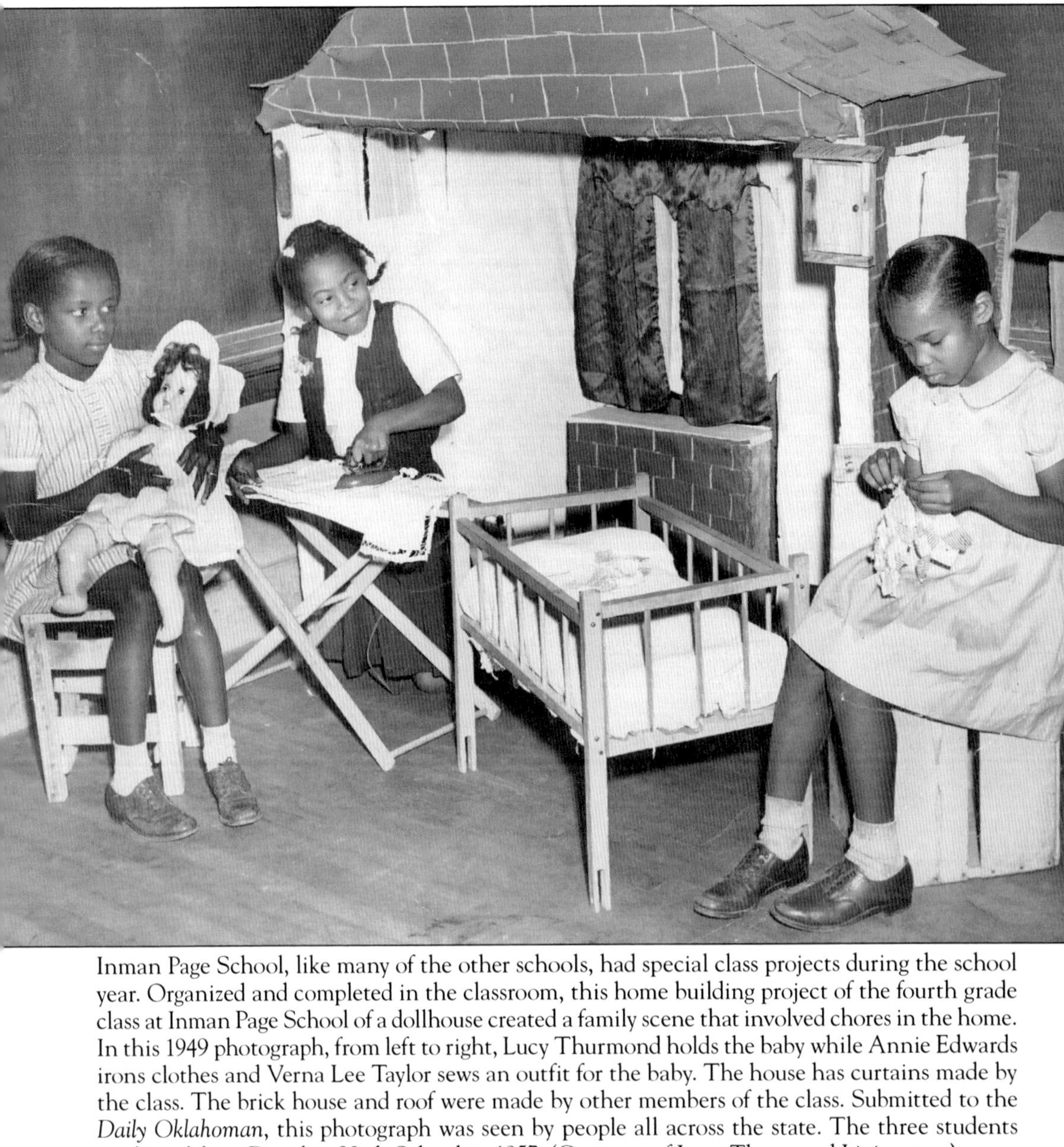

Inman Page School, like many of the other schools, had special class projects during the school year. Organized and completed in the classroom, this home building project of the fourth grade class at Inman Page School of a dollhouse created a family scene that involved chores in the home. In this 1949 photograph, from left to right, Lucy Thurmond holds the baby while Annie Edwards irons clothes and Verna Lee Taylor sews an outfit for the baby. The house has curtains made by the class. The brick house and roof were made by other members of the class. Submitted to the *Daily Oklahoman*, this photograph was seen by people all across the state. The three students graduated from Douglass High School in 1957. (Courtesy of Lucy Thurmond Livingston.)

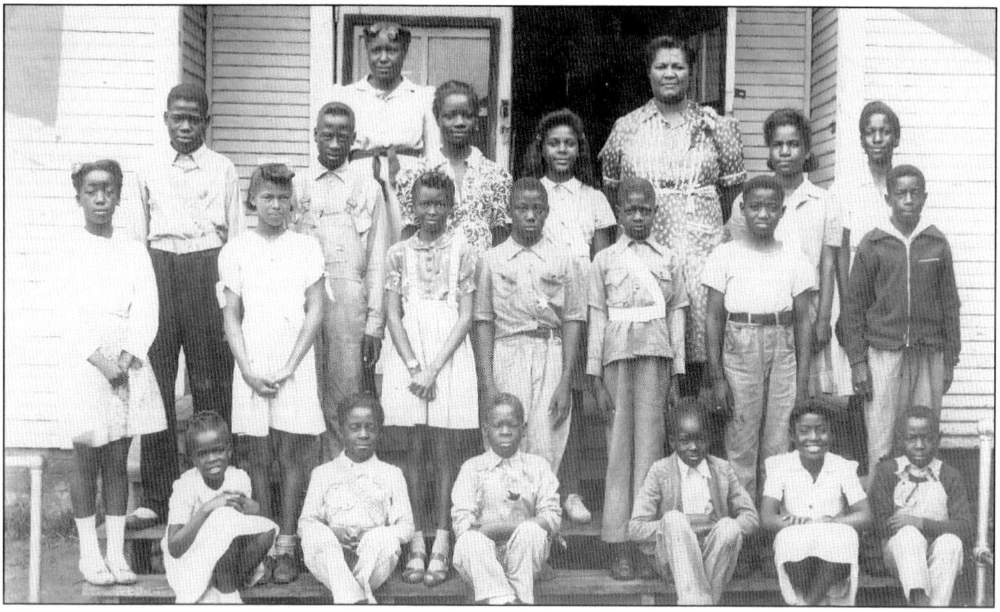

Choctaw Elementary School was established in 1914 in east Oklahoma City in a mostly rural area. One school organized and met in the basement of Avery Church. Many were soon out of business for various reasons. The Oklahoma City Separate Schools that closed after a short time were Sandtown and Packing Town Elementary Schools. Other elementary schools moved into buildings previously occupied by white students. Choctaw Elementary School continues to this day. The above photograph shows Choctaw Elementary students in 1923 with their two teachers, Mattie Williams (fourth row, left) and Leona Palmer (fourth row, right). The photograph below shows Choctaw teachers Ida Jordan (fourth row, left) and Leona Palmer (fourth row, right). (Both, courtesy of Leonardo DeBose, from the Freddie Stephens Collection.)

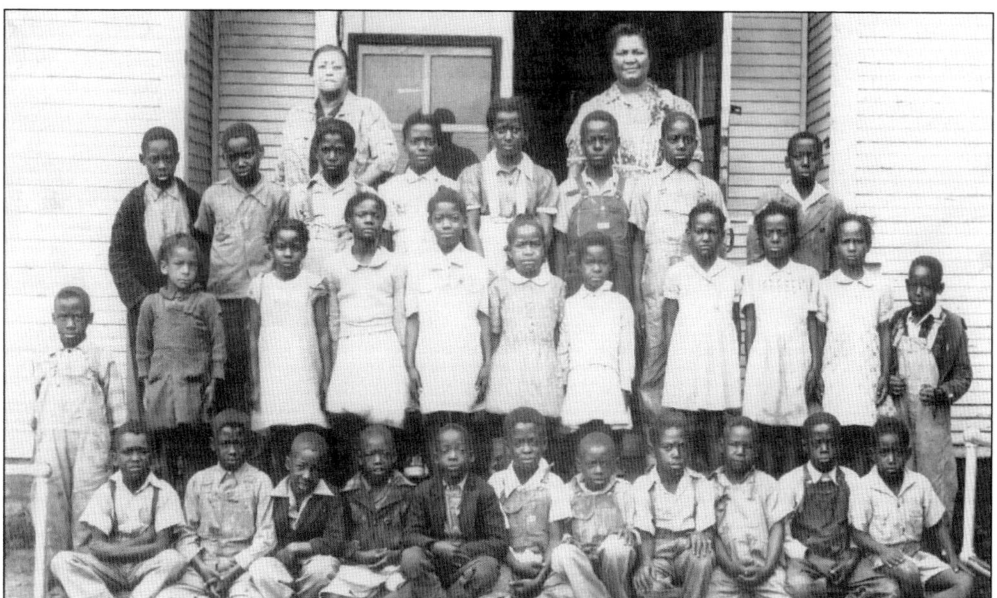

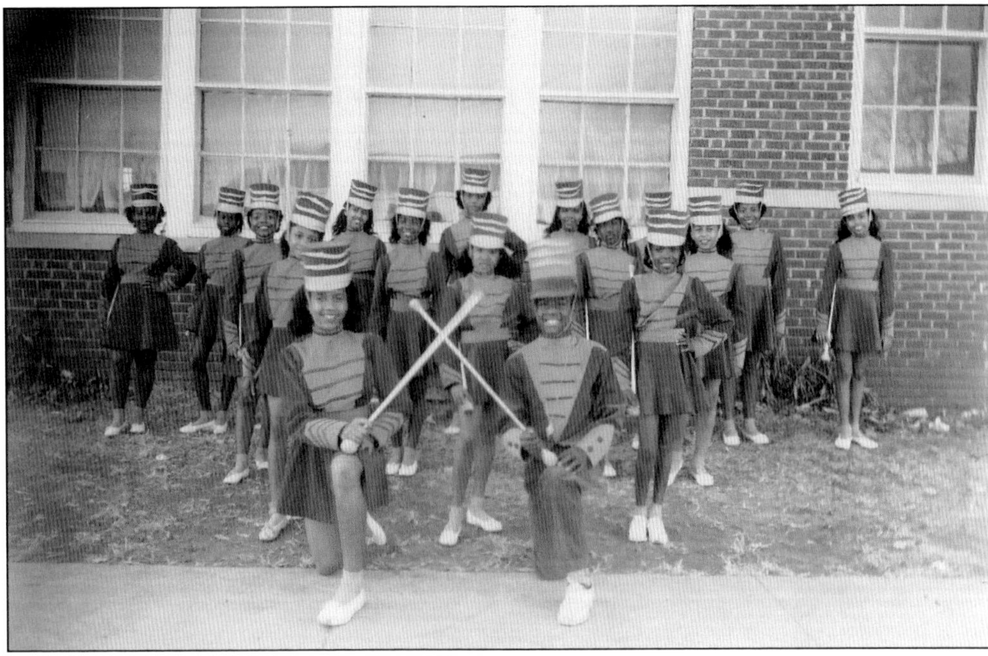

Dunbar Elementary School, located at 1432 Northeast Seventh Street in Oklahoma City, was named for African American poet Paul Lawrence Dunbar. It served a growing population of African Americans in first through sixth grades and was a feeder school to Frederick A. Douglass High School. Consistent with the education model, music was required at all Oklahoma City Separate Schools. The photograph above features the band with their head majorette and drum major in front. Uniforms, like the ones shown, were required for all bands to participate in school-related events. The Oklahoma Negro Band Association held competitions and provided recognition to individual band members, such as the Award of Merit shown below. (Above, courtesy of Bonita Forrest Edwards; below, courtesy of Lucy Thurmond Livingston.)

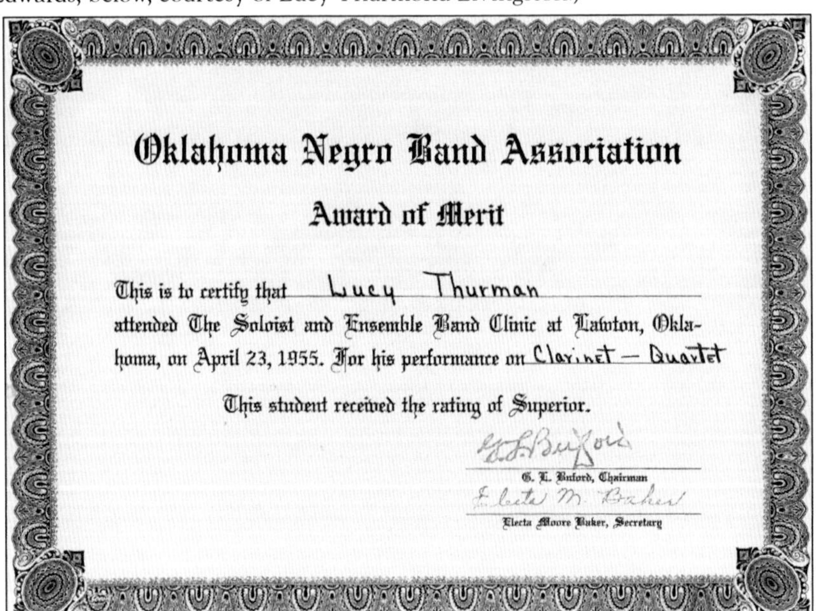

Oklahoma Negro Band Association

Award of Merit

This is to certify that Lucy Thurman attended The Soloist and Ensemble Band Clinic at Lawton, Oklahoma, on April 23, 1955. For his performance on Clarinet – Quartet

This student received the rating of Superior.

G. L. Buford, Chairman

Electa Moore Baker, Secretary

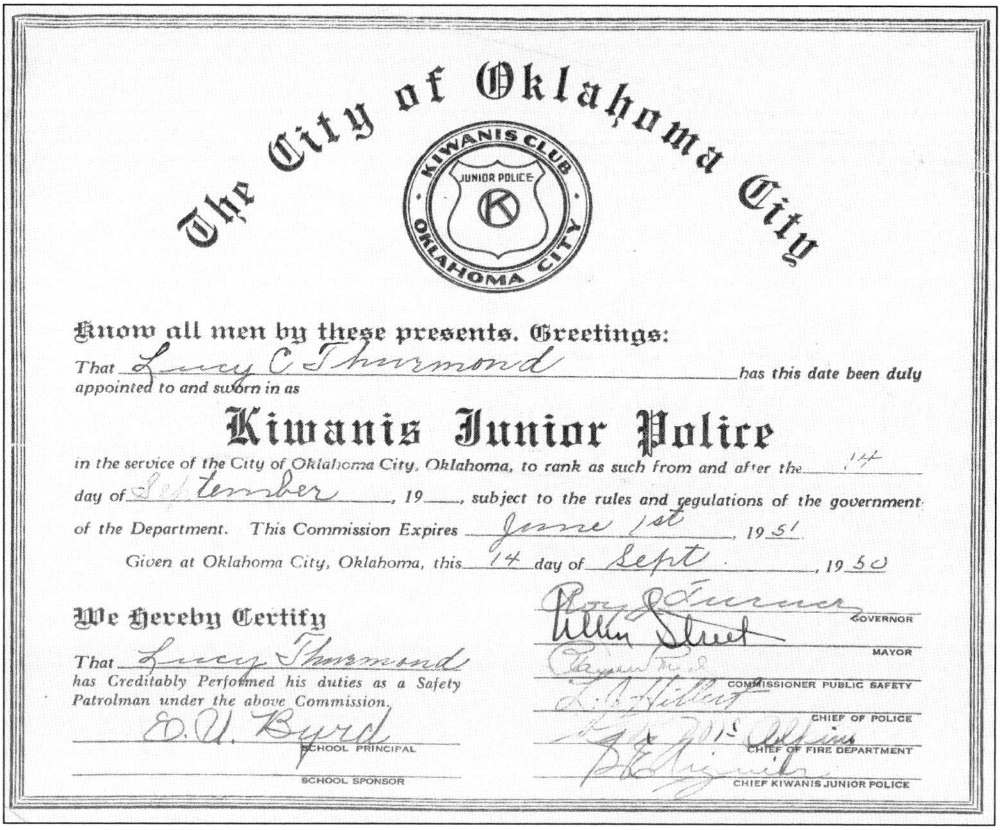

The City of Oklahoma City

KIWANIS CLUB · JUNIOR POLICE · OKLAHOMA CITY

Know all men by these presents. Greetings:

That Lucy C. Thurmond has this date been duly appointed to and sworn in as

Kiwanis Junior Police

in the service of the City of Oklahoma City, Oklahoma, to rank as such from and after the 14 day of September, 19__, subject to the rules and regulations of the government of the Department. This Commission Expires June 1st, 1951.

Given at Oklahoma City, Oklahoma, this 14 day of Sept, 1950

We Hereby Certify

That Lucy Thurmond has Creditably Performed his duties as a Safety Patrolman under the above Commission.

E. U. Byrd
SCHOOL PRINCIPAL

SCHOOL SPONSOR

GOVERNOR

MAYOR

COMMISSIONER PUBLIC SAFETY

CHIEF OF POLICE

CHIEF OF FIRE DEPARTMENT

CHIEF KIWANIS JUNIOR POLICE

By the 1940s and through the early 1970s, reward systems from the larger community recognized excellence, leadership, service, and participation in their programs to encourage students, parents, and teachers. Many clubs and organizations supporting these collaborations were organized in all schools, beginning with elementary schools. Special school assemblies were held to recognize participants. The Daughers of the American Revolution honored good citizenship in the schools, and the Kiwanis Club recognized service to Oklahoma City through its Junior Police program. (Both, courtesy of Lucy Thurmond Livingston.)

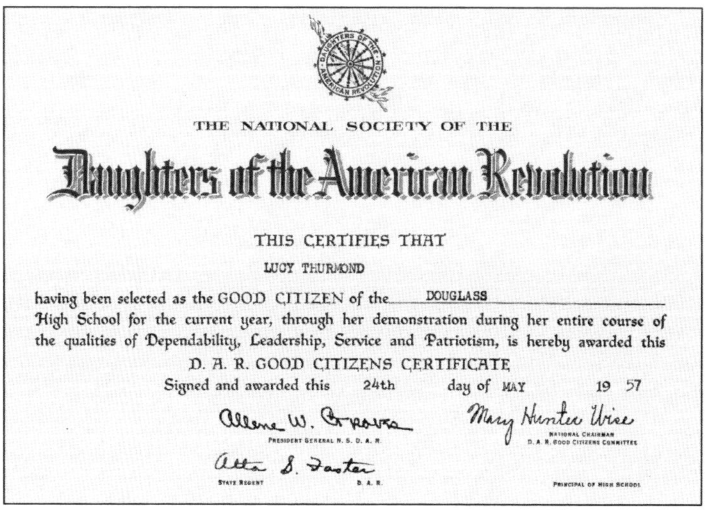

THE NATIONAL SOCIETY OF THE

Daughters of the American Revolution

THIS CERTIFIES THAT

LUCY THURMOND

having been selected as the GOOD CITIZEN of the DOUGLASS High School for the current year, through her demonstration during her entire course of the qualities of Dependability, Leadership, Service and Patriotism, is hereby awarded this

D. A. R. GOOD CITIZENS CERTIFICATE

Signed and awarded this 24th day of MAY 19 57

Allene W. Groves
PRESIDENT GENERAL N. S. D. A. R.

Mary Hunter Wise
NATIONAL CHAIRMAN D. A. R. GOOD CITIZENS COMMITTEE

Atta S. Foster
STATE REGENT D. A. R.

PRINCIPAL OF HIGH SCHOOL

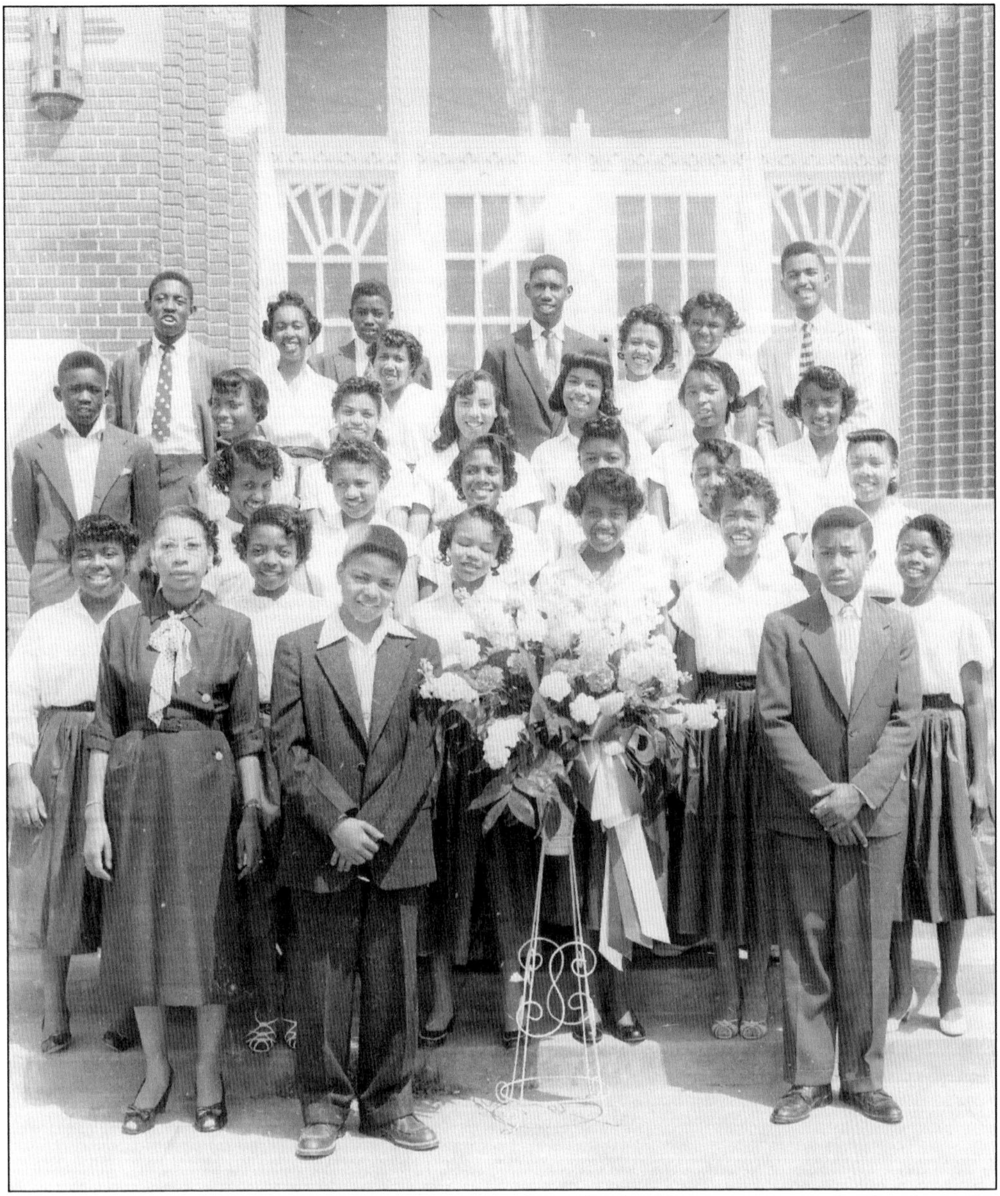

Ruth Evelyn Macklin Allen was born in 1913 and taught for 33 years at several schools in the Oklahoma City Public Schools District. She taught English, French, and social studies at Douglass High School and took a leadership role in developing the growing student body. She started the CAVANIPP Club to aid English students. The acronym captured the eight parts of speech (conjunction, adverb, verb, adjective, noun, interjection, pronoun, and preposition). From left to right, club members are (first row) Ruth Allen (sponsor), Don E. Benefee, and Wesley Gude; (second row) Mary Bunn (president), Barbara Langston, Ruby Darling, Wanda Davis, Patricia Moore, and Helen Brown; (third row) Janetta Robinson, Lois J. Reed, Wilma Bradley, Barbara J. Henry, Patricia Lewis, and Bonita Davis; (fourth row) Charles Hodge, Janice Bennet, Patricia Parker, Patricia Buckner, Betty Braggs, Lue Anna Watkins, Gladys Williams, Judith Neal, and Edith Smith; (fifth row) Curtis Dodson, Sherrill Mitchell, George Martin, Roy Lee Benford, Barbara Downey, and Don Muse. (Courtesy of Nannette Allen.)

Three

Genius in the Making

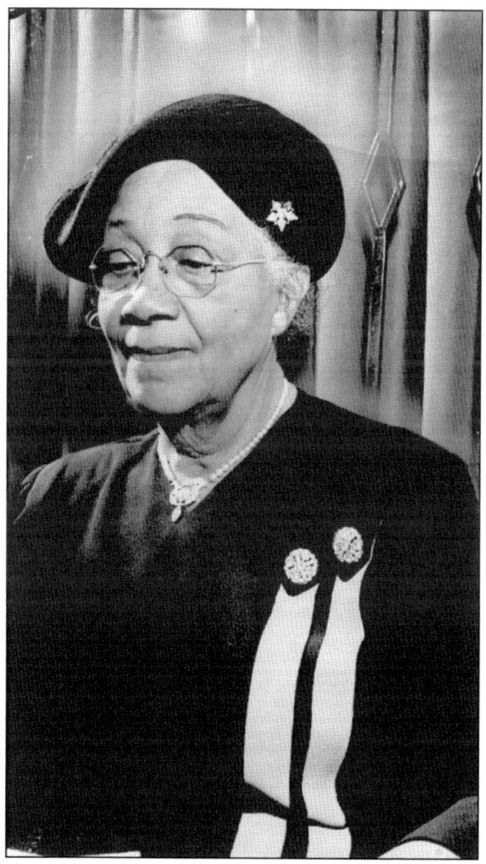

Zelia N. Page (Breaux) was 15 years old when she organized the music department for Langston University. At age 18, she received her bachelor of music degree from Langston. She was supervisor of music for the Oklahoma City Separate Schools for 25 years. Breaux was world renowned and was inducted into several music halls of fame. Step "Buddy" Anderson, one of her students, remembered her as having turned Oklahoma City into a musical town more than anyone else. (Courtesy of the Oklahoma Historical Society.)

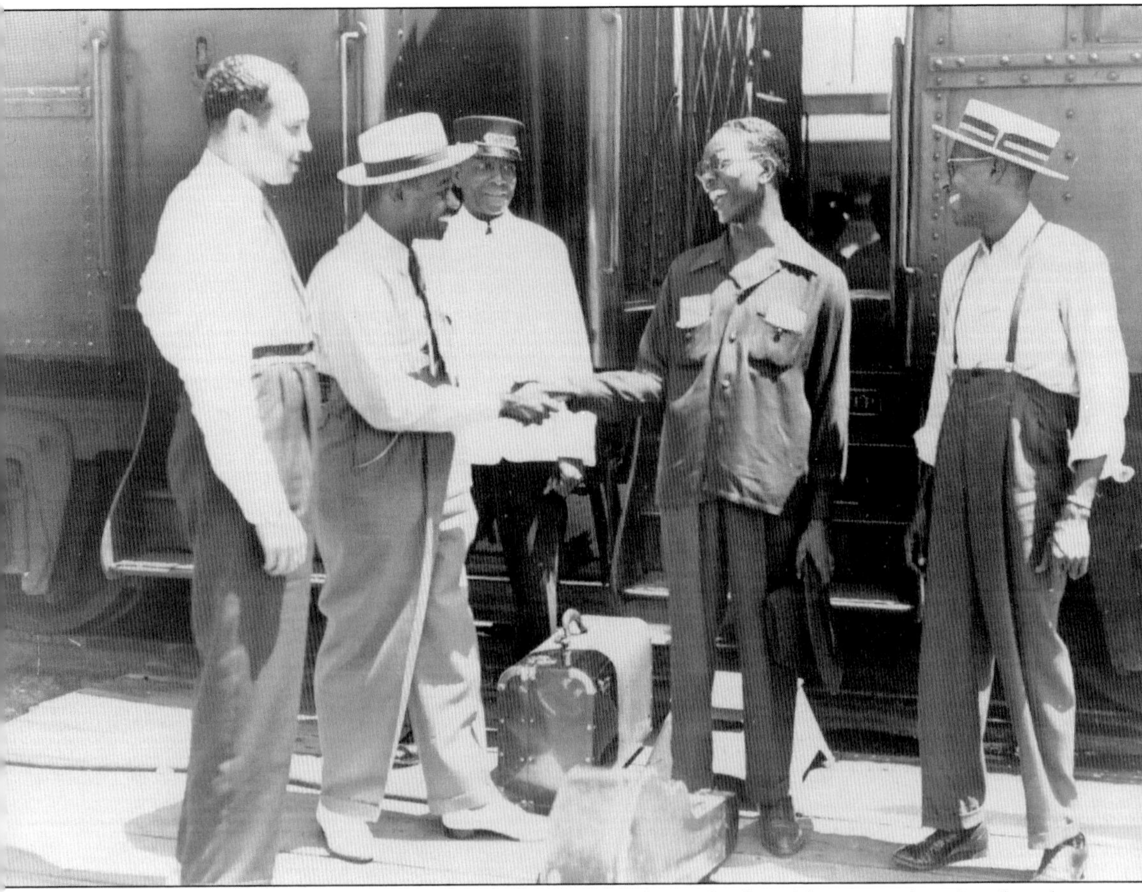

Zelia Breaux's Douglass High School student Charles "Charlie" Christian played in bands in Oklahoma City and toured through states as far as the Dakotas, earning a reputation for his unusual, powerful playing on the electric guitar. He and his musical family were well known in Oklahoma City. Soon word reached Benny Goodman about his talent. Goodman's brother-in-law John Hammond flew from New York to Oklahoma City to hear Christian play. Hammond promised Christian he would send a train ticket for him to join Hammond and Goodman in Beverly Hills. On August 14, 1939, the 23-year-old Christian is seen with his friends at the Oklahoma City train station as he heads to California. From left to right, trumpeter Henry Butler looks on as trumpeter James Simpson gives Christian a farewell handshake. Older brother Edward (right) and a train porter look on. (Courtesy of the Black Liberated Arts Center Inc.)

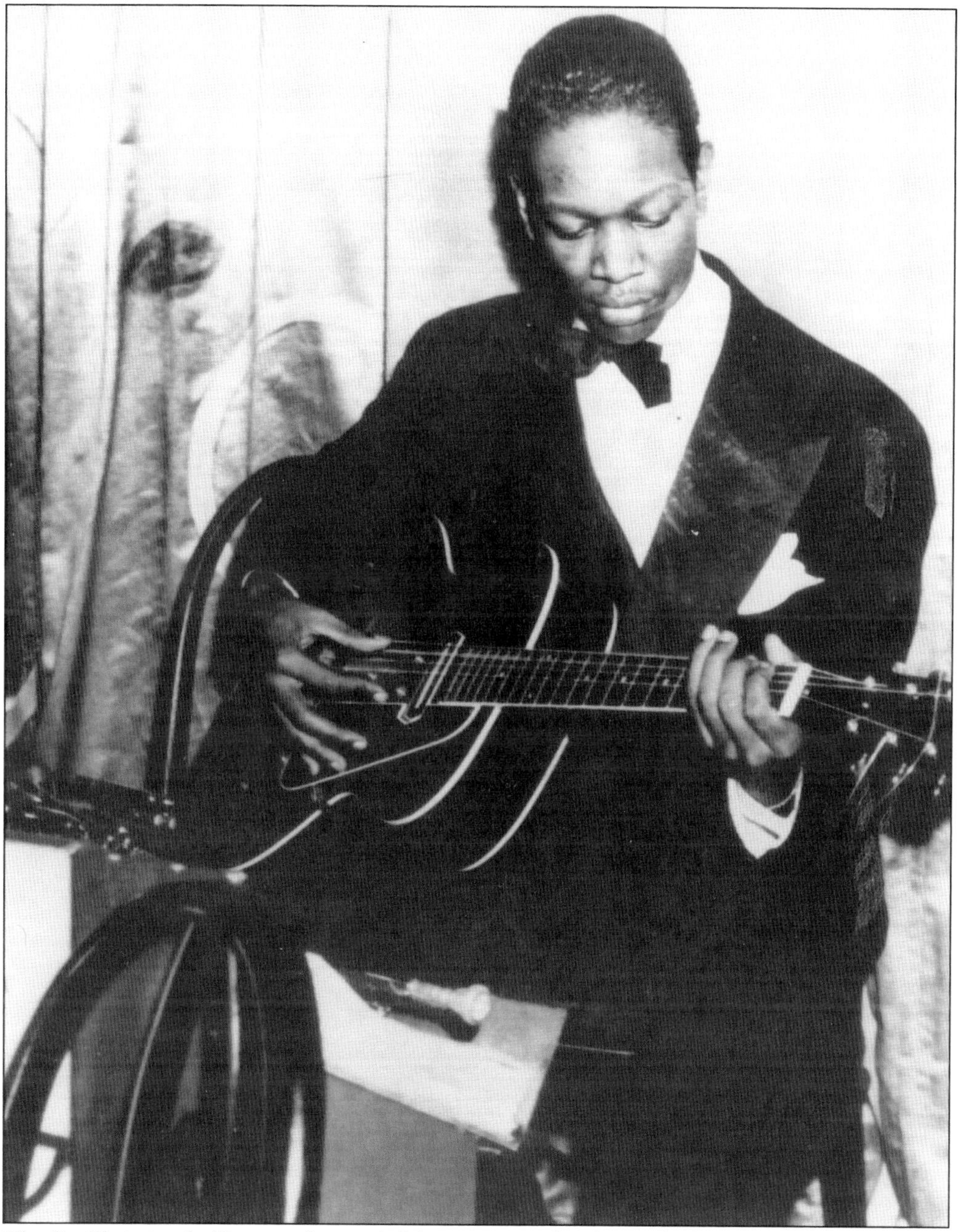

Charlie Christian holds one of several Gibson guitars that he made famous. He was often seen with the ES-150 and ES-250. Other times, he played the Gibson L7. The stylish young man would often appear in advertisements promoting Gibson guitars and Adams hats. Christian was the talk of the guitar world, winning jazz polls from international critics in the short two and a half years he toured with Benny Goodman. In a rare letter, he wrote to his guitarist friends encouraging them to amplify their guitars and to keep playing good guitar music, with a promise that others would soon notice, acknowledge them, and pay them "well for the music that would feed their stomachs and hearts." Christian is known as the "Father of Bebop" and the father of the single-string solo on the electric guitar. (Courtesy of the Black Liberated Arts Center Inc.)

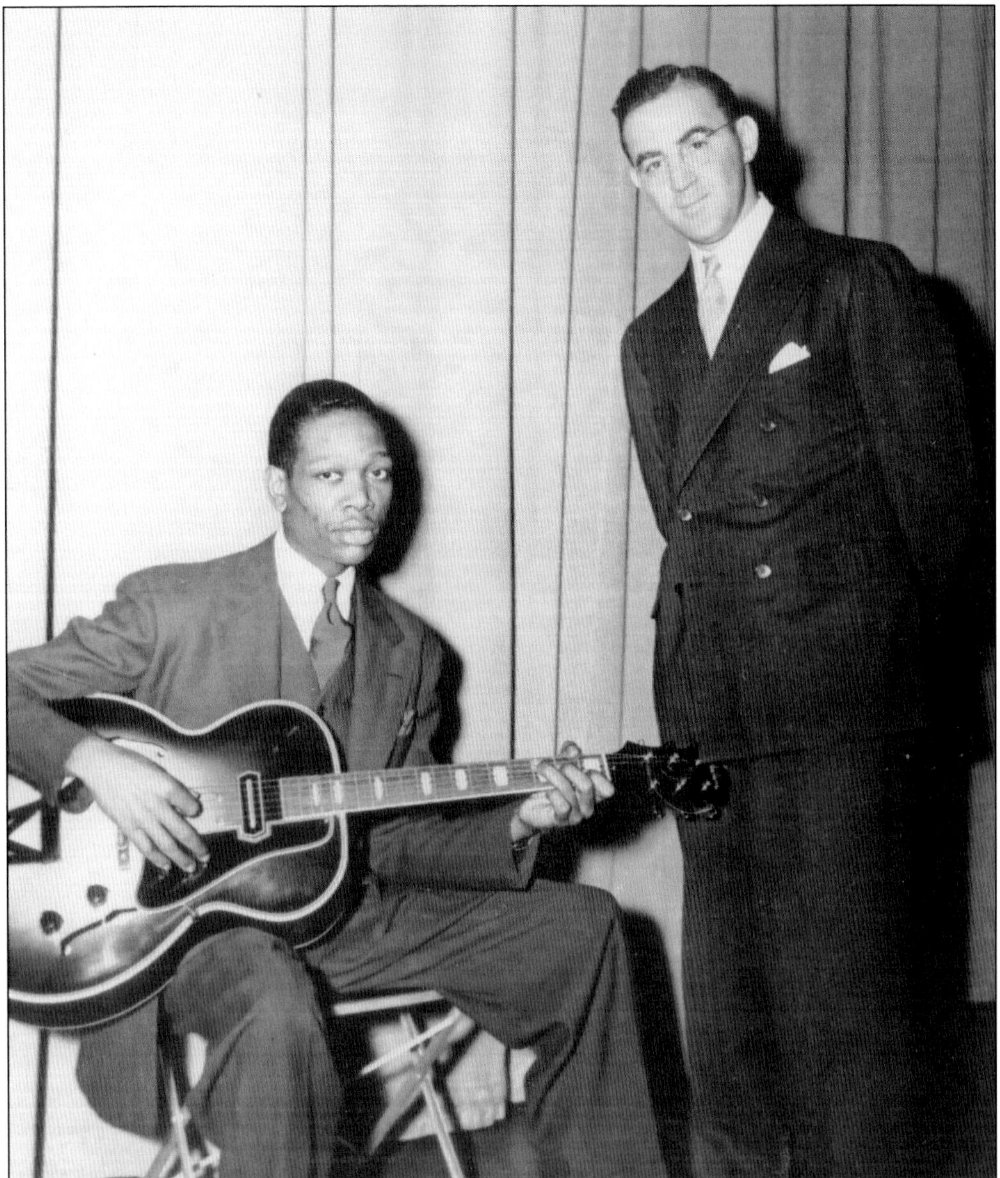

Charlie Christian almost lost his place in history when he showed up at Victor Hugo's Supper Club in Beverly Hills, California, for a rehearsal with Benny Goodman's band. Unimpressed with the young man from Oklahoma wearing his best outfit and cowboy boots, Benny Goodman let his brother-in-law John Hammond know that Christian could not play with his band. Additionally, Goodman was concerned about what his patrons would think, as Count Basie and Lionel Hampton were already band members and three black people might not sit well with them. Goodman played the first half of the show without Christian. Hammond knew Goodman always took a dinner break and visited with his patrons. During dinner, Hammond sneaked Christian onto the band stand. Returning, Goodman was annoyed to see Christian there and decided to eliminate him by putting him on the spot as he called "Rose Room" for the next number. Christian knew that song well. Patrons took to the dance floor and gave Christian 45 minutes of encores. Charlie Christian was on his way. (Courtesy of the Black Liberated Arts Center Inc.)

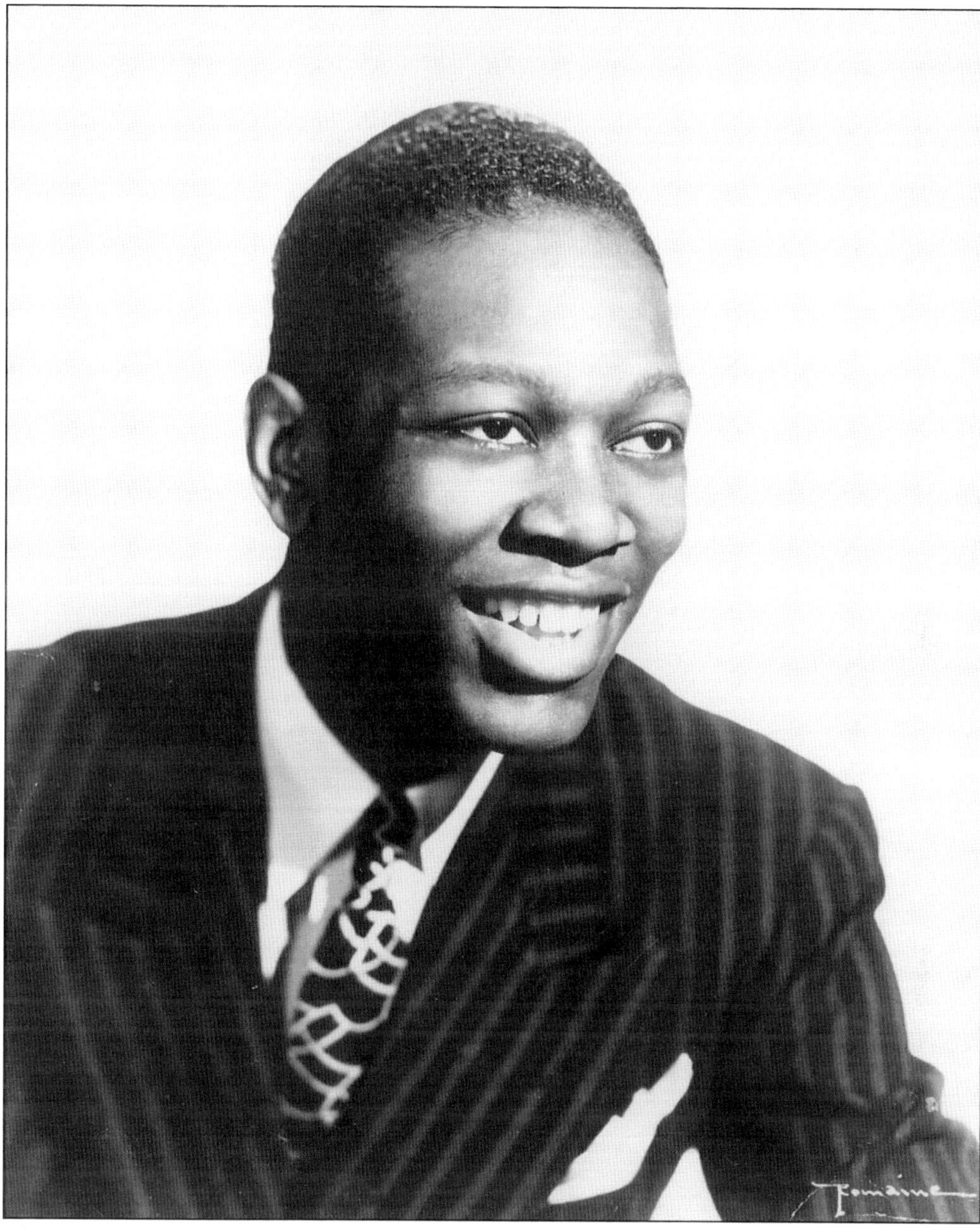

Charlie Christian died at 25 from tuberculosis at Seaview Hospital in New York City. Though he had only been on the national scene for a short time, he crammed his schedule full of musical engagements from coast to coast, playing with all the greats of the time. Christian played night and day in places like Minton's Bar and Grill following performances with Goodman on Broadway in the musical *Swinging the Dream*. He recorded at Columbia Studios and did radio shows. Christian also practiced with Goodman before hitting the road to perform the next gig. He collapsed on stage in Toledo, Ohio, and never returned. To this day, people from other countries journey to Bonham, Texas, to lay a wreath on his grave out of respect for him. (Courtesy of the Black Liberated Arts Center Inc.)

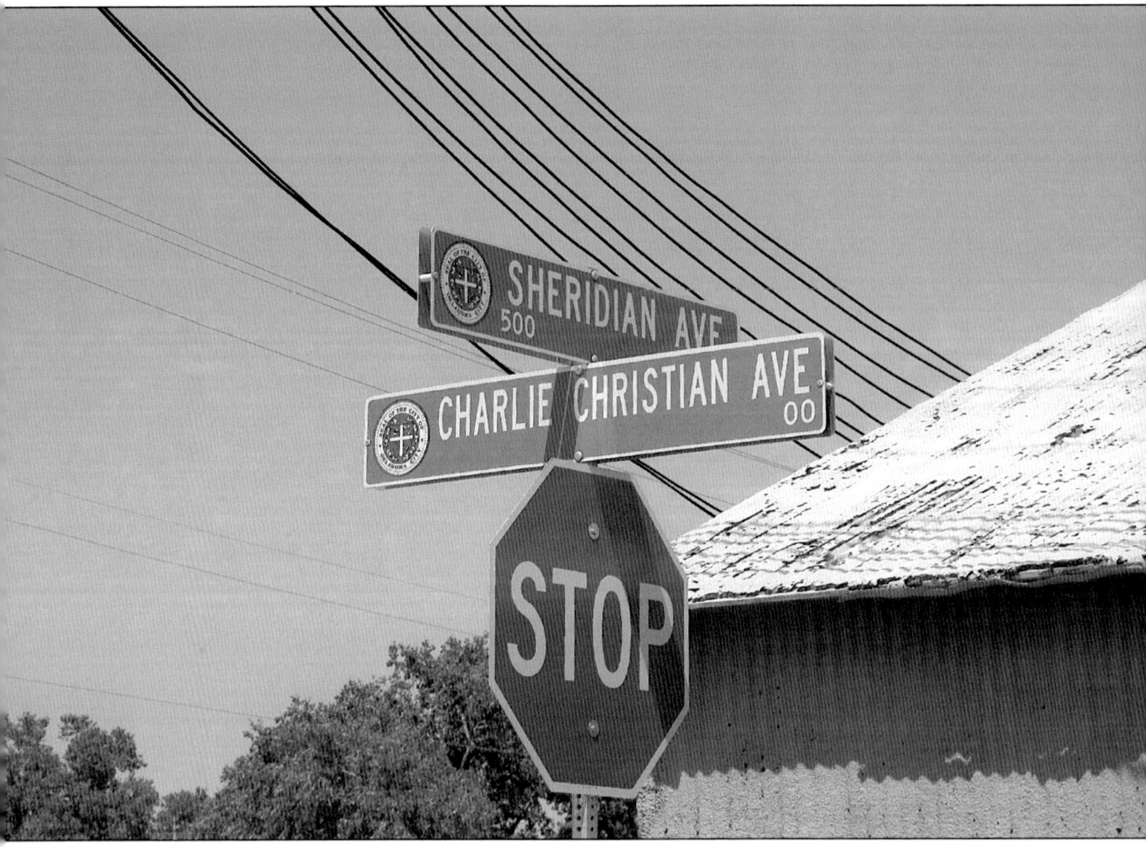

Charlie Christian Avenue, located near "Deep Deuce" in Oklahoma City, commemorates the international icon's legacy. Christian has been inducted into every major music hall of fame around the world; he is a member of the Oklahoma Hall of Fame and Ertegun Jazz Hall of Fame in New York City, among others. College courses and workshops continue to teach his music. Festivals, parades, and other events celebrate him. Seventy-five years after his death, feature articles about him and his music continue to appear on newsstands and websites in many countries. (Photograph by Levi McCullogh, courtesy of the Black Liberated Arts Center Inc.)

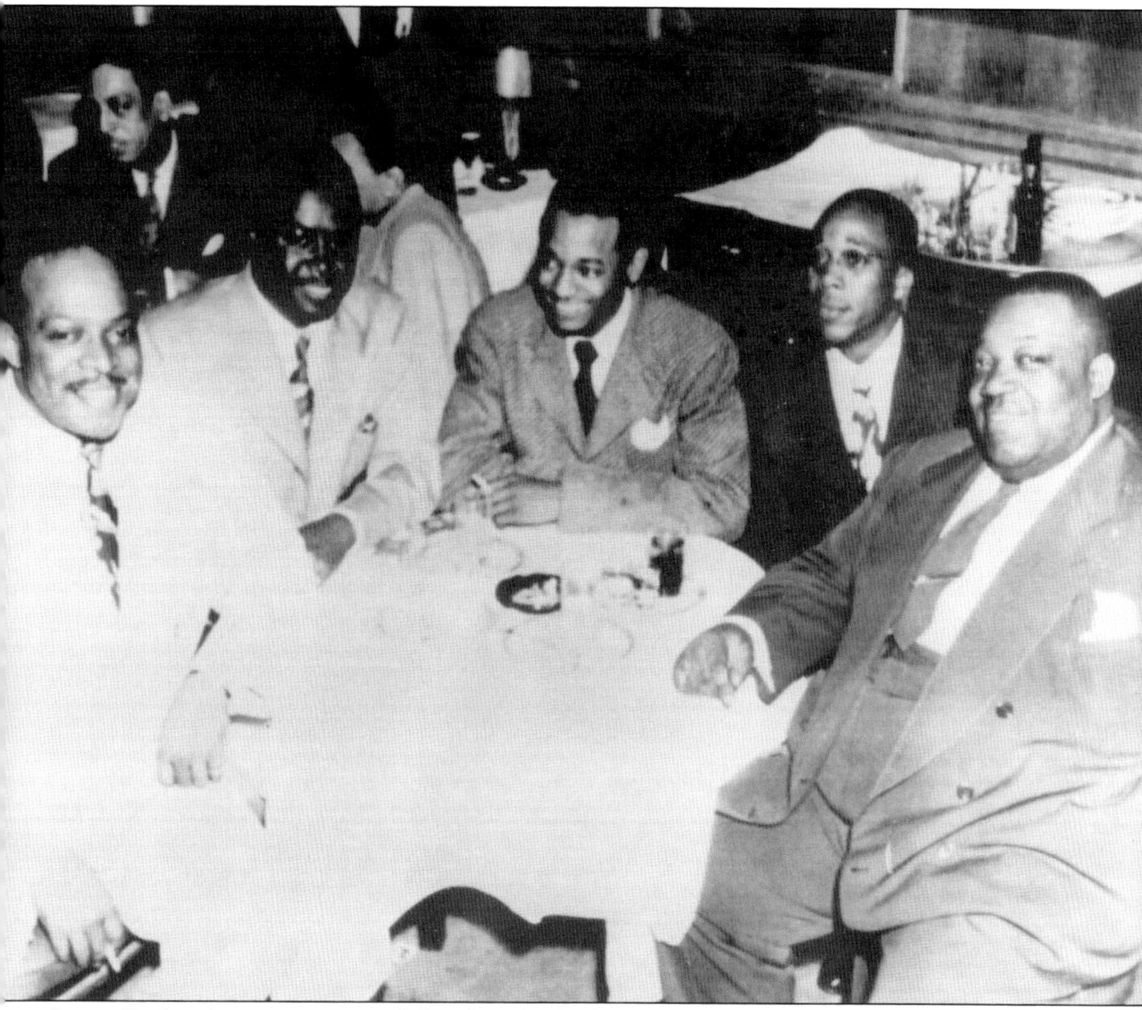

Jimmy Rushing's uniqueness was defined on the back cover of his recording *The Jazz Odyssey of James Rushing ESQ.* Irving Townsend, the writer of the cover, wrote, "He has been a part of jazz in the four cities having most to do with the development: New Orleans, Kansas City, Chicago and New York." Rushing was best known for the song "Mister Five By Five," written by Don Raye as a tribute to him. The song, also his nickname, describes him as being a short, rotund man. Best known for "I'm Going to Chicago" and "Good Morning Blues," he became known as the "Greatest Blues Shouter" in the world. The US Postal Service issued a Jimmy Rushing postage stamp in 1994. He died of leukemia on June 8, 1972. On one of his rare visits back home, the Douglass High School graduate is seen at far right with Charlie Christian to his left. (Courtesy of the Black Liberated Arts Center Inc.)

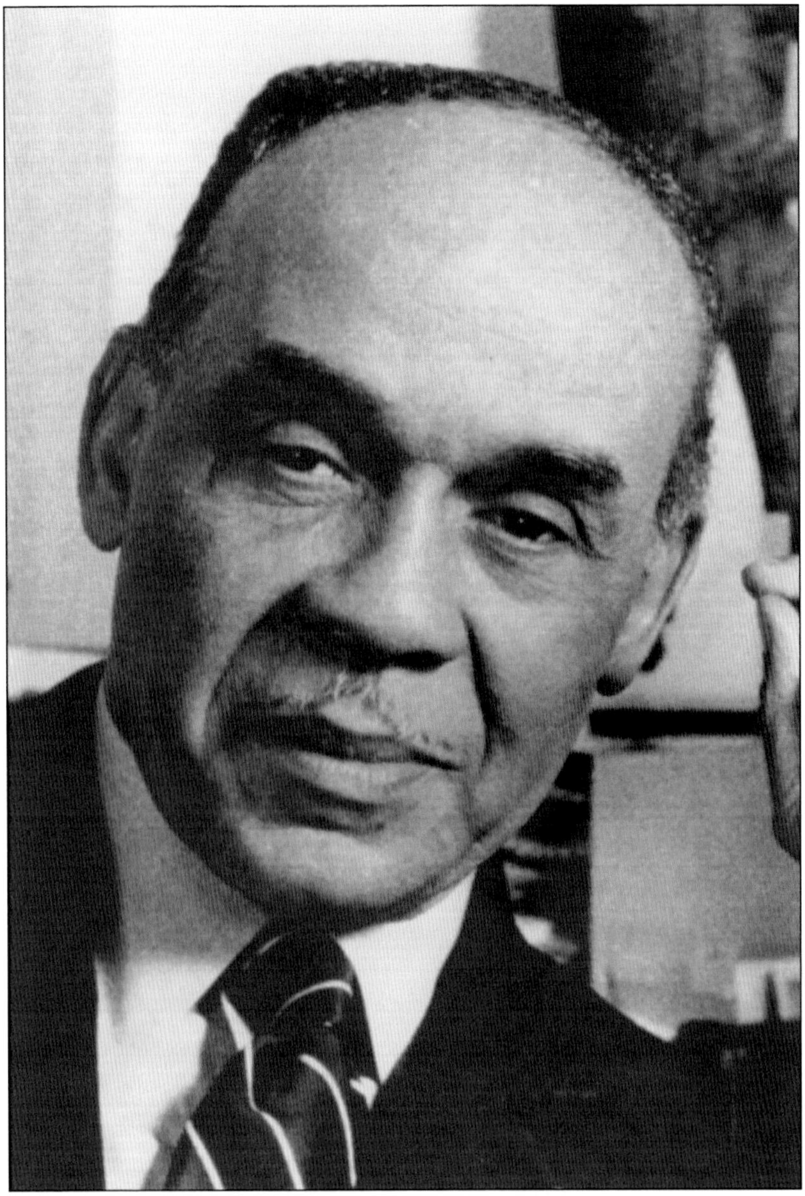

A critic at the *New Leader* said of Ralph Waldo Ellison, "His mind is unfailingly interesting." Zelia N. Page Breaux, Ellison's music teacher at Douglass High School, probably agreed. She made Ellison a captain in her band and encouraged him to pursue music further. As Ellison made his way to Tuskegee College in Alabama armed with a music scholarship and the clothes on his back, he was determined to become an orchestra conductor. Hitchhiking his way from Oklahoma City to Tuskegee, he arrived and enrolled in college. He soon discovered an interest in literature while working in the library. Ellison made several trips to New York City to help pay college expenses, and while there met famous African American writers who persuaded him to write articles for local papers. His interest was further piqued when he and his brother Herbert suddenly found themselves homeless after his mother's death. To overcome the depression of his mother's death, he was encouraged by a local attorney to start writing again. (Courtesy of Oklahoma Hall of Fame.)

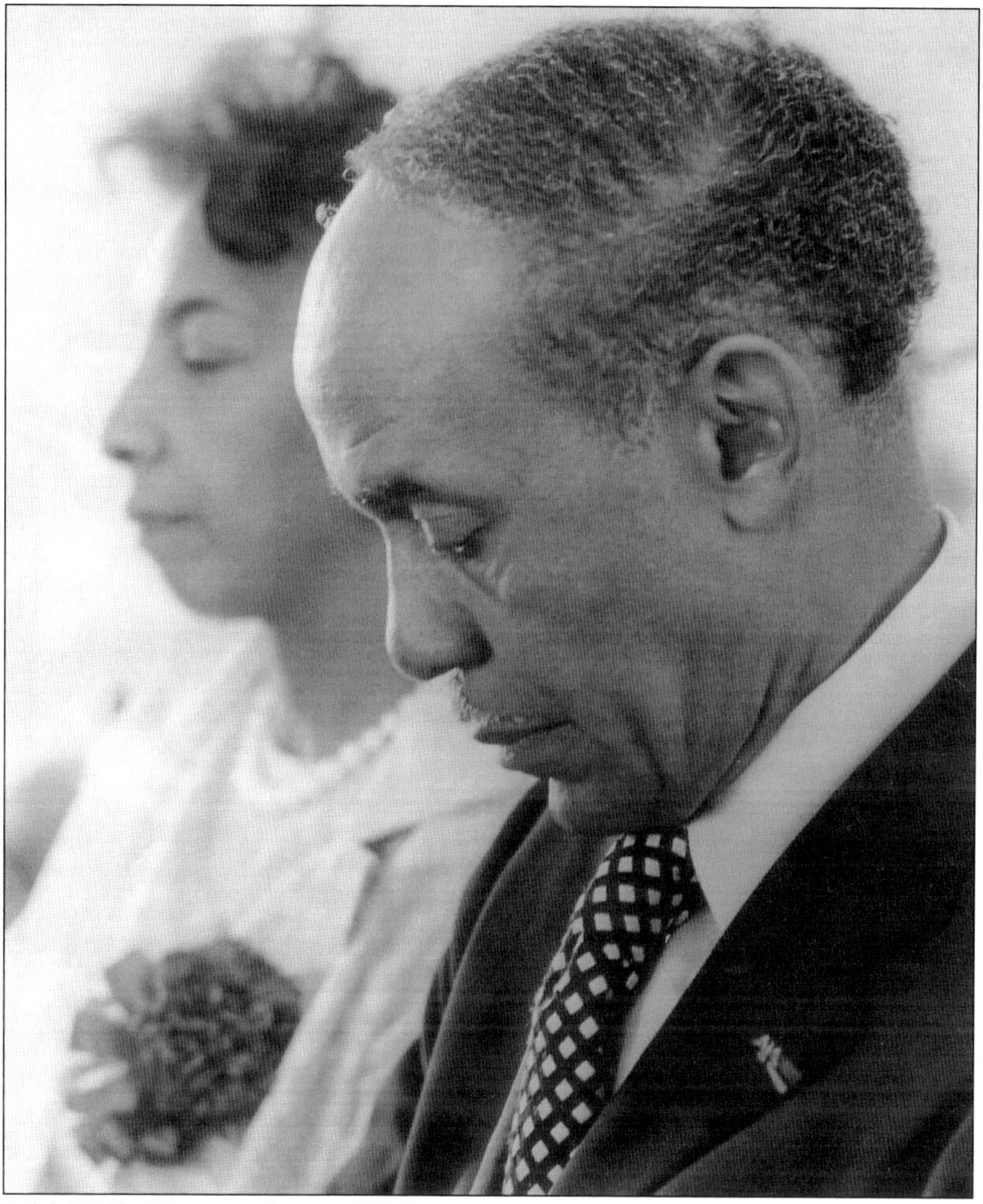

Ralph Waldo Ellison was born in Oklahoma City in 1913 or 1914. The youngster was with his father when a block of ice fell on him, puncturing his stomach and causing him to bleed to death. Ellison's mother was left to raise her two sons alone. Often she would bring home magazines from work, which she gave to Ellison. He often went to church with her and noted that she really loved church music but also loved jazz. When he began to write his first novel, *Invisible Man*, he relied on the discipline and rhythm of the music he learned. Among his favorite authors were Emerson and Dostoyevsky. *Invisible Man* won the National Book Award in 1953, and Ellison was an acclaimed author of the 20th century. Ellison was an author, literary critic, and educator, though he never finished college. He died on April 16, 1994. He is shown here with Oklahoma secretary of state Hannah Atkins during his induction into the Oklahoma Hall of Fame. (Courtesy of Oklahoma Hall of Fame.)

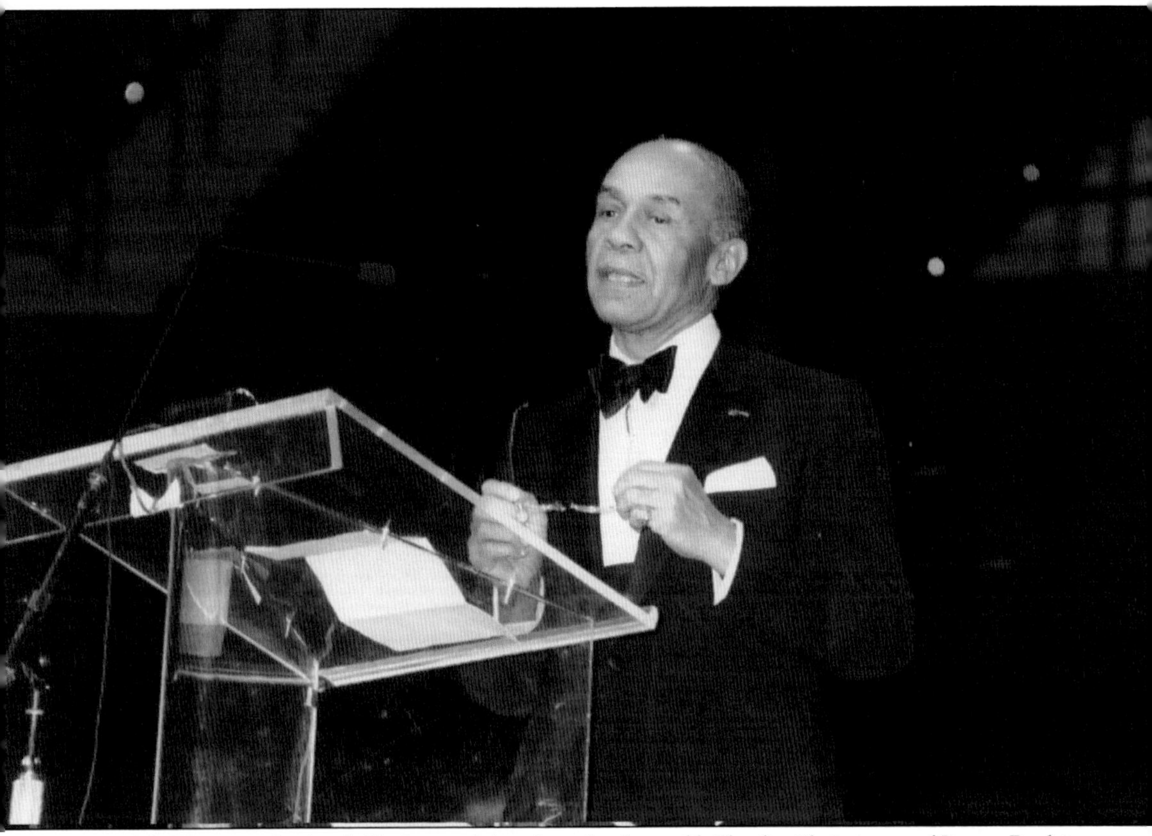

Ralph Ellison, in his book *Shadow and Act*, describes himself, Charlie Christian, and Jimmy Rushing as "Renaissance Men" whose identities were rooted in culture and intellectualism. In this book, Ellison wrote about his Oklahoma City friends, family, classmates, and others. He described how jazz music affected the lives of African Americans in and around Deep Deuce. There is a sense of the classical music that Zelia N. Page Breaux taught in the life of Charlie Christian, for instance. Christian, his father, and his brothers played light classics as they strolled through neighborhoods in the white community to supplement the family income. Jazz and blues were considered low-class forms of expression, according to Ellison. In defining Oklahoma music, he described a duality in the music experience—classical, which was "correct," and the rest as eclectic, unconscious, and "jazzy." When author Anita Arnold of Oklahoma asked Ralph Ellison for permission to use *Invisible Man* in her early writings of Charlie Christian, he referred her to *Shadow and Act* as the appropriate book to use. Here, Ellison makes his acceptance speech during his induction into the Oklahoma Hall of Fame. (Courtesy of the Oklahoma Hall of Fame.)

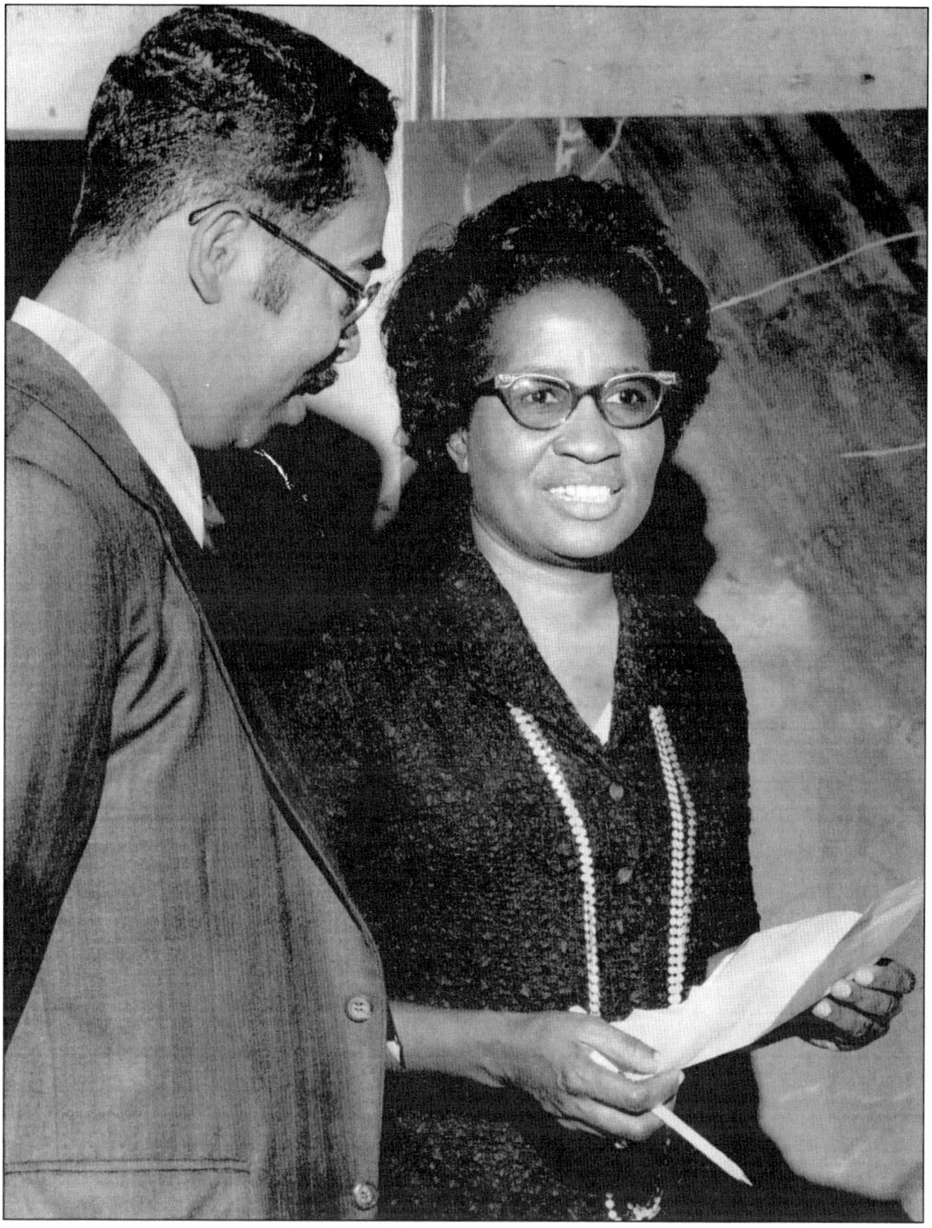

Clara Mae Shephard was born May 3, 1923, in rural Okfuskee County, Oklahoma. Her parents, Ezell and Isabell Shephard, would never have imagined that she would begin a career as a teacher at Douglass High School or run for president of the United States. She did. Her father kept telling her that one day there would be no segregation, and she would experience freedom to go anywhere she pleased. They could not imagine that their daughter would become renowned, nationally, as a civil rights leader, one who would be in the history books of America with scholarships, memorials, and other celebrations in her honor. Clara received her bachelor of arts in mathematics from Langston University in 1944. By 1950, she was a teacher in the Department of Natural Sciences and Mathematics, headed up by Wyatt F. Jeltz, with F.D. Moon as her principal. She is pictured with Sen. E. Melvin Porter during one of her civil rights events. (Courtesy of the Oklahoma Historical Society.)

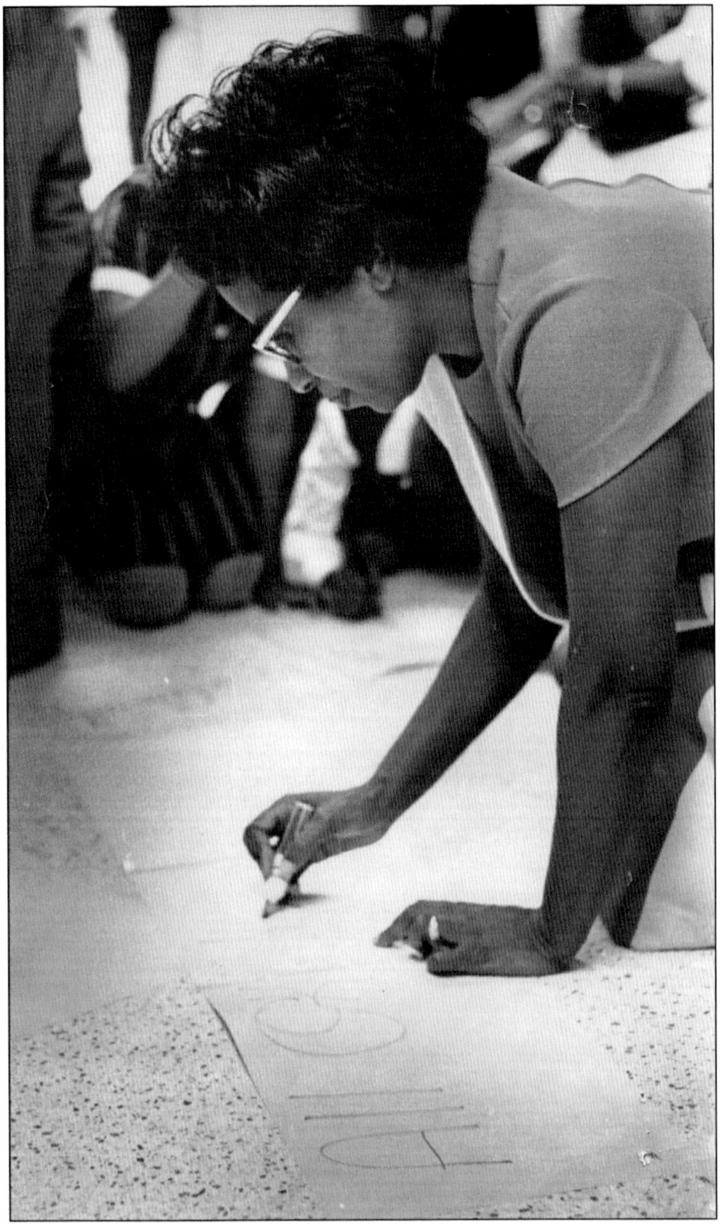

In 1957, Clara Luper was a history teacher at Dunjee High School when she became advisor to the Oklahoma City NAACP Youth Council. By this time, Martin Luther King Jr. had begun his civil rights work in America. Moved by his work, she wrote and staged a play, *Brother President*, that garnered an invitation from the New York City chapter of the NAACP to bring the play to New York. After experiencing the freedom to eat in restaurants and enter other places in New York, the group faced Southern hostility as they made their way back home. Luper decided then to do everything she could to destroy segregation in Oklahoma. At a youth council meeting, young people asked how they could get involved to correct the wrongness of segregation. A plan was made to go to Katz Drug Store with no less than six people and sit at the counter, placing an order for a hamburger and Coke, a favorite meal of Americans. She led the students, with a few adults accompanying them. (Courtesy of the Oklahoma Historical Society.)

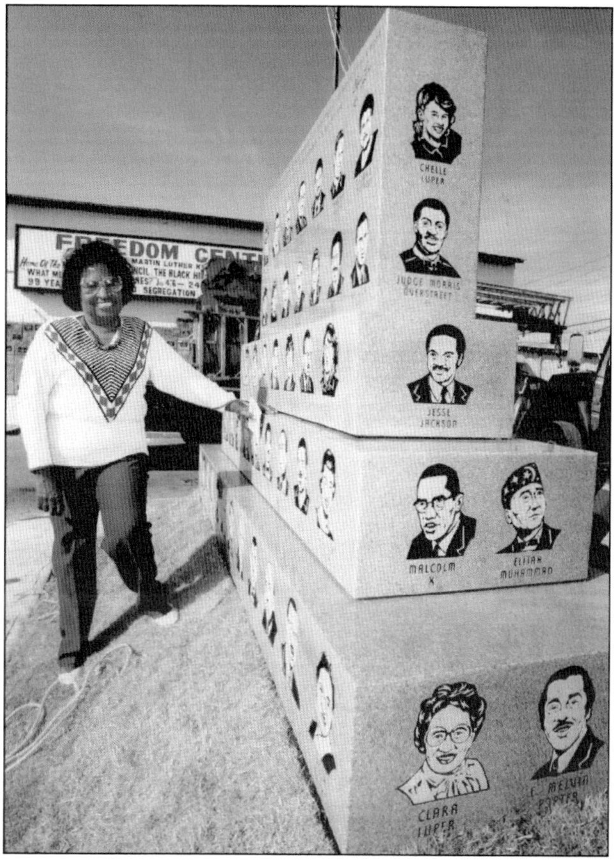

Clara Luper's civil rights movement in Oklahoma City lasted from 1958 until 1964 and led to the integration of restaurants, banks, corporations, theaters, hotels, and churches. Being sensitive to the wishes, needs, and desires of her young participants, Luper told them to bring school work and to read during the sit-ins. When Roger Countee told her he wanted to become a doctor, she advised him to "memorize all the bones, the vessels, the veins and the arteries in the body." Countee did and became one of the top brain surgeons in America. Luper created a monument that sits in front of her Freedom Center as a memorial to those who participated. A portion of the monument shows Countee, located between Martin L. King Jr. and Supreme Court justice Thurgood Marshall. (Right, courtesy of Jane Countee and Oklahoma Historical Society; below, courtesy of Levi McCullough.)

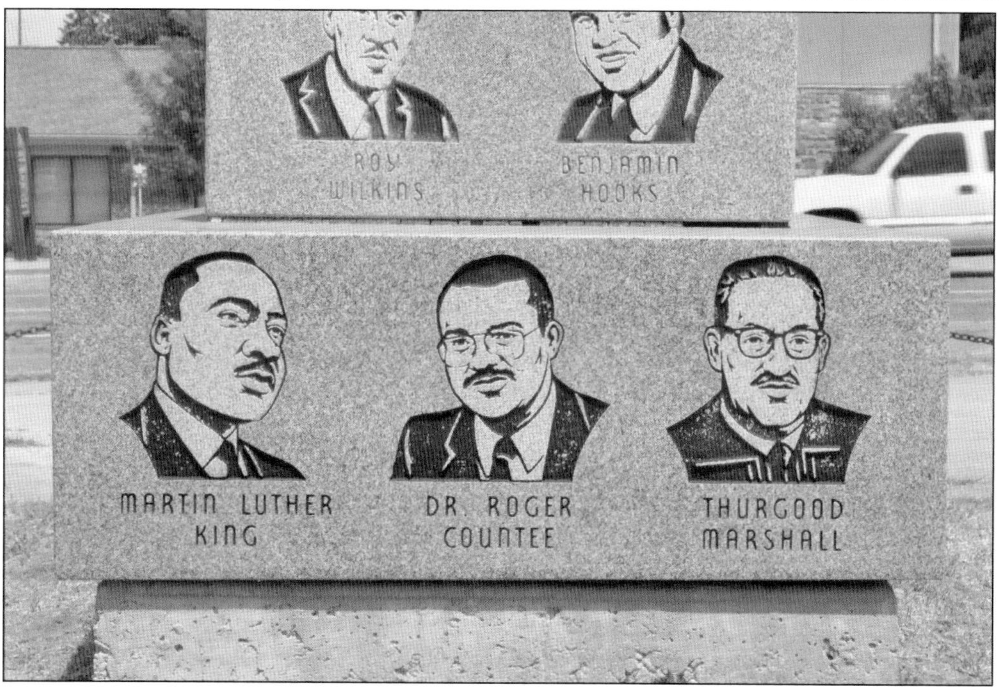

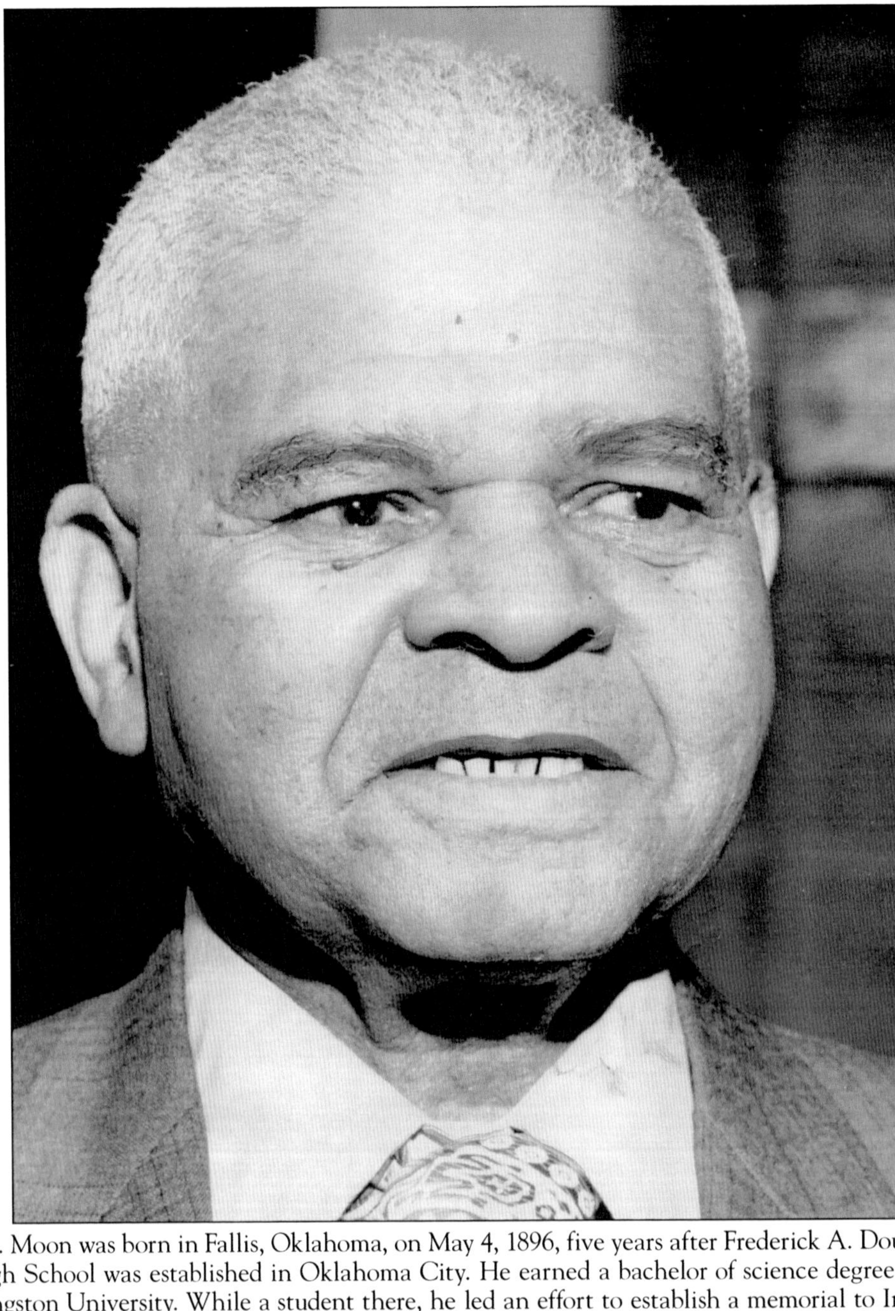

F.D. Moon was born in Fallis, Oklahoma, on May 4, 1896, five years after Frederick A. Douglass High School was established in Oklahoma City. He earned a bachelor of science degree from Langston University. While a student there, he led an effort to establish a memorial to Inman Page, Langston's first president. Moon earned a master's degree from the University of Chicago in 1938 after traveling to the university during summers. He later encouraged all teachers under his leadership who did not have advanced degrees to follow his example in completing a master's degree. He began his teaching career in 1921 and gained accreditation for his school, growing it from a junior high school to a high school. He became president of the Oklahoma Association of Negro Teachers in 1931. As principal at Wewoka's Douglass High School, he gained accreditation for that school. In 1940, Moon became principal of Frederick A. Douglass High School in Oklahoma City. (Courtesy of the Oklahoma Historical Society.)

Four

The Model is the Dream

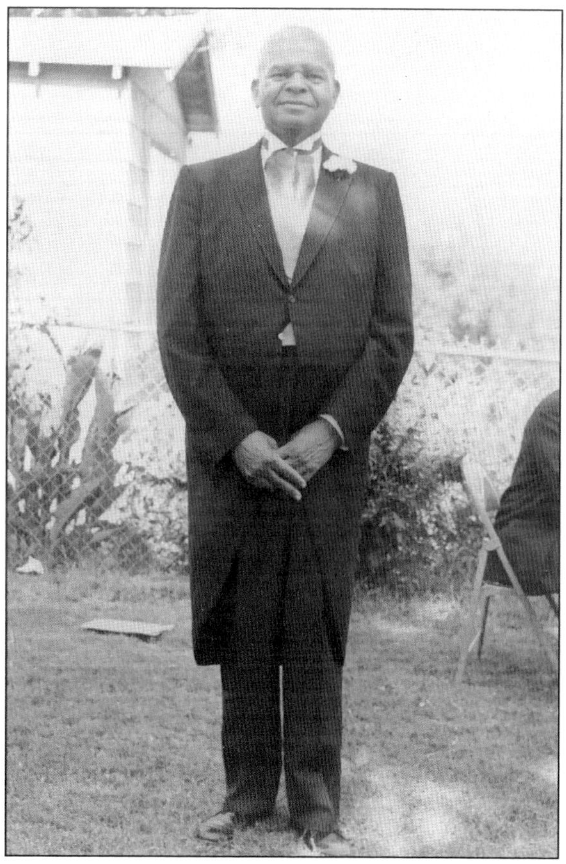

The "dreamer" was Frederick Douglass Moon, principal of Douglass High School when his dream became reality. Moon had dreamed of the day when he could move his students into a more spacious, modern facility. He had pursued a model of education that embraced each student and served their needs. This photograph captures his mood. (Courtesy of Deola Harris.)

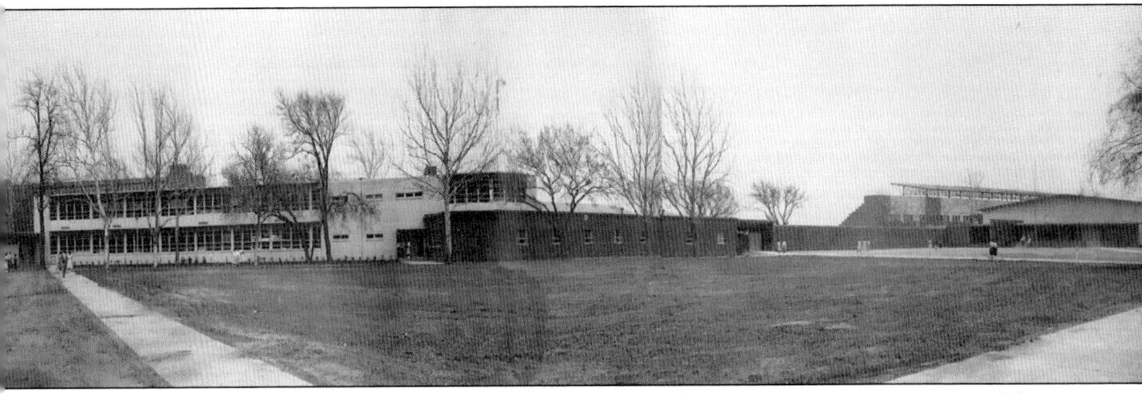

On May 1, 1955, the model became a reality for the African American community. The new Frederick A. Douglass High School, at 900 North Eastern Avenue, sat on about 40 acres of land formerly Oklahoma's state fairgrounds. After the successful passage of three bond elections, from 1945 until 1953, and with support and effort from the Citizens' Action Committee, the Interdenominational Ministerial Alliance, and the Negro Chamber of Commerce, the land was purchased and construction began. According to the dedication program, the school was built at a cost of $2,769,365.46. The beautiful, modern, and functional plant was meant for both high school and community use. A history of the school lists eight principals prior to F.D. Moon becoming principal in 1940: Jefferson Davis Randolph, J.W. Sharpe, G.F. Porter, J.H.A. Brazelton, T.R. Debnam, Dr. S.R. Youngblood, Dr. Inman Page, and C.O. Rogers. (Courtesy of Edwina Littlepage, from the Joe Littlepage Collection.)

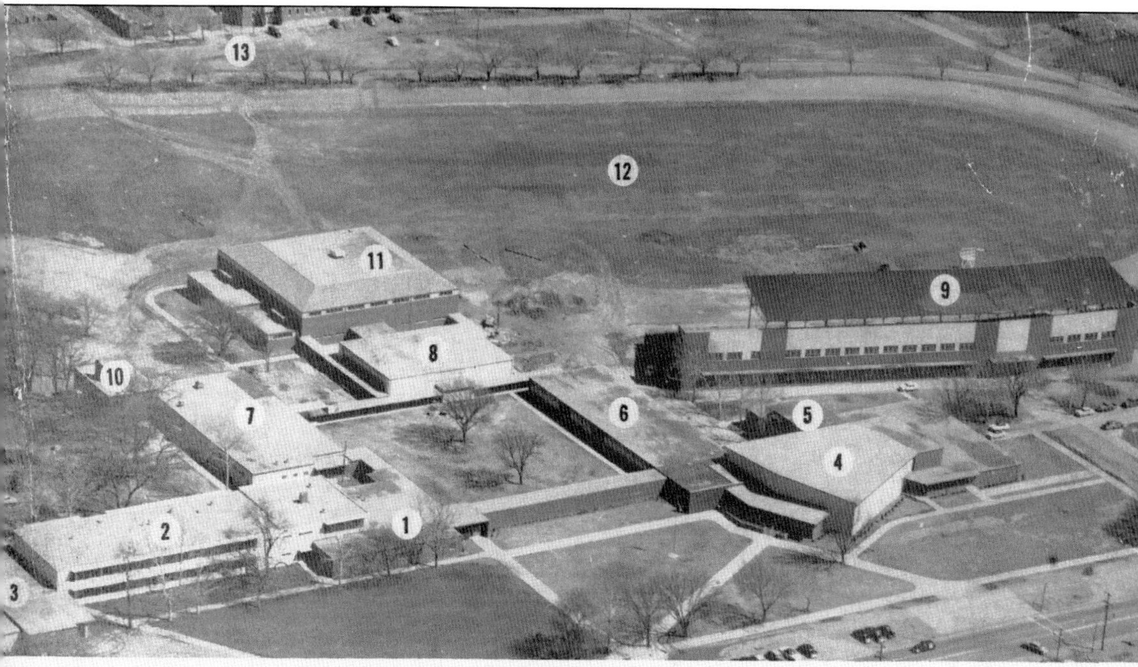

Aerial View of Douglass High School

1. Administration Office
2. Classrooms
3. Library
4. Auditorium
5. Little Theatre
6. Home Economics
7. Cafeteria
8. Swimming Pool
9. Stadium
10. Heating Plant
11. Gymnasium
12. Athletic Field
13. Vocational Building

N.L. George, of Oklahoma City Public Schools, wrote an objective of the new plant: "[It] is based on the educational needs of the youth and adults who use the plant. . . . It is a safe shelter . . . spaces are provided for tools of instruction for the community . . . a creative environment technologically controlled . . . and is the pride of the community as a symbol of the power of public education." Frederick Moon stated his objectives: "We make provisions for the academic and vocational needs of youth in the same institution. We offer . . . math courses to qualify students for entering schools of engineering. We meet modern language and science requirements . . . in the art of public speaking we are almost nationally known . . . In the field of music and other fundamental fields, students needs are met . . . English, . . . Negro History." (Courtesy of Edwina Littlepage, from the Joe Littlepage Collection.)

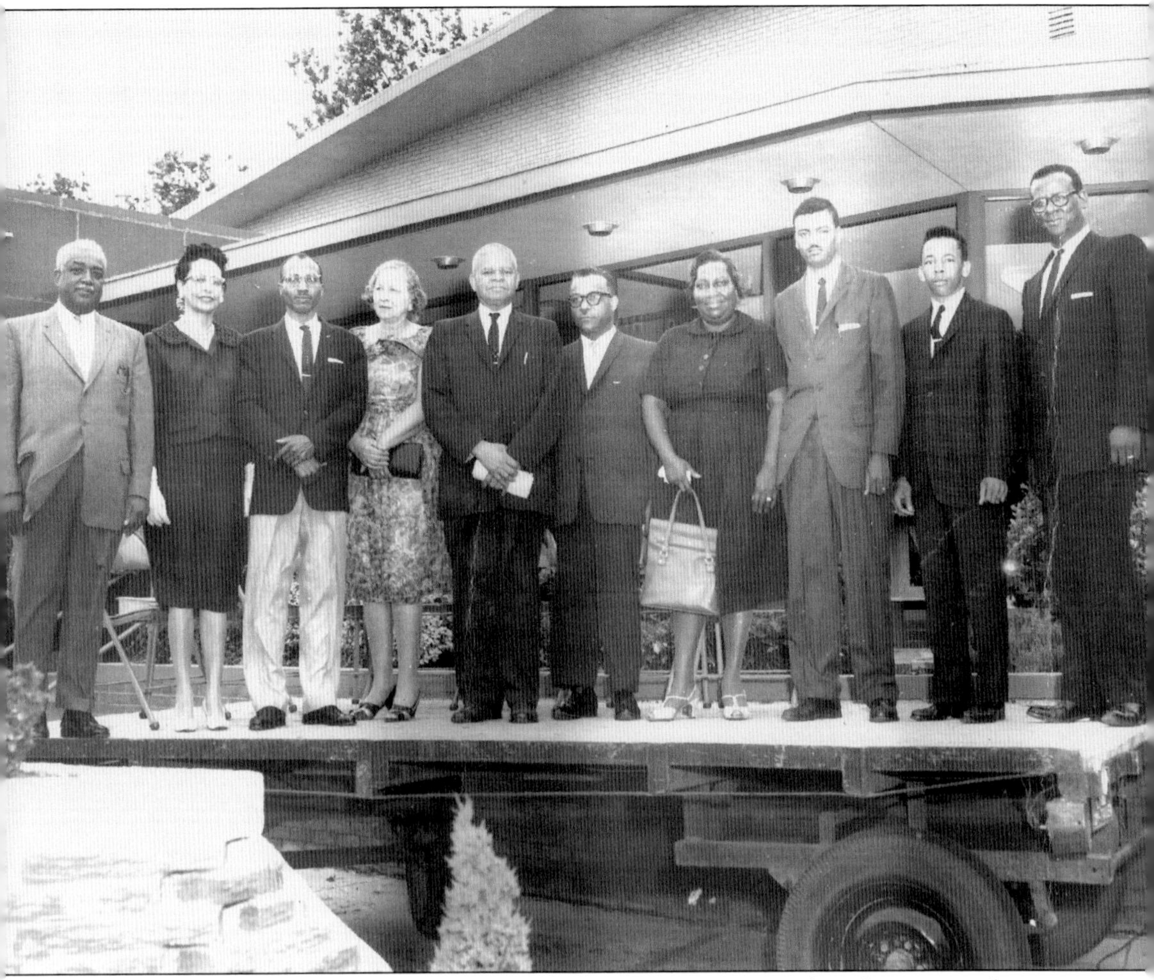

As the new building was being dedicated, photographers were recording the event with pictures to be used in the media, yearbooks, and in the archives of Frederick A. Douglass High School. Taking in all of the festivities from a prime spot atop a flatbed in front of the new 1,300-seat auditorium is a group of individuals who were part of the support system that helped make the dream come true. From left to right are Bert V. Watkins (elementary school principal), Geneva Johnson (longtime secretary to F.D. Moon), H.H. Sharp (driver's education instructor), T. Odessa Temple (geometry and trigonometry teacher), F.D. Moon (principal), Rev. W.K. Jackson (pastor of St. John Missionary Baptist Church), Margaret Dabney (art instructor), Leonardo DeBose (1955 Douglass High School graduate), Joe Littlepage (1959 Douglass High School graduate), and Maurice Benefee (upholstery instructor). Two thousand people attended the dedication. (Courtesy of John Temple.)

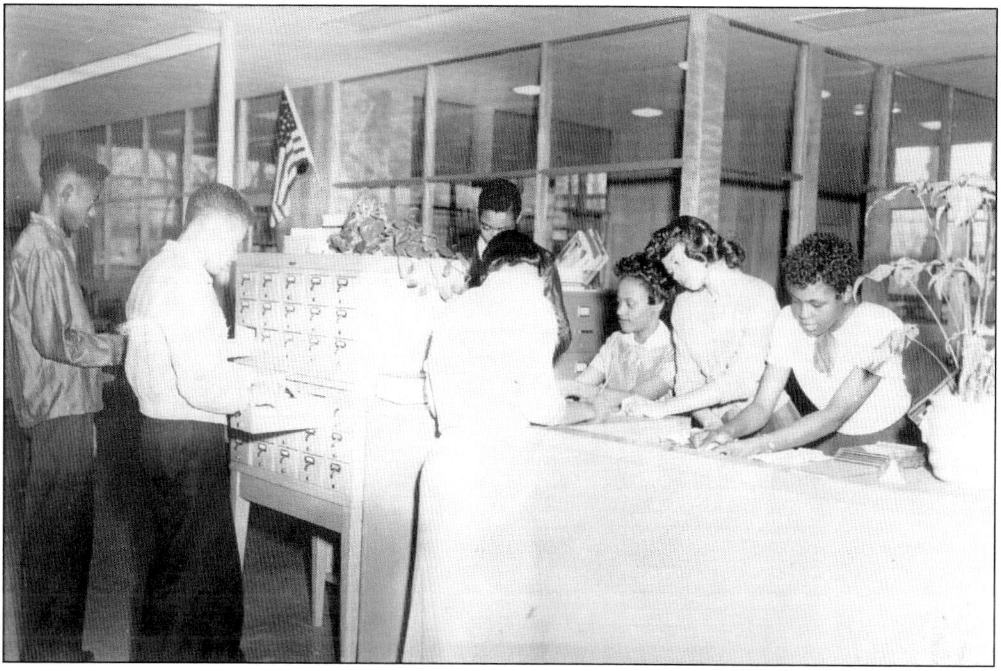

Above, a group of students is learning to use the new state-of-the-art library in 1959. Students used the library for research in developing essays, for history and science projects, and for other special assignments. Among the 12,000 varied books in the library was the F.D. Moon Memorial Book Collection. It was considered the materials center for providing books, pamphlets, pictures, films, filmstrips, and other materials. Students also had opportunities to work in the library after school under the tutelage of the librarian. The Library Club was formed to promote friendship, create interest in librarianship as a career, and stimulate the exchange of ideas. Below, F.D. Moon is shown on stage at Douglass High School as he hosts guests from the Oklahoma Library System, whose purpose was to encourage students to read and celebrate National Library Week. (Both, courtesy of Brenda Seward Johnson, from the Walter Seward Collection.)

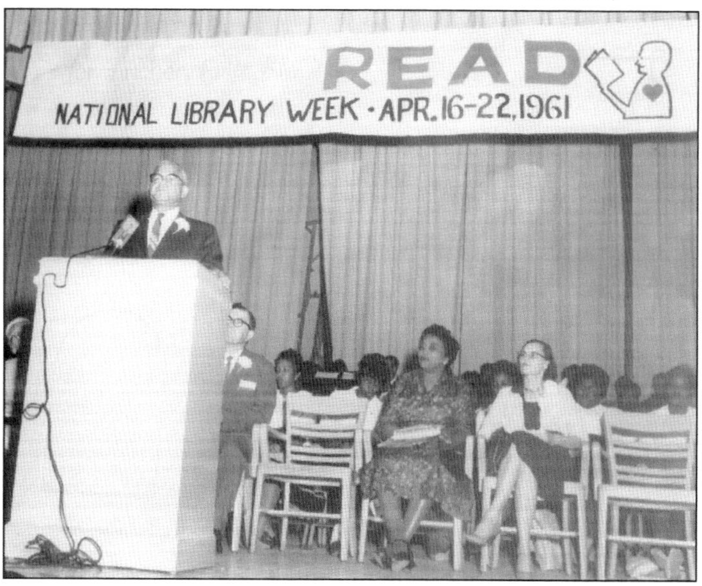

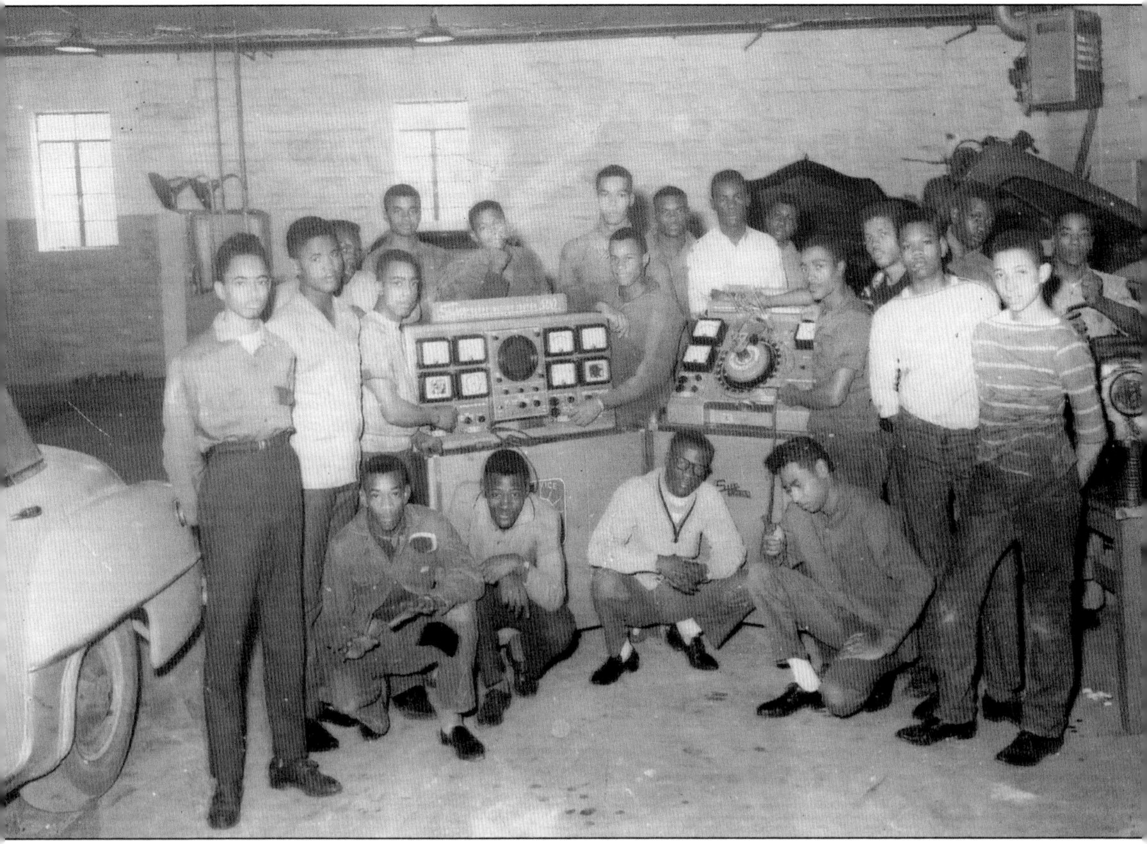

Douglass High School had an auto mechanics class as far back as 1950 in the Department of Industrial Arts. The department's purpose was to prepare students to fit into the economic pattern of American life. By 1961, each trade within the department had its own goal. Auto mechanics had the goal of providing students valuable experience and training in the successful operation and upkeep of automobiles. Also, students who demonstrated knowledge and skill in the basic fundamentals of auto mechanics were permitted to receive additional training by actually repairing community cars and their own cars. Trade and industrial awards during the Southwestern Exposition of Science and Industries at Oklahoma City's fairgrounds in 1956 were given to 36 students in auto mechanics, cosmetology, brick masonry, drafting, printing, and upholstery. Of the 36 awards, three were superior ratings, seven were excellent, and the rest were good. (Courtesy of Brenda Seward Johnson, from the Walter Seward Collection.)

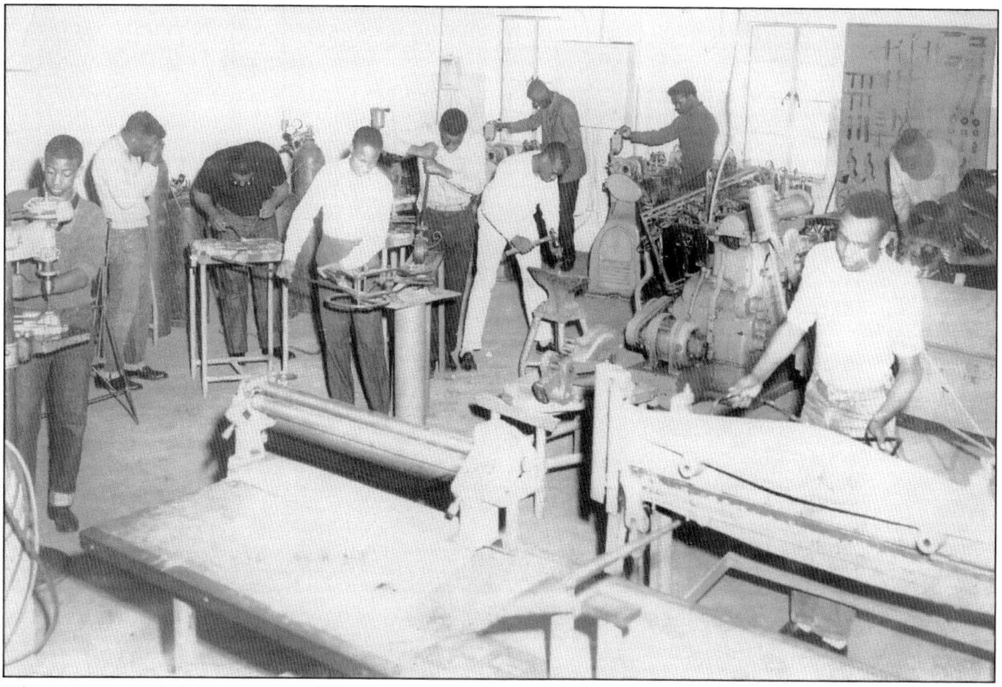

The purpose of the general welding class, taught by Walter E. Seward, was to provide interested students with adequate training and knowledge necessary to become successful business operators or employees in this field. Seward, like other teachers who taught more than one course in the Douglass curriculum, also taught photography. Members of the welding class, as other classes at Douglass, often used their skills and talents to benefit the school. This class made beautiful decorative house number signs for students, faculty, and the community. Funds raised by this project and other projects in the department were given as a gift to Douglass High School. (Both, courtesy of Brenda Seward Johnson, from the Walter Seward Collection.)

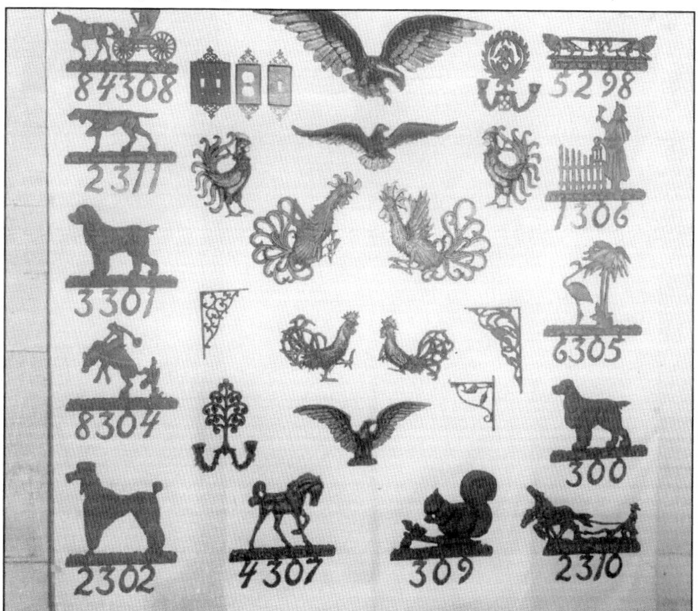

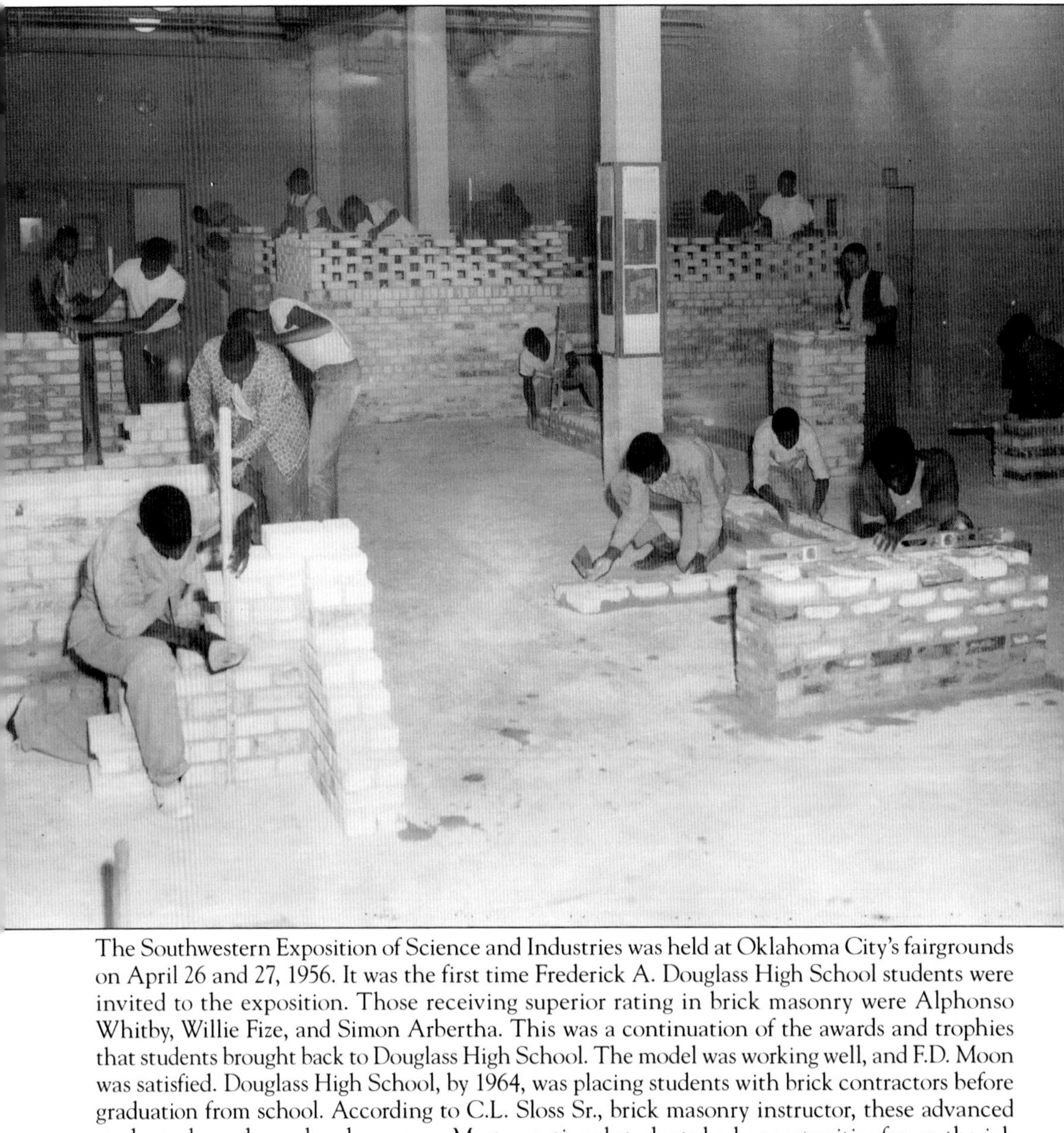

The Southwestern Exposition of Science and Industries was held at Oklahoma City's fairgrounds on April 26 and 27, 1956. It was the first time Frederick A. Douglass High School students were invited to the exposition. Those receiving superior rating in brick masonry were Alphonso Whitby, Willie Fize, and Simon Arbertha. This was a continuation of the awards and trophies that students brought back to Douglass High School. The model was working well, and F.D. Moon was satisfied. Douglass High School, by 1964, was placing students with brick contractors before graduation from school. According to C.L. Sloss Sr., brick masonry instructor, these advanced students showed speed and accuracy. Most vocational students had opportunities for on-the-job training. Willie Fize made a career as a master brick mason. Building scaffolds and laying brick were parts of the trade. This photograph shows students working with bricks. (Courtesy of Brenda Seward Johnson, from the Walter Seward Collection.)

Hillard H. Sharp, who has an annual golf tournament named after him by the Douglass High School class of 1972, was the driver's education instructor in 1961, but in 1950, he taught barbering and shoe repair. He had a bachelor of science degree. In the photograph at right, Sharp instructs a young lady on the proper use of a simulator car as a resource tool to learn how to drive a car. Below, he teaches some students how to change a flat tire and check the oil on a car. (Both, courtesy of Brenda Seward Johnson, from the Walter Seward Collection.)

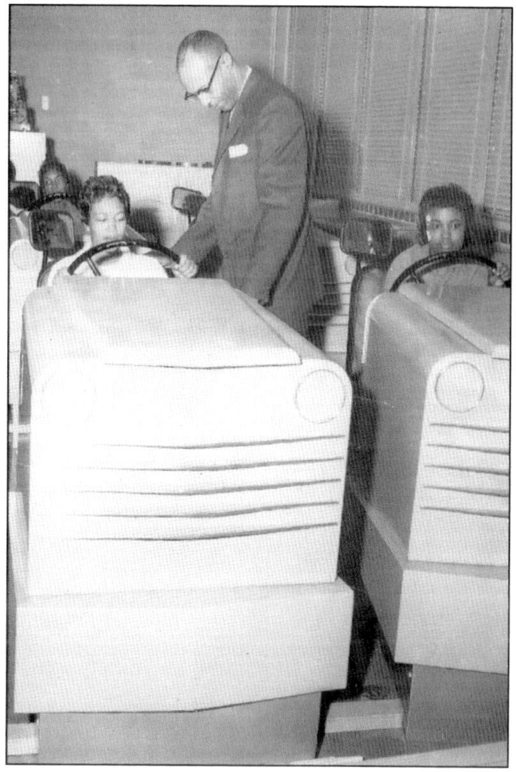

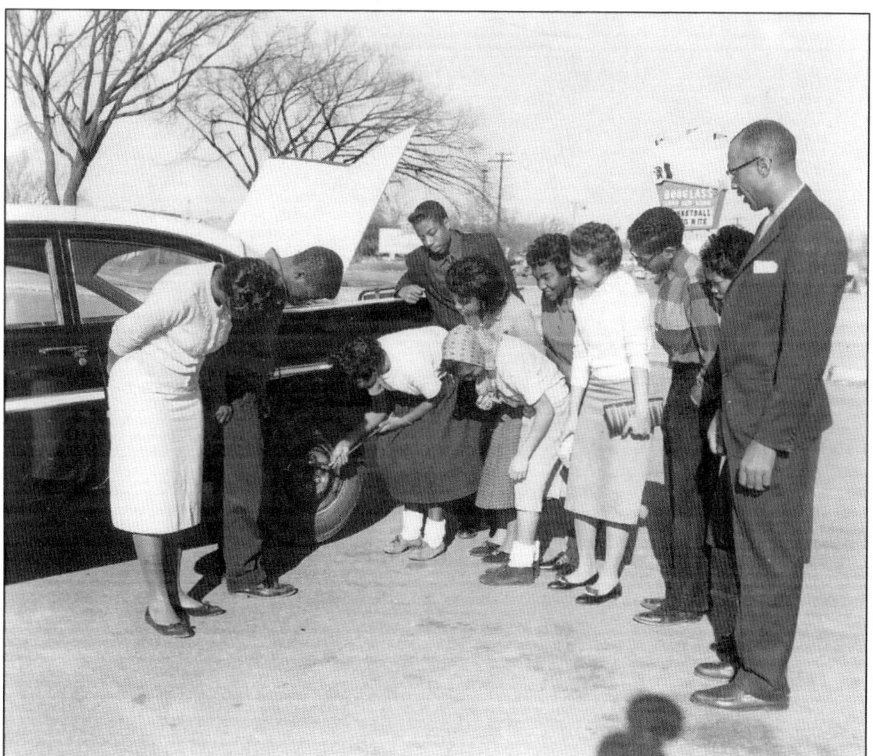

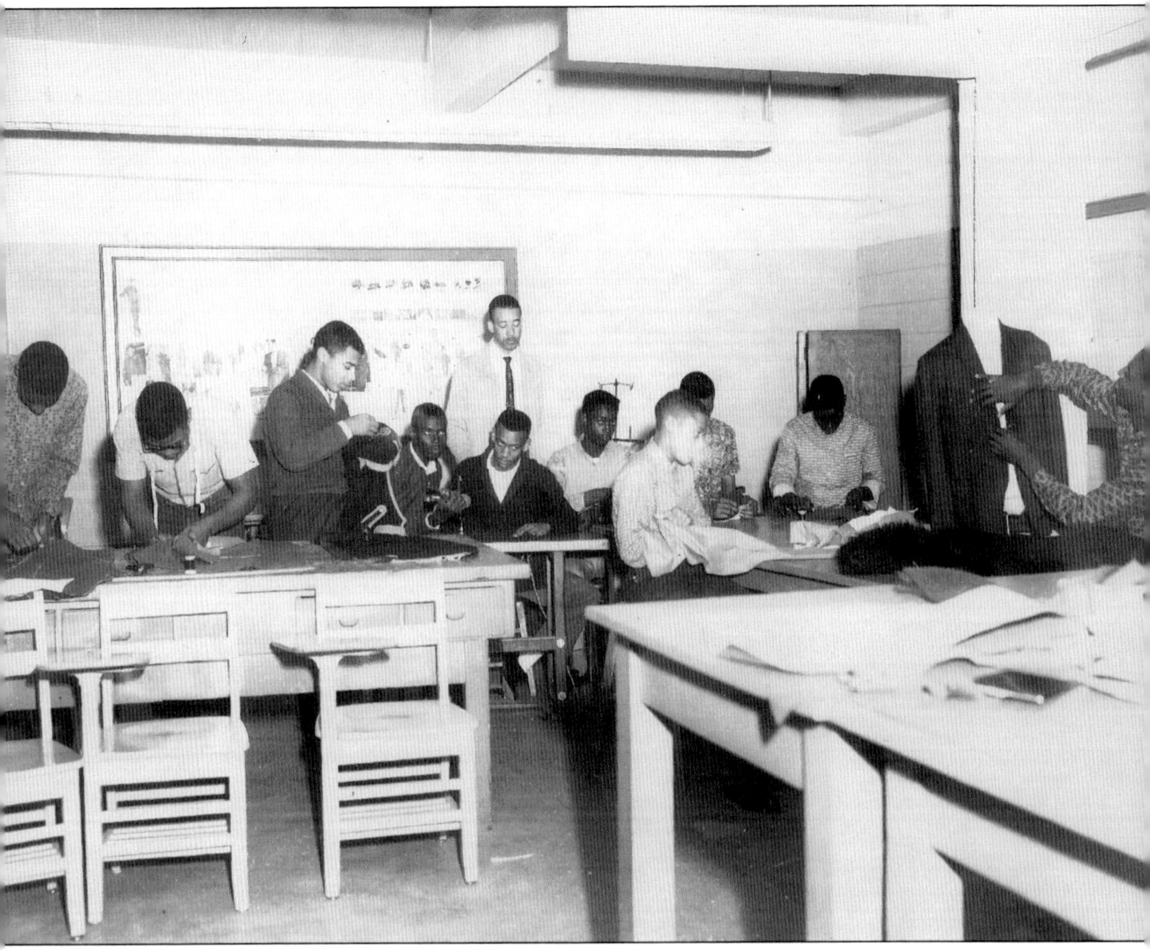

Douglass High School instructor L.O. Alexander was a career teacher in tailoring. In his class, students learned that trouser assembly, machine pressing, and steam ironing pressing were part of creating a professional image. Students were also taught to design their own clothes as well as clothes for members of their family or people in other classes. Emphasis on the finely finished "tailored look" was a goal of the class. Several students who mastered the tailoring class established their own tailoring businesses. One well-known tailor from the Douglass High School class of 1957 was Anderson Davis. This photograph shows students engaged in various phases of the tailoring process. Alexander's aim was to get students prepared for life, including looking good. (Courtesy of Brenda Seward Johnson, from the Walter Seward Collection.)

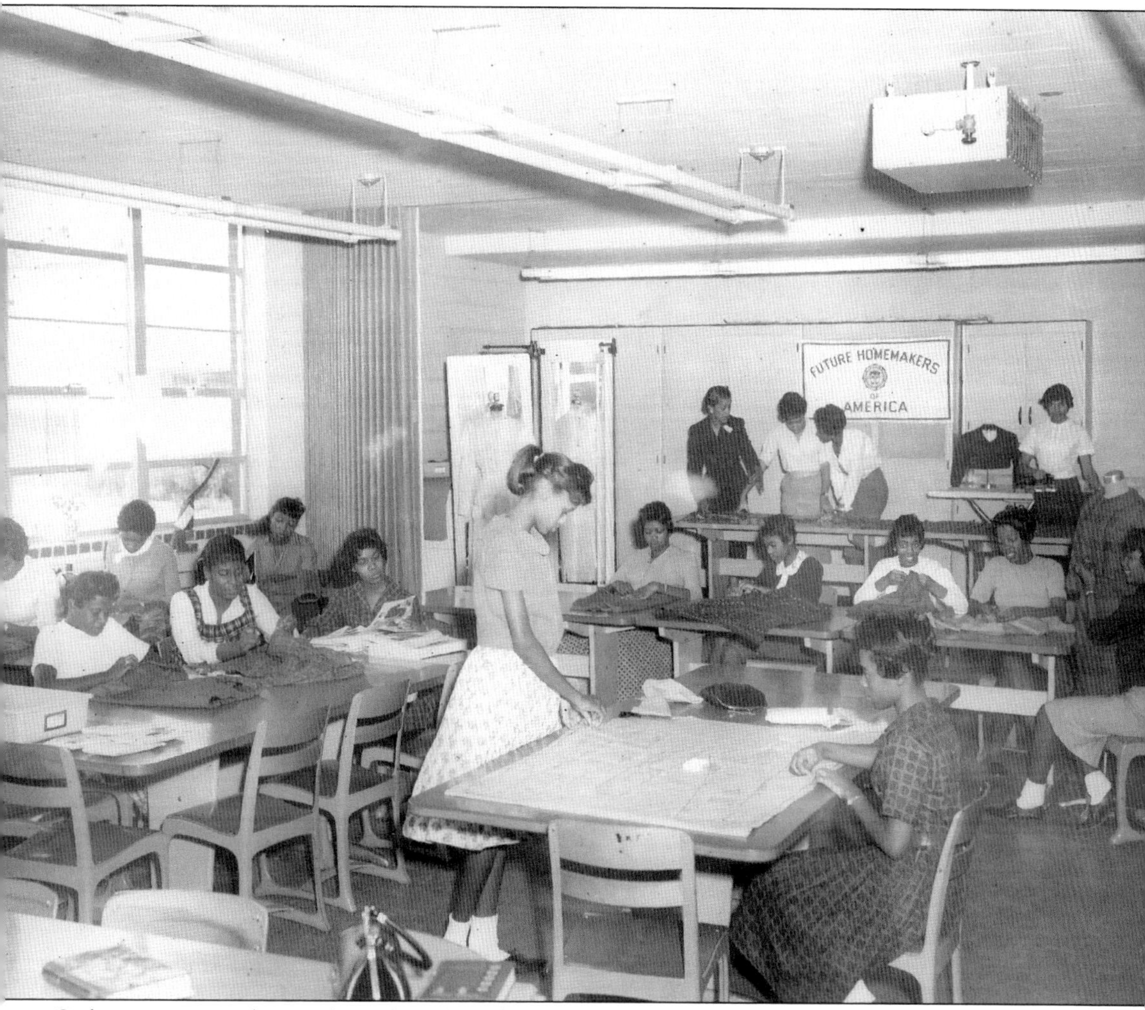

Girls were prepared to graduate from Douglass High School with options to succeed. Whatever the direction in life, basic homemaking was always a good option, and Douglass offered classes in both clothing and cooking. In cooking, students cooked by recipe; however, nutrition was essential in planning menus and meals. The goal of the Department of Home Economics was to guide each student into becoming their own best self. Each teacher understood that their responsibility was to satisfy the needs and interests of the student. Jesse J. Moore was the cafeteria manager and taught commercial cooking in 1950. Students in that class were divided into station service and were responsible for desserts, entrees, salads, and beverages to ensure a well-balanced, nutritious meal. The Future Homemakers of America club enhanced the students' class experiences. Zelma R. Love was the department head. This photograph was taken in a sewing class. (Courtesy of Brenda Seward Johnson, from the Walter Seward Collection.)

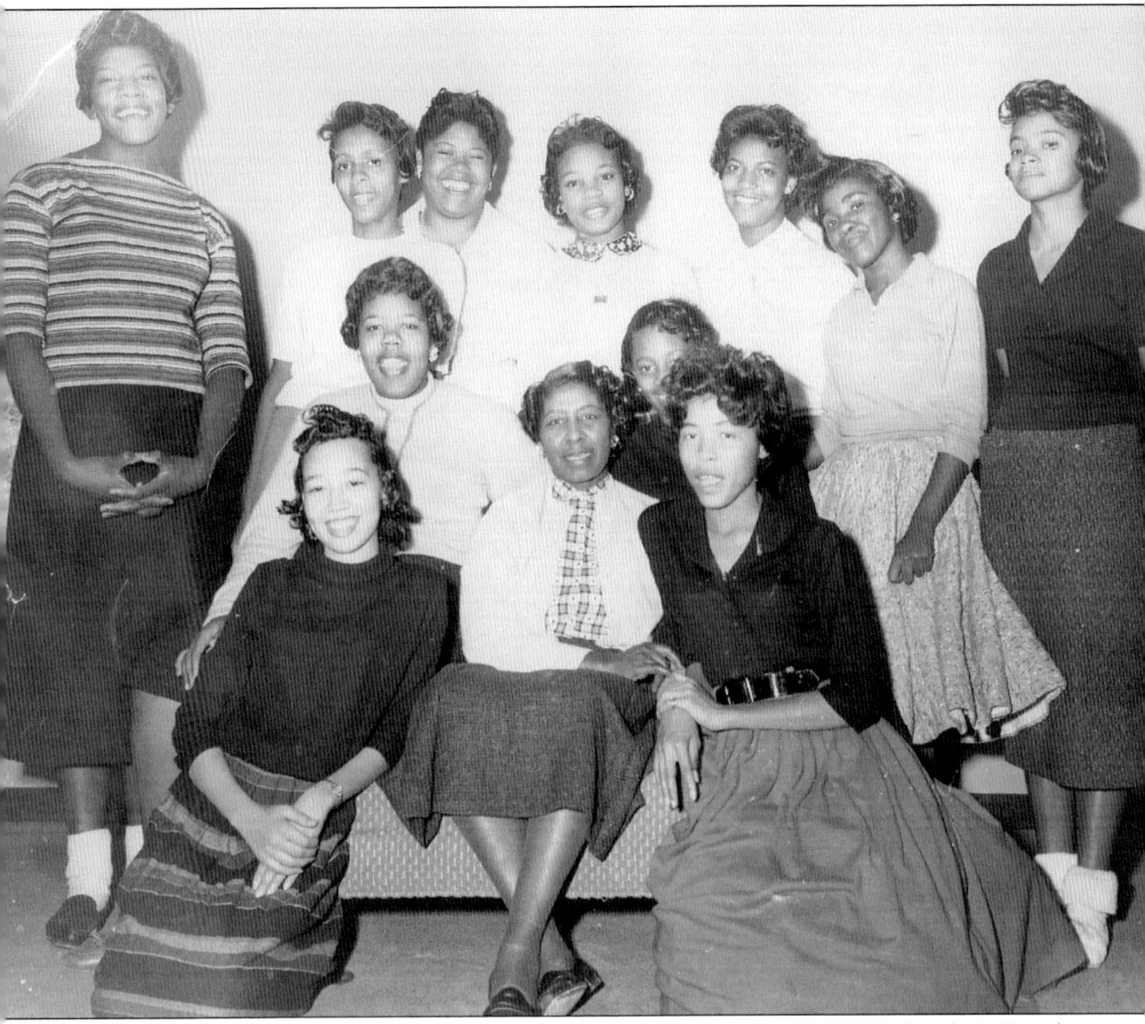

Jesse J. Moore was club sponsor for the Future Homemakers of America at Frederick A. Douglass High School. She is seated at center. Courses in homemaking were designed to shape and develop attitudes, values, and skills necessary to affect home and community life. Advanced homemaking taught how to make clothes from a pattern. At Thanksgiving and Christmas, the club gave baskets of food to the needy. Boxes were prepared and given to the Red Cross to send overseas to the needy as well. (Courtesy of Brenda Seward Johnson, from the Walter Seward Collection.)

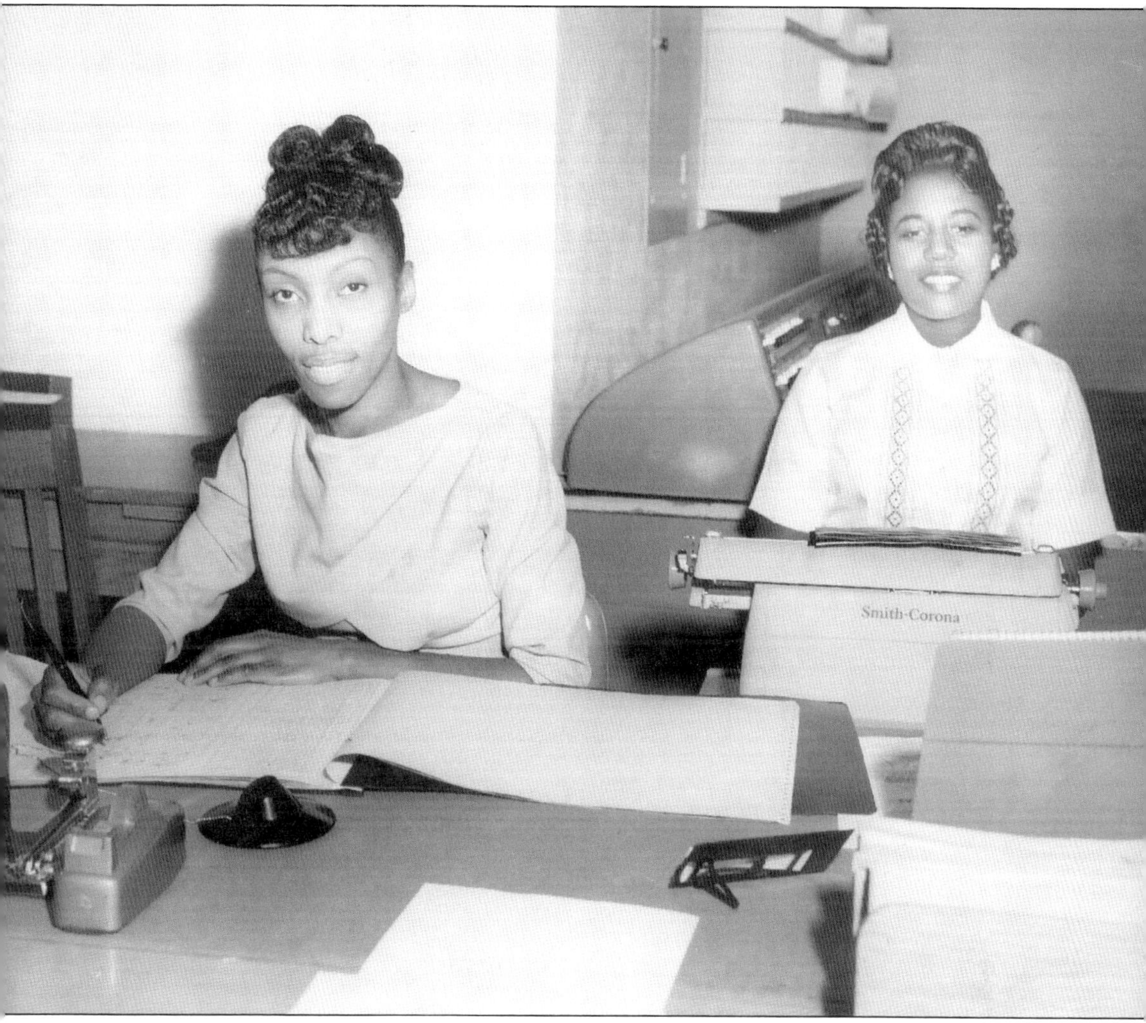

Vice Principal Wyatt Jeltz became pivotal in the continuing success of Douglass High School as F.D. Moon looked forward to retiring. The fame of the school spread, and Jeltz's responsibilities increased. To keep pace, he increased his secretarial staff to handle the workload. Shown here are Helena Tate (left) and Lorine Turner. Jeltz said, "Without them, work could not go on for suitable records would be missing." (Courtesy of Brenda Seward Johnson, from the Walter Seward Collection.)

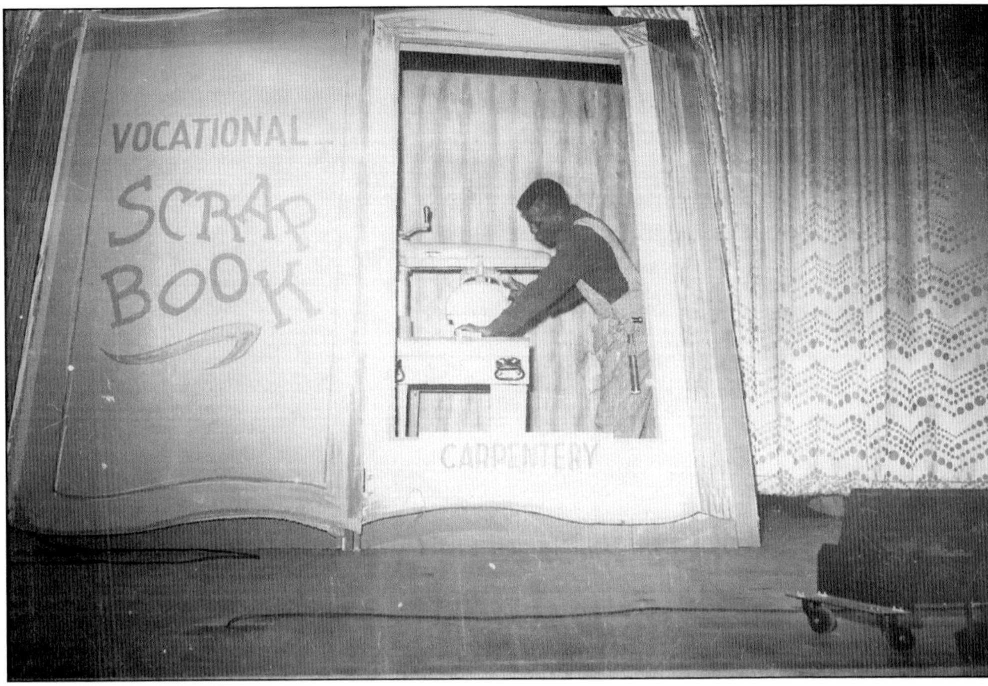

Principal Moon kept teachers and students engaged through annual recognition programs. The Department of Industrial and Vocational Arts showed creativity in many of its program presentations. Above, a student sets the stage with a scrapbook that pictures each class exhibit. The photograph below shows student banners that announce each of the departments for this recognition program. Also shown below are, from left to right, (seated) F.D. Moon, Paul L. Strong (department head), and two unidentified men. They are focused intently on the speaker at the podium. (Both, courtesy of Brenda Seward Johnson, from the Walter Seward Collection.)

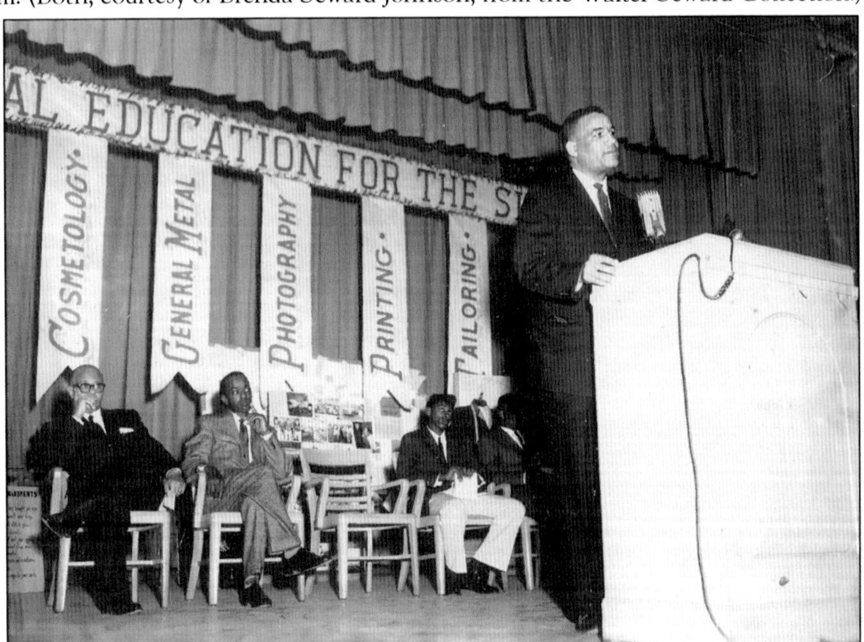

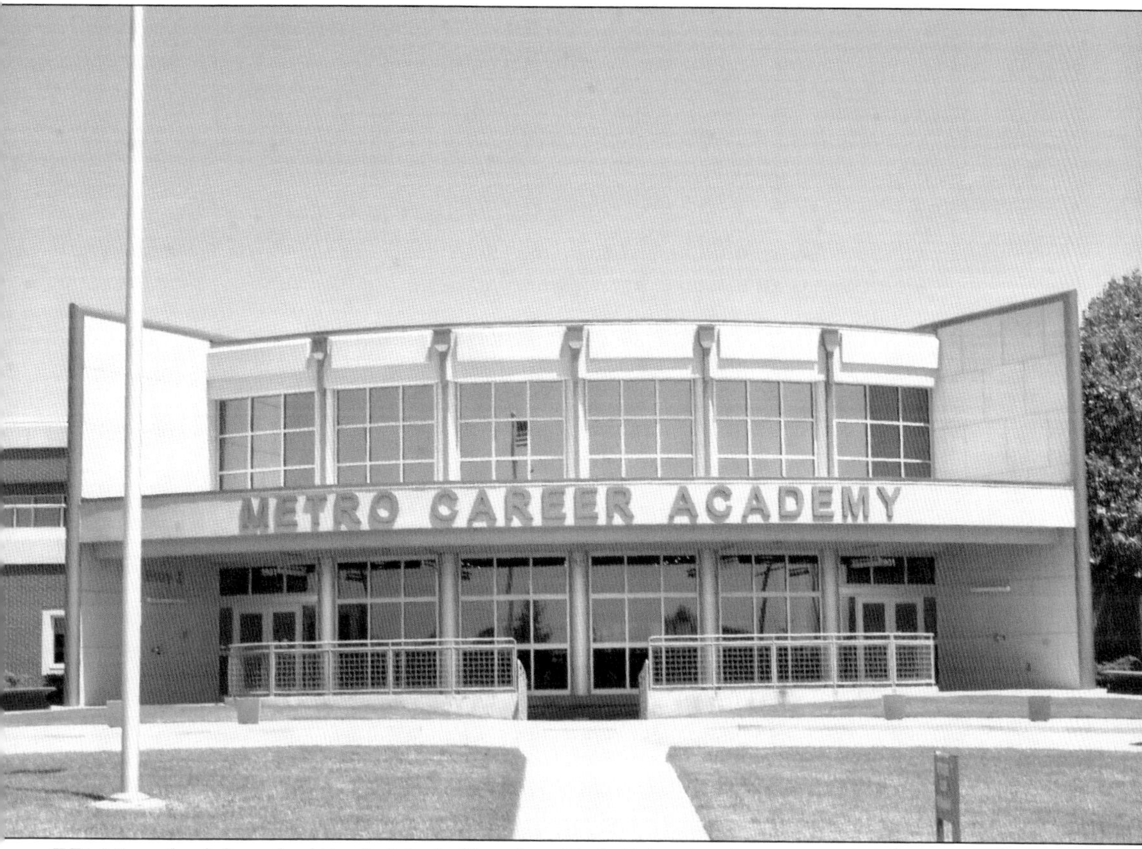

F.D. Moon had described Frederick A. Douglass High School as being a comprehensive school system that prepared students and adults for life, both academically and vocationally. From 1936 until 1961, Douglass High School offered more than 15 courses in the trades, including tailoring, barbering, upholstery, vocational printing, vocational carpentry, welding, electricity, metal work, driver's education, brick masonry, auto mechanics, industrial arts, photography, commercial cooking, and cosmetology. By 1970, when the Oklahoma Metro Technology system was established, there were few remnants of the Department of Vocational and Industrial Arts at Frederick A. Douglass High School. Students or adults who wish to take courses in these areas now must attend one of the four Metro Tech Centers scattered around Oklahoma. Patterned after the F.D. Moon legacy, the theme of the Metro Tech Centers is "Preparing for Life." No vocational courses are offered at Douglass today. (Photograph by Levi McCullough, courtesy of the Black Liberated Arts Center Inc.)

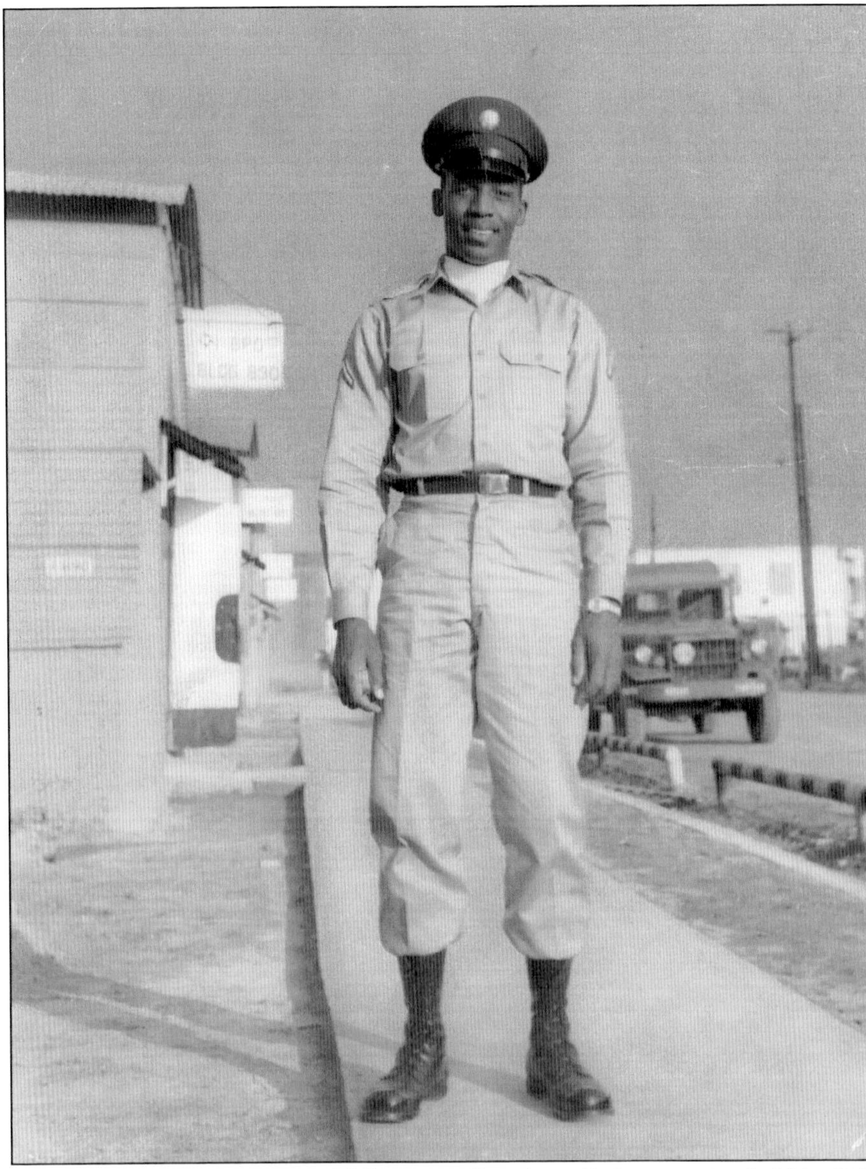

An alumni association was organized following a Douglass all-class reunion held in California and attended by graduates from all over America who expressed concerns about the state of affairs at Douglass High School. Freddye Williams, a Douglass graduate and Oklahoma state representative, wrote a column in the *Black Chronicle* entitled, "Weep for Dear Old Douglass." It was said that Williams meant that the "real glory of Douglass is gone." She said real accomplishment was academics. On December 2, 1987, six former Douglass graduates met to form the National Oklahoma City Frederick A. Douglass Alumni Association. The founders were Sherman Carthen, Johnny Hawkins, James Hotchkins, Joyce Jackson, Charles Morgan, and Horace Stevenson. At the next meeting, Sherman Carthen was elected president of the organization with the original six joined by Freddye Forest Clark, Michael Baldwin, Louise Diggs, Londa Jane Howard, Linzetta Jones Carter, Herman S. Nichols, Lonza Owens, Carolyn Sanders, Bill Ward, Geneva Williams, and Principal Ron Poole. Two weeks later, a constitution had been written and ratified. Pres. Sherman Carthen, a military veteran, is shown above. (Courtesy of Sherman Carthen estate.)

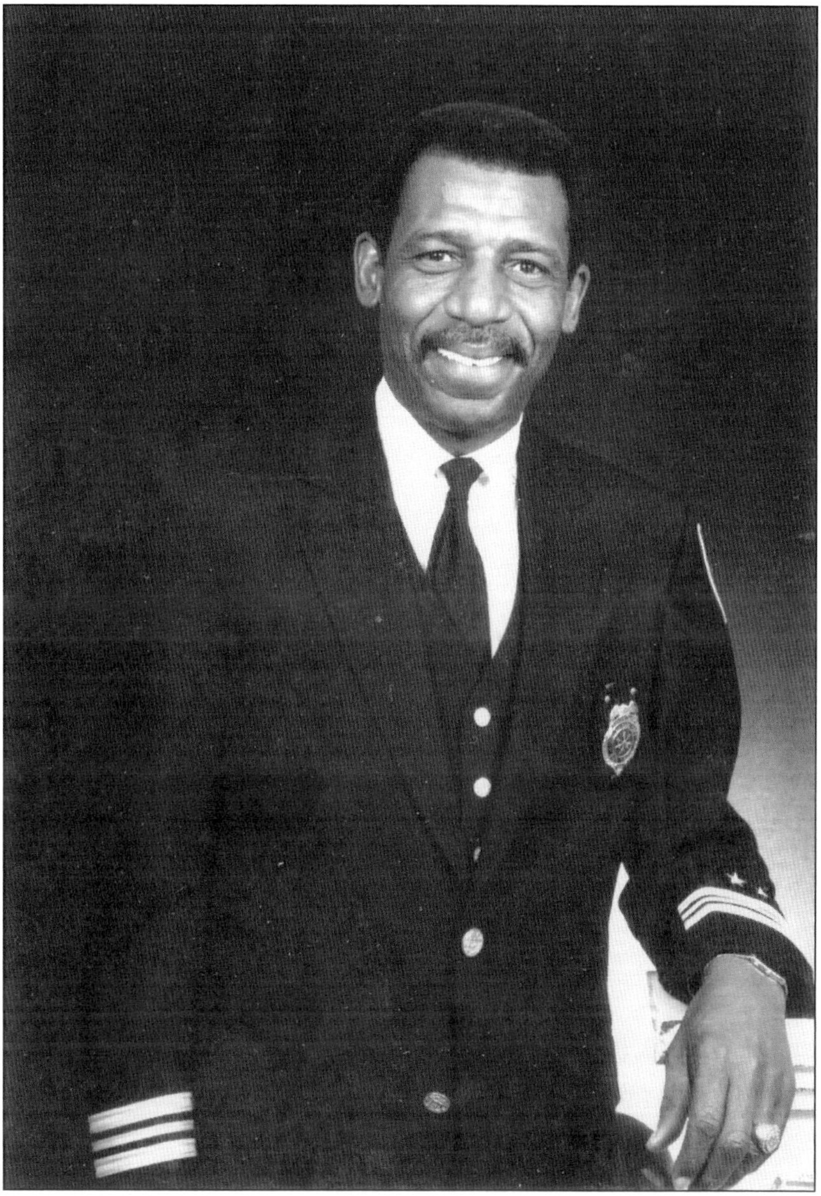

Sherman Massey Carthen was born July 4, 1938, in Oklahoma City. Fondly known as Jimmy, he graduated from Douglass High School in 1956. Carthen was active in his father's and grandmother's church, Church of the Living God, PGT. He was a singer and orator at the National Church Conferences. Carthen considered himself a "Mighty Trojan" and forever loved "Dear Old Douglass." He was a member of the Douglass High School Marching Band, which always attracted thousands of excited spectators. As founding president of the National Oklahoma City Frederick A. Douglass High School Alumni Association, Carthen led the group to establish its purpose "to foster pride and integrity, inspiring alumni to devote their talent and resources in preserving the welfare of Douglass High School." This forward thinker facilitated the burial of a time capsule on the front lawn of the high school in 1991. His wealth of experience organizing family reunions was helpful in the many class reunions that became a tradition of Douglass. (Courtesy of Sherman Carthen estate.)

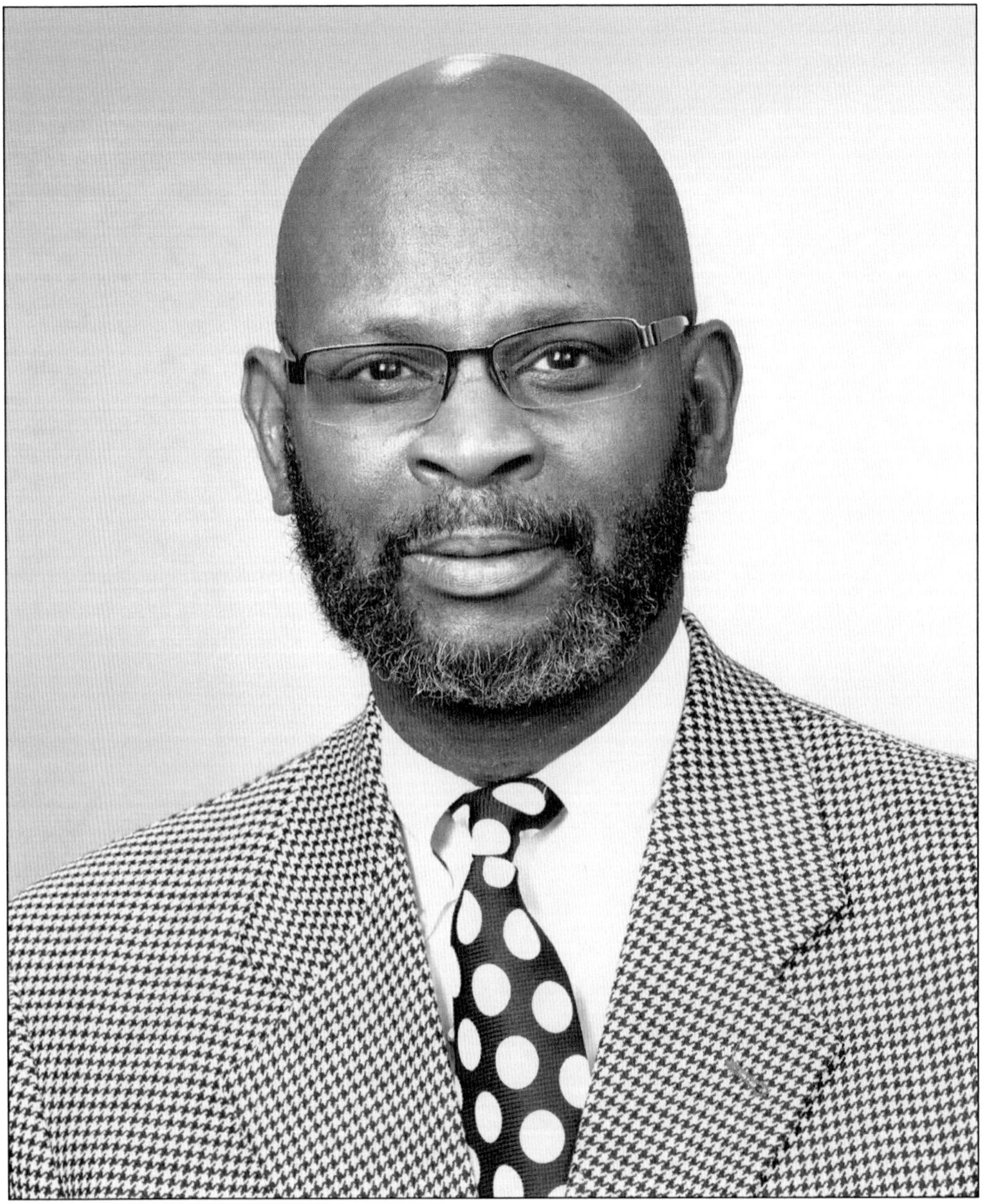

James Johnson, a Douglass High School graduate, has served in the Oklahoma Department of Commerce since 1989, recruiting in the life sciences, biotechnology, automotive, and energy industries. He began his professional career as a retail broker for Merrill Lynch, and later for Smith Barney. Johnson worked to develop the Central City Industrial Park in Oklahoma City for Oklahoma City Northeast Inc. He was founding president of the Oklahoma City Metropolitan Area Council of Better Investing and is a past member of the National Investors Association's Advisory Board. He served as president of the National Oklahoma City Frederick A. Douglass High School Alumni Association for more than 20 years. He is a member of the advisory board of directors of The Foundation for Oklahoma City Public Schools. He is the grandson of W.J. and Frances Edwards. His mother, Maxine Johnson, was Walter Edwards's youngest daughter. (Courtesy of James Johnson.)

Five

Standards and Expectations

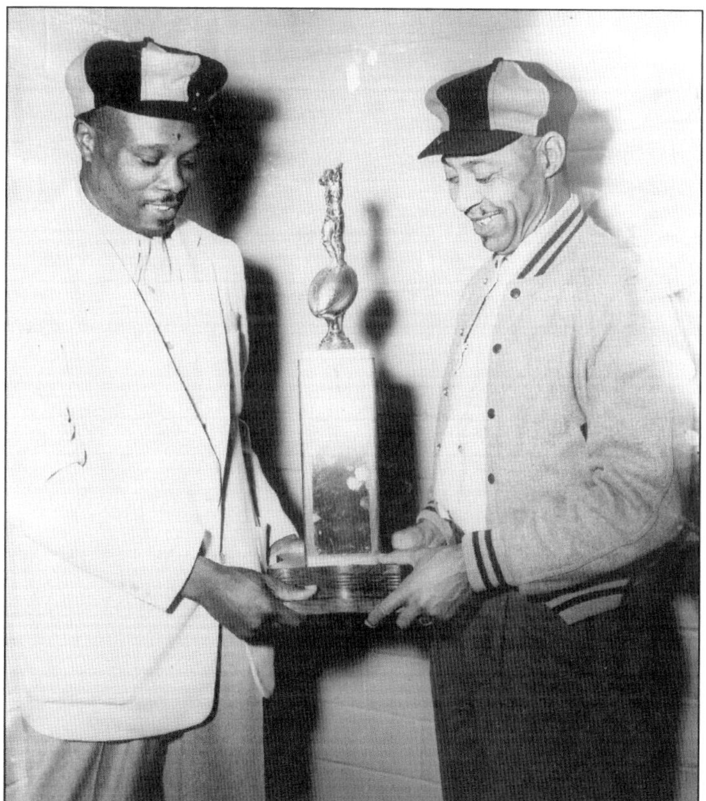

Excellence and trophies were indicators of standards and expectations at Frederick A. Douglass High School in all departments. Coaches Jake Diggs, left, and Moses "PiYi" Miller, right, hold the football trophy earned by the Trojans as reigning champions of the 1955–1956 AA Conference. (Courtesy of Bonita Forrest Edwards.)

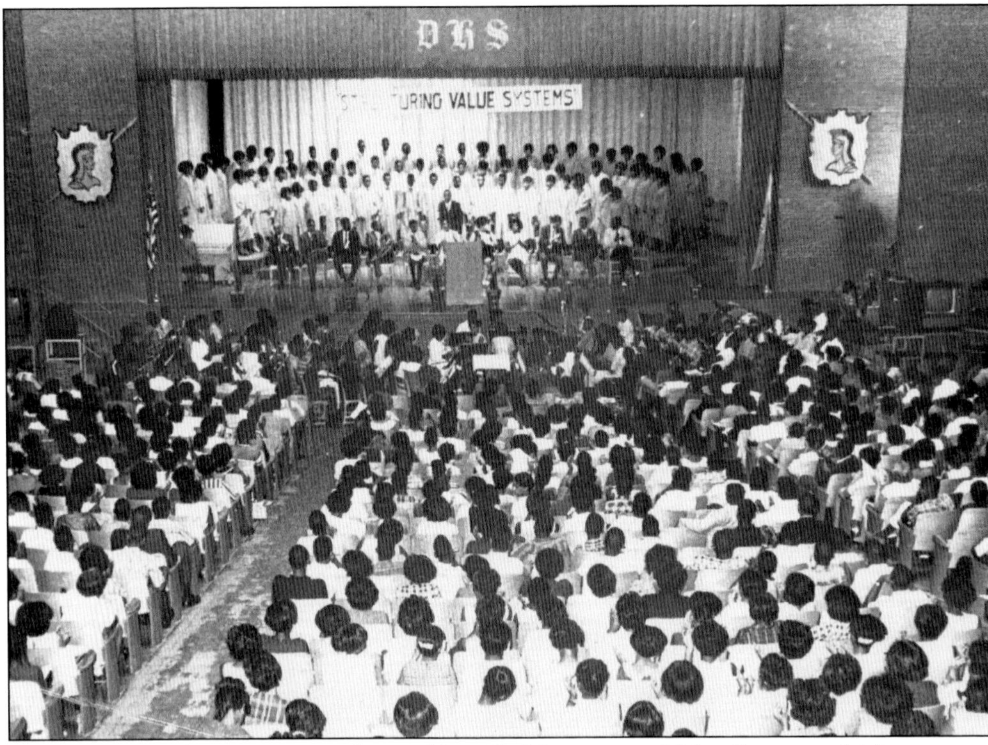

Above, students listen in a special assembly called Structuring Value Systems, which supported the goals and objectives of Douglass High School. Below, the Honor Society conducts a meeting in the library. Pictured are, from left to right, (first row, seated) Lee Etta Edwards, Sondra Sanders, Brenda Pierce, and Sandra Battle; (second row) Pauline Daniels, Saundra Thompson, Patricia Burks, Gayle Smith, Peggy Patterson, Euzerla Rice, Kathryn Tease, Joyce Battle, and Edwina Richardson; (third row) James Reed and Charles Walker. (Both, courtesy of Brenda Seward Johnson from the Walter Seward Collection.)

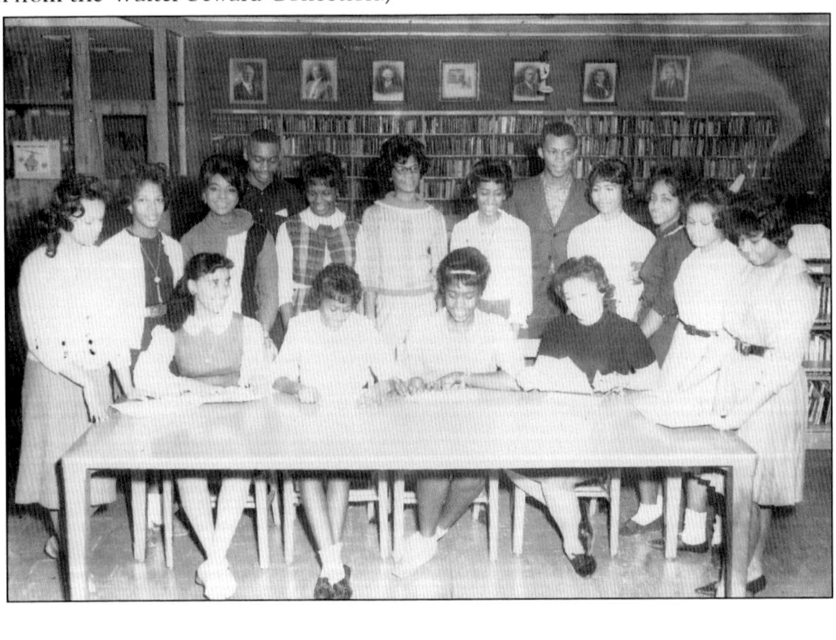

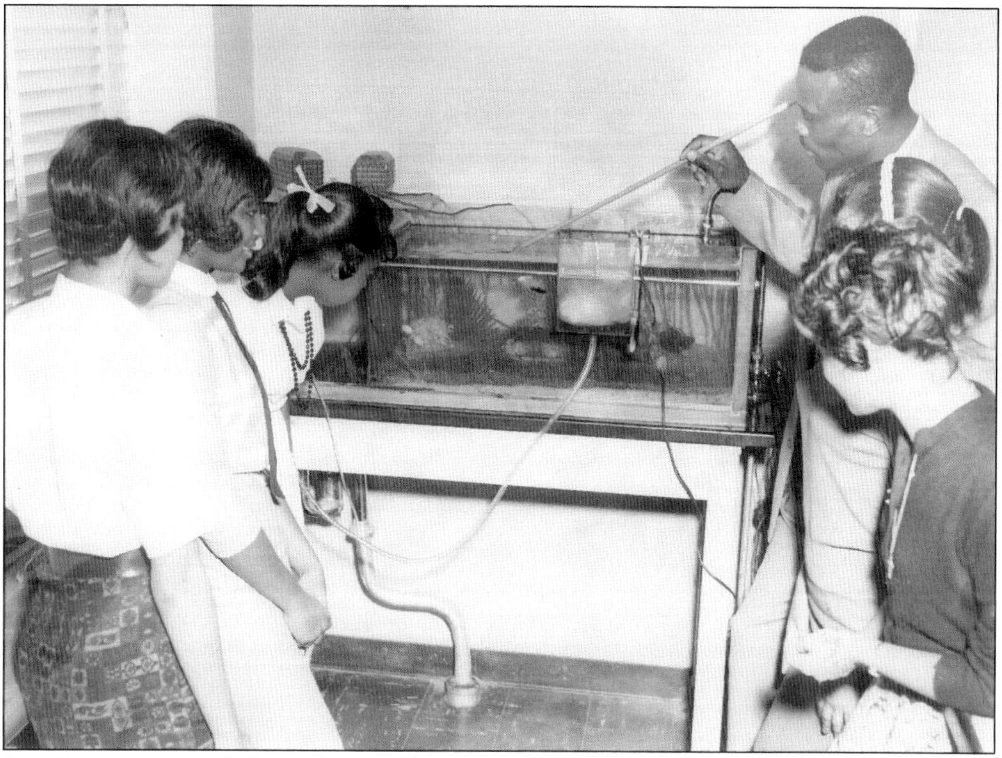

Jake Diggs is pictured above showing three students how life exists under water in one of the two biology classes. Diggs was also the track and football coach. Teachers were expected to take leadership in academics and school organizations. Diggs would become principal of Douglass High School in 1970. Below, Hurlan Dulan, chemistry instructor, demonstrates the chemical action of substances to members of his class. Douglass students were expected to compete and win at the state science fair and at the Interscholastic Meet each year. (Both, courtesy of Brenda Seward Johnson, from the Walter Seward Collection.)

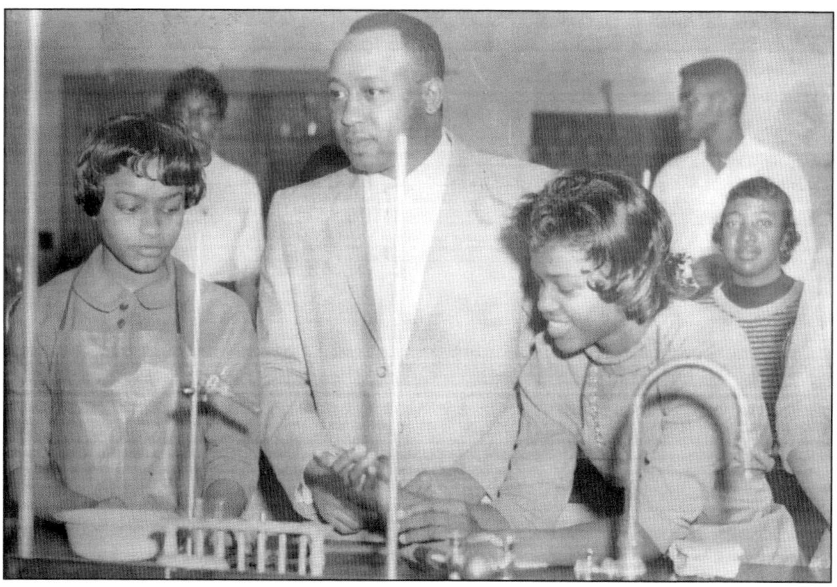

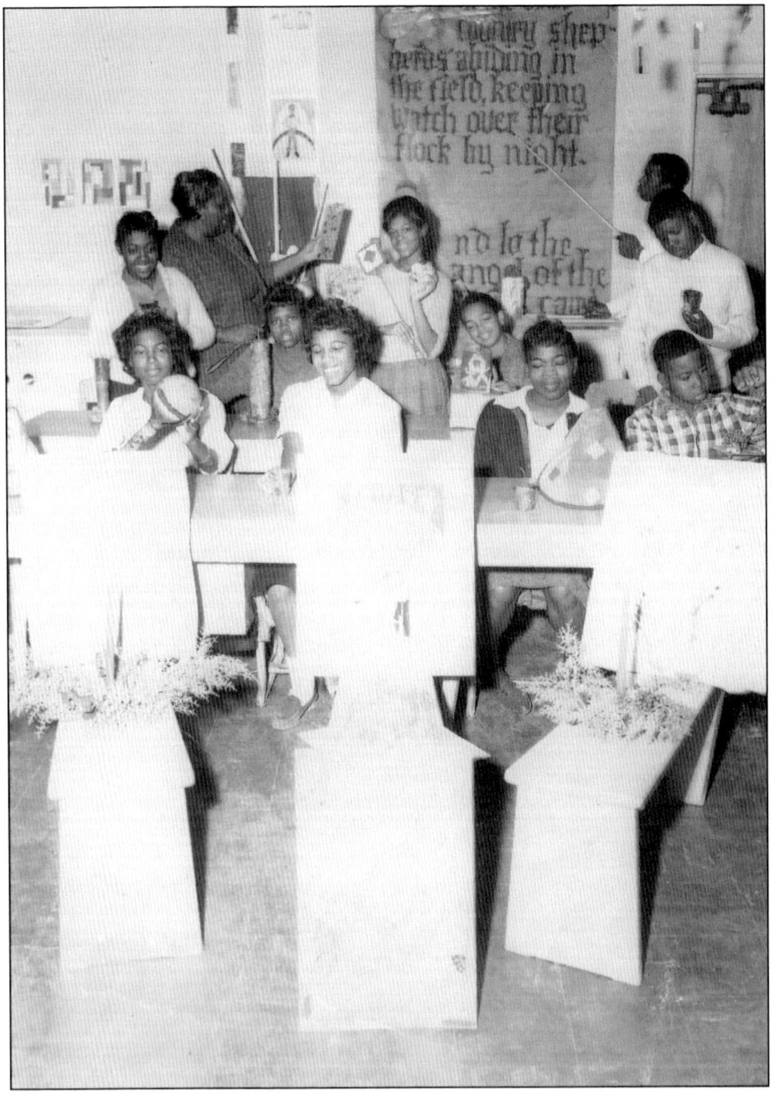

In the photograph at left, Margaret Dabney stands at left in the back of the classroom. The art class is creating stage decorations for an upcoming Christmas play to be held at the Douglass High School auditorium. After the new school opened in 1954, all Douglass graduations took place in the auditorium. Below, French Club members, taught French by Dr. Evelyn Strong, also music director at Douglass High School, stand in front of the school. Dr. Strong stands at far left. (Both, courtesy of Brenda Seward Johnson, from the Walter Seward Collection.)

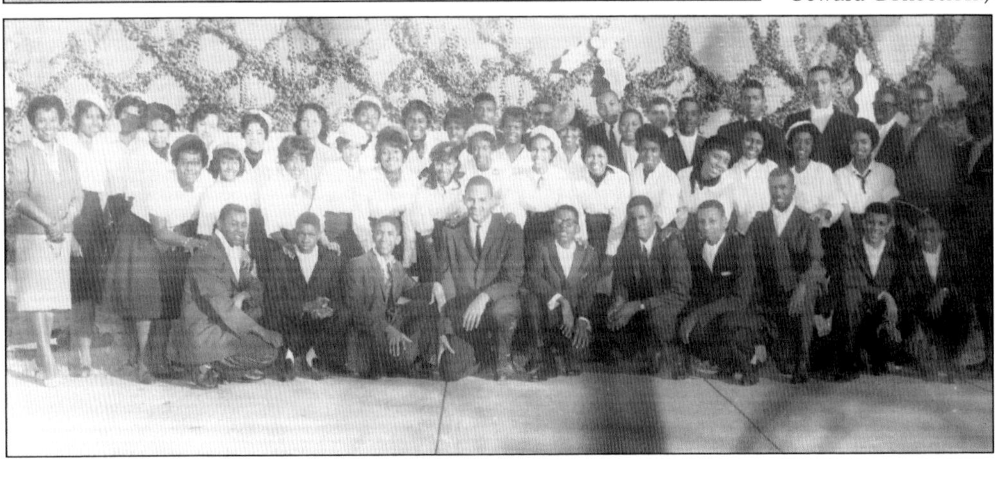

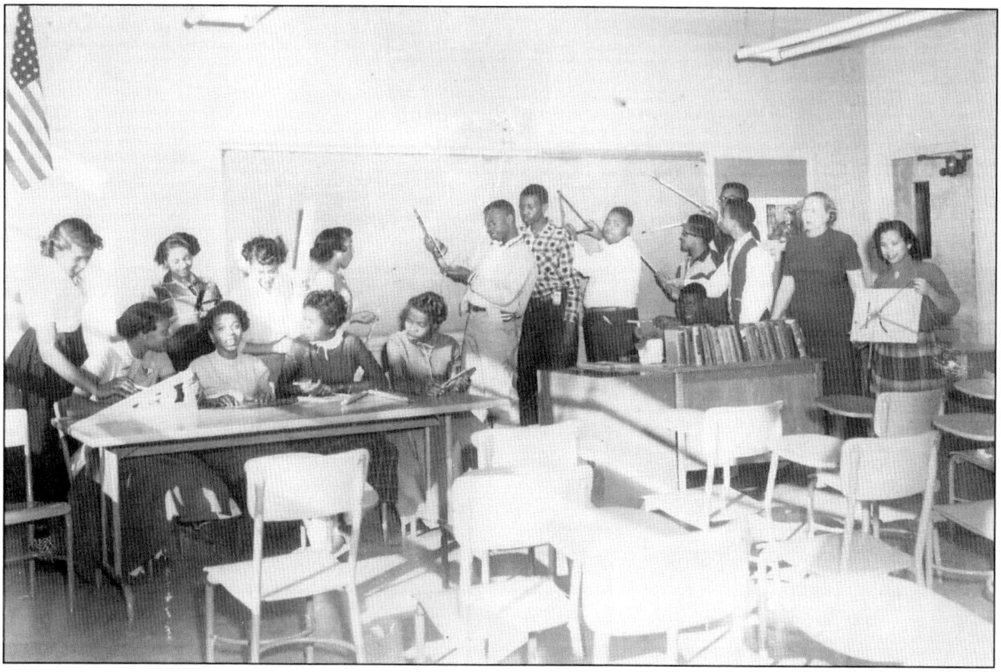

Above, Odessa Temple, geometry, trigonometry, and beginning calculus instructor, stands in the right corner of the room near a student wearing a plaid dress. She is watching as students demonstrate a lesson on triangles. Below, students in a biology class study seven life functions, seen on a chart in the left corner of the room. The functions are listed as sensation, food getting, motion, excretion, respiration, reproduction, and nutrition. (Both, courtesy of Brenda Seward Johnson, from the Walter Seward Collection.)

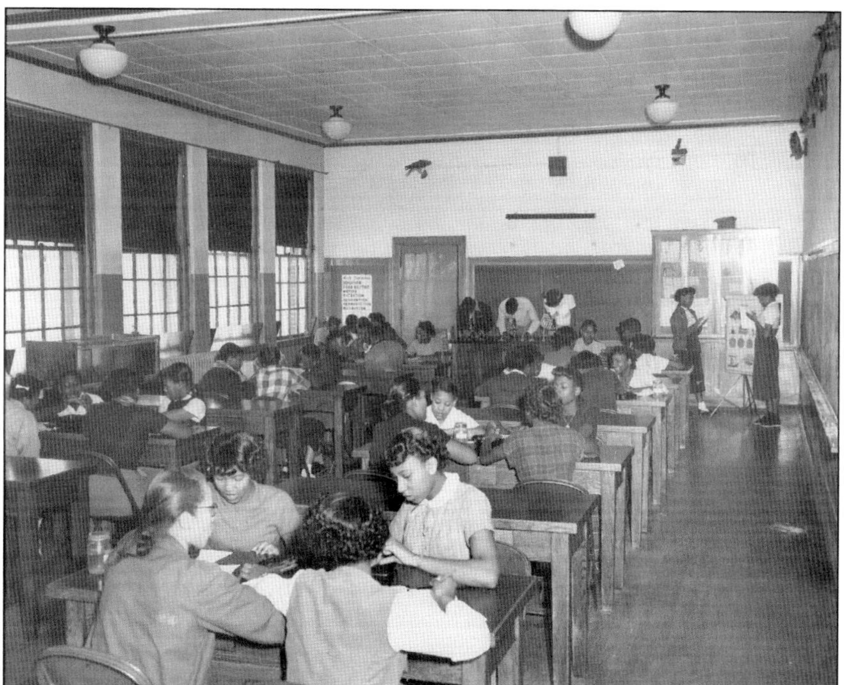

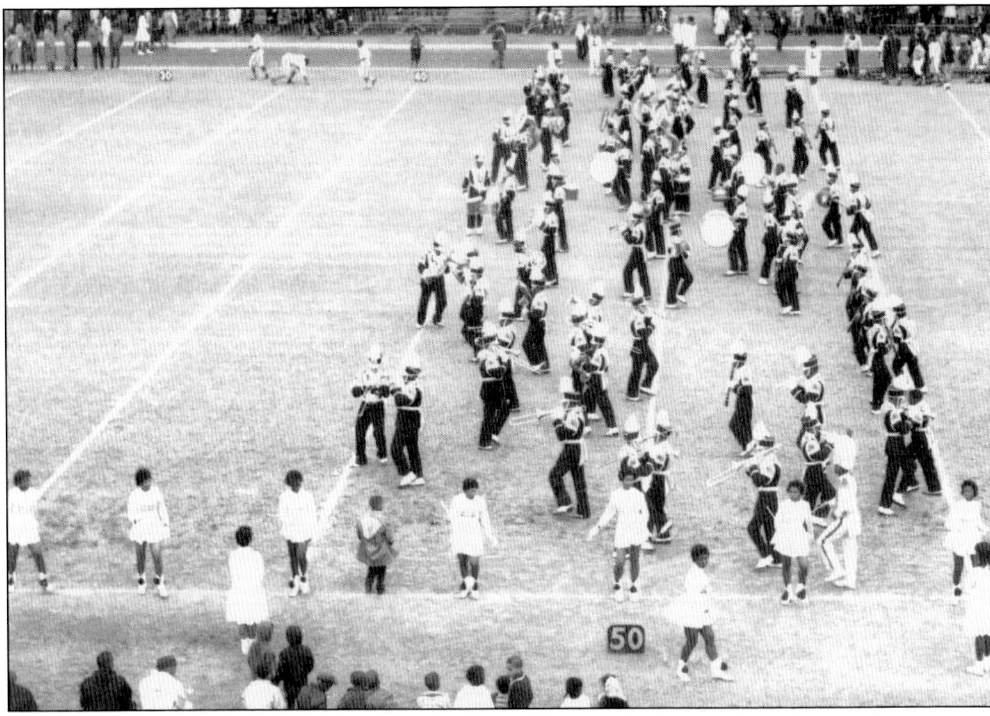

In the image above, the marching band, led by drum major Willard Pitts, moves into formation at the 50-yard line during a half-time performance at Douglass Stadium. In the 1950s, the marching band dominated competitions in Oklahoma. Individual band members often received superior or excellent awards from judges. Floats at festivals in Oklahoma City and at Douglass were always exceptional. Shown below is a Douglass float in an Oklahoma Day parade on Northeast Fourth Street. America was always reflected in activities and celebrations at Douglass. (Both, courtesy of Brenda Seward Johnson, from the Walter Seward Collection.)

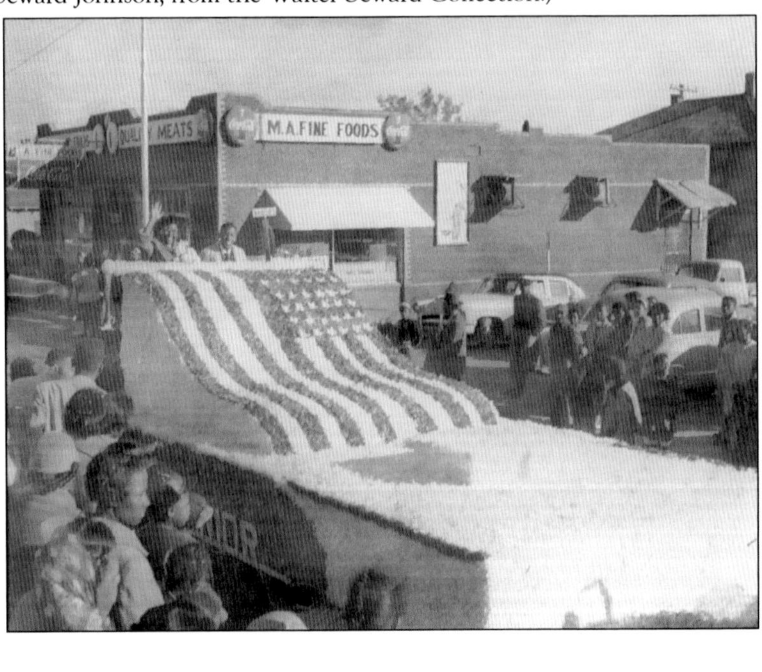

Six

"The Dean of Negro Education"

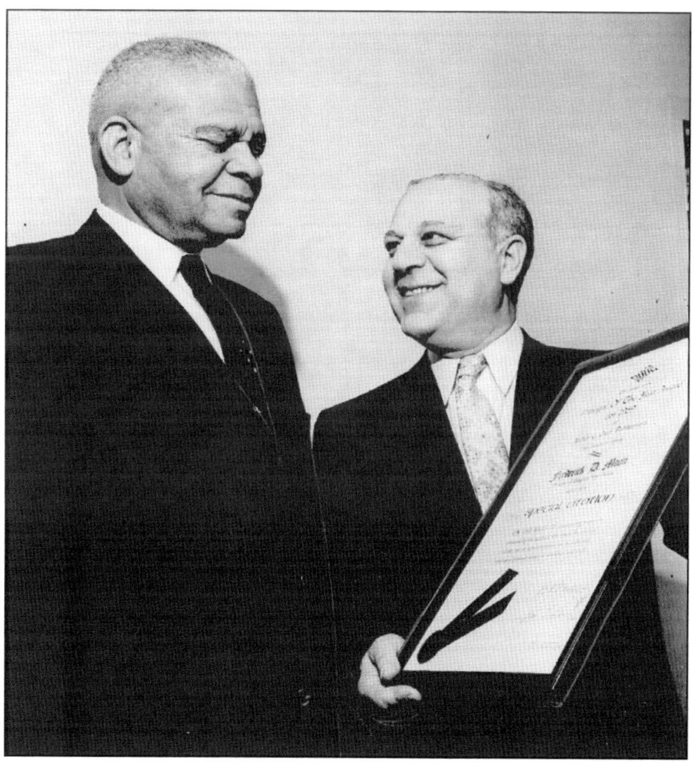

The *Saturday Evening Post* called him "the Dean of Negro Education" because of the many honors Principal F.D. Moon received. One of the highest honors he received was an award given him in the first National Principal of the Year competition. Here, Ben Brodinsky, editor in chief of Croft Publications, who flew from Connecticut to Oklahoma City, congratulates Moon after Gallup Polls identified him as one of 13 excellent principals in America. (Courtesy of Oklahoma Historical Society.)

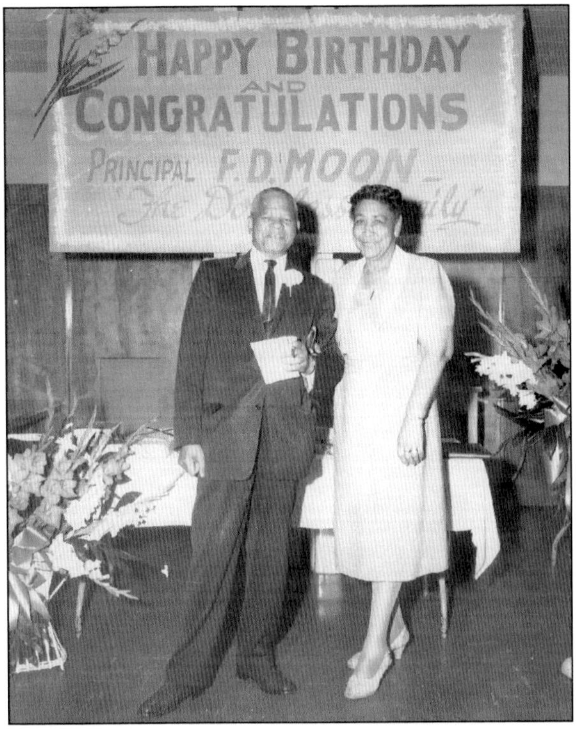

By the time F.D. Moon had finished building his "Moon Model" education system, he was nearing retirement age. Moon had earned the respect of his teachers, students, and the education world. Here, Moon enjoys the big birthday celebration the school gave him. At left, he poses with the dean of girls, Thelma Boyd Wilson-Tillman. Below are, from left to right, W.F. Jeltz (vice principal), E.C. Moon Sr. (brother), Leotia Moon (wife), F.D. Moon, and Sara Jane Bell (librarian). (Both, courtesy of Deola Harris.)

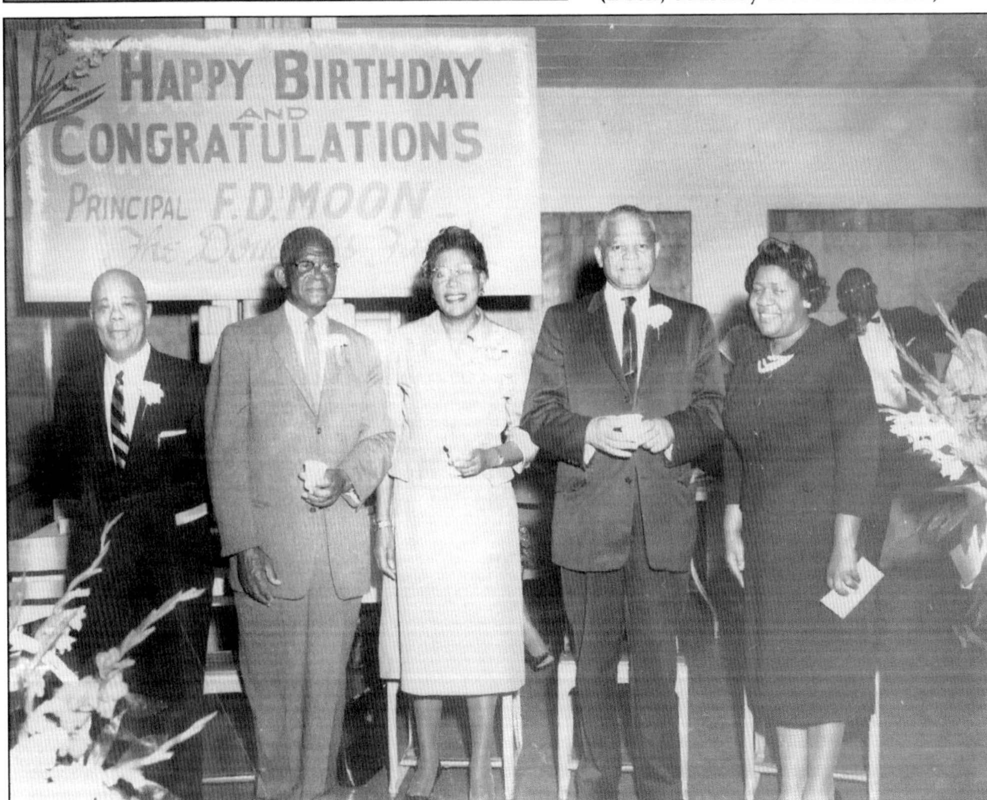

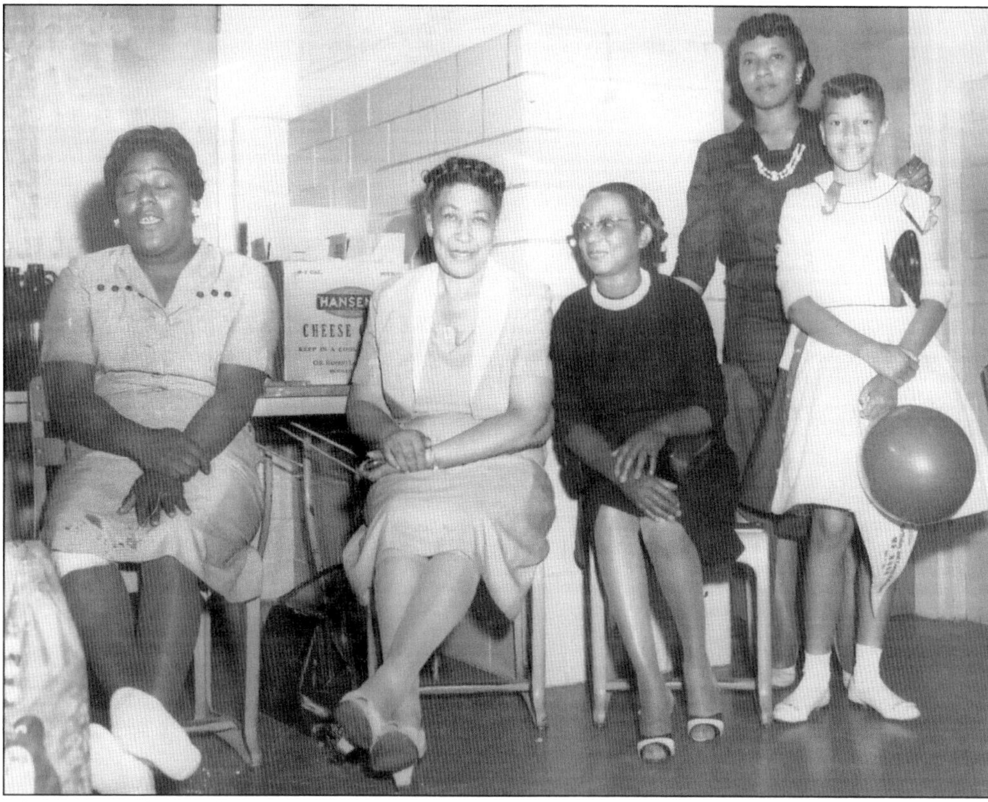

Above, after the birthday celebration, key planners of the birthday party relax in a corner of the kitchen. From left to right are Erma Moore (cosmetology instructor), Thelma B. Wilson-Tillman (dean of girls), Geneva Johnson (Moon's longtime secretary), and an unidentified woman and girl. Below is another memorable celebration—F.D. Moon Recognition Day—planned for the soon to be retired principal. The steps to the stars show the accomplishments of Moon during his career in Oklahoma City. He stands at the microphone as the band and students look on. (Both, courtesy of Deola Harris.)

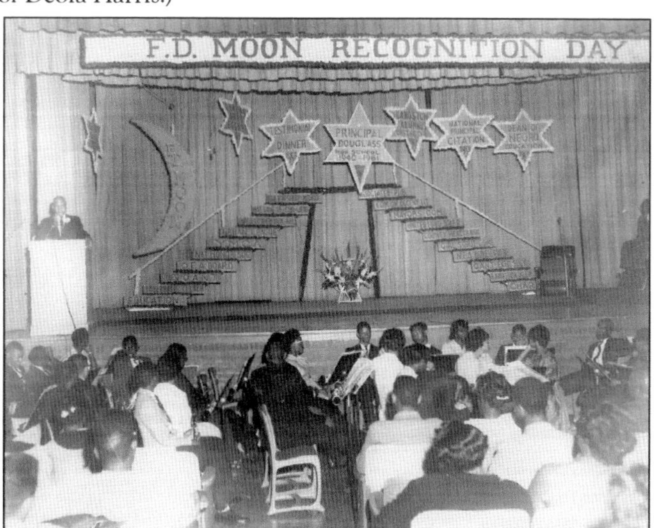

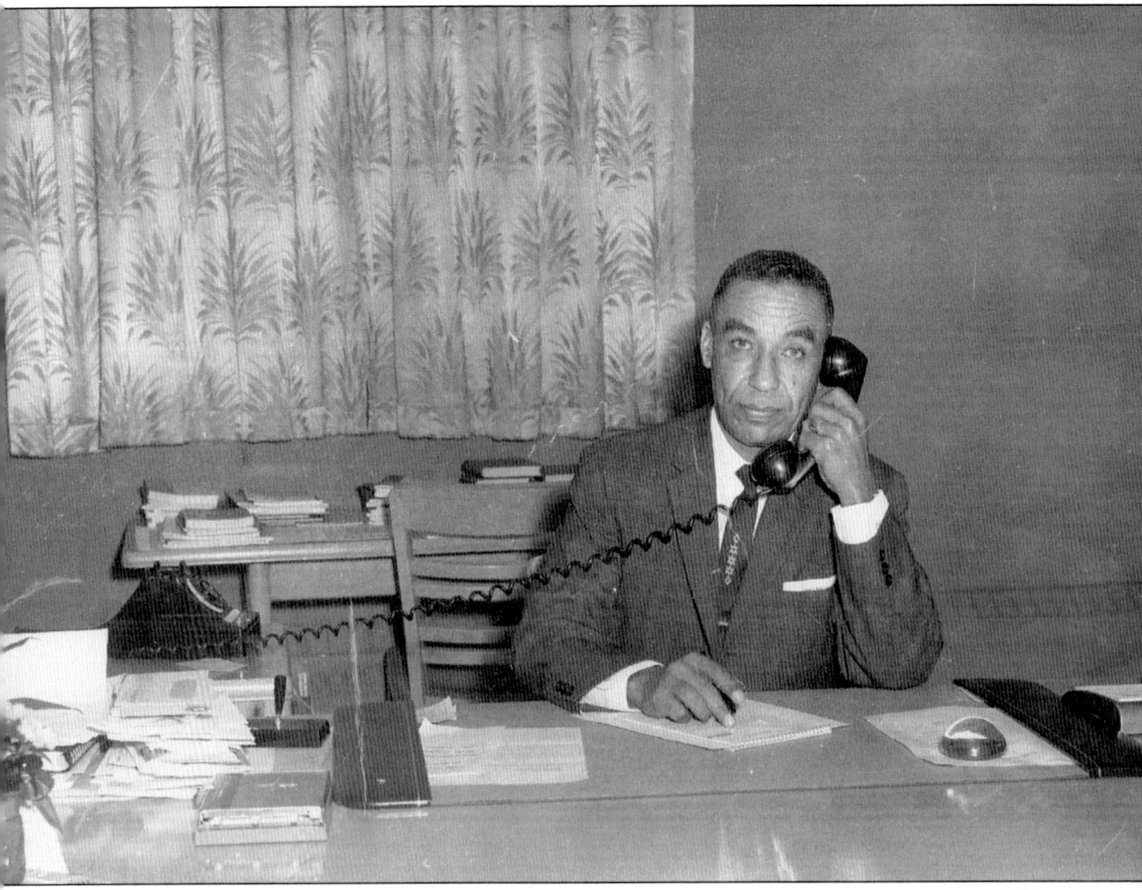

O.M. McDaniels became principal of Frederick A. Douglass High School in 1962. According to the yearbook, "Mr. O. M. McDaniels, Principal, has already enriched the lives and characters of all members of "The Douglass Family," with his seasoned experience, patience, wisdom and excellent leadership." He had more than 1,500 students and 62 faculty members to lead. (Courtesy of Brenda Seward Johnson, from the Walter Seward Collection.)

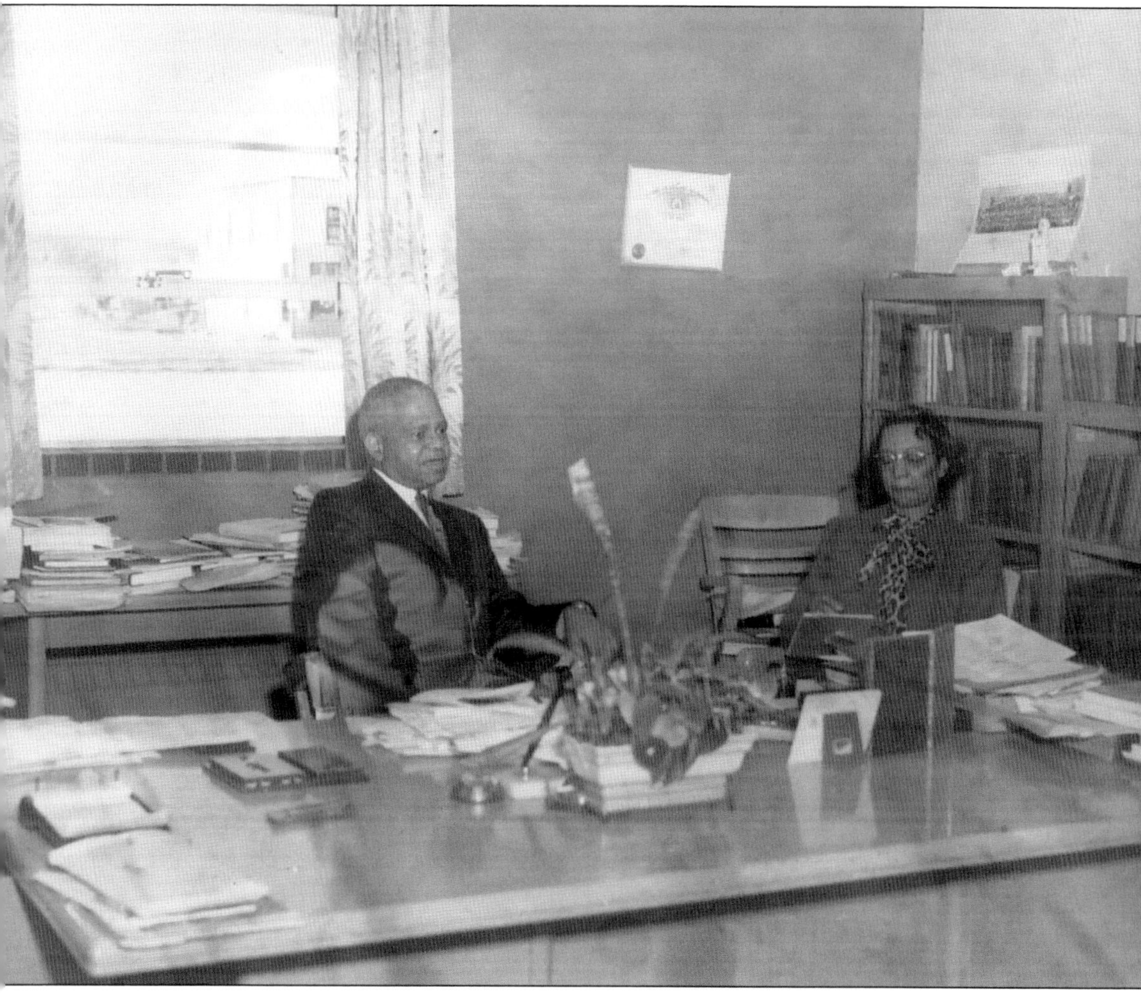

F.D. Moon is seen with his longtime secretary/financial secretary Geneva Johnson in his office before his retirement, prior to O.M. McDaniels assuming leadership of Douglass High School. By 1955, Moon had formed an Administrative Council that included Geneva Johnson, the vice principal, chairmen of the nine departments, the librarian, the dean of boys, and the dean of girls. (Courtesy of Brenda Seward Johnson, from the Walter Seward Collection.)

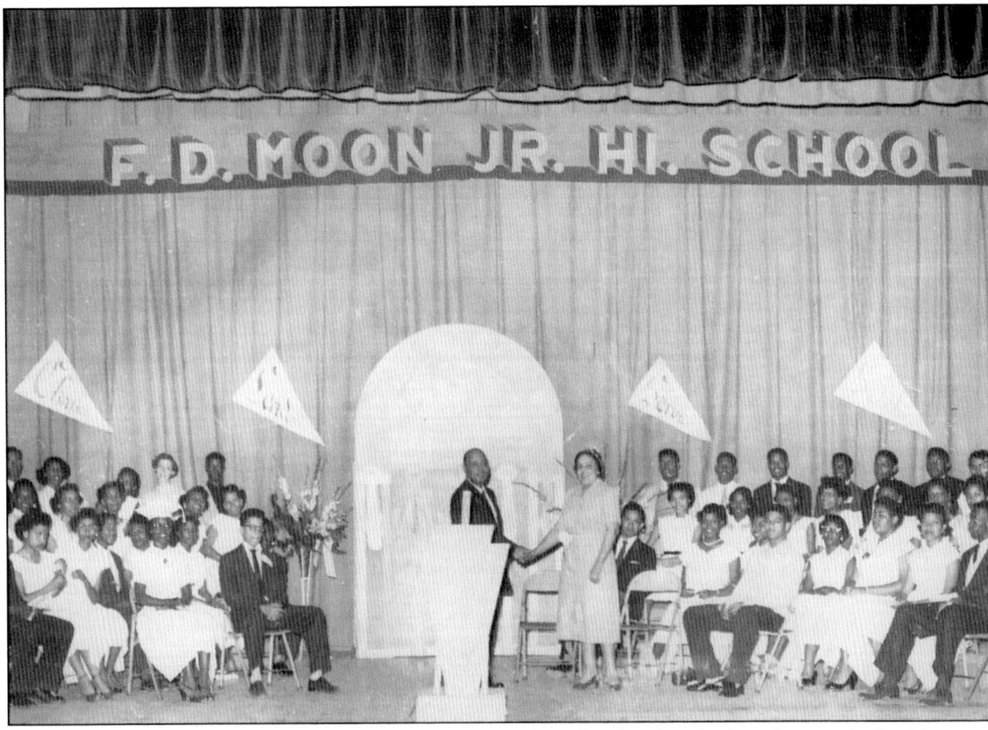

Shortly before F.D. Moon retired from Douglass High School, school officials—with the blessings of the community—began naming school buildings after him. Over a period of 40 years, there were four buildings that had the name F.D. Moon placed on them. The above photograph shows a name dedication ceremony for the first building, which was the first Douglass High School where he was principal. The photograph below shows the F.D. Moon Center, located near the Douglass High School he built. The image was taken by photographer Levi McCullough. (Both, courtesy of the Black Liberated Arts Center Inc.)

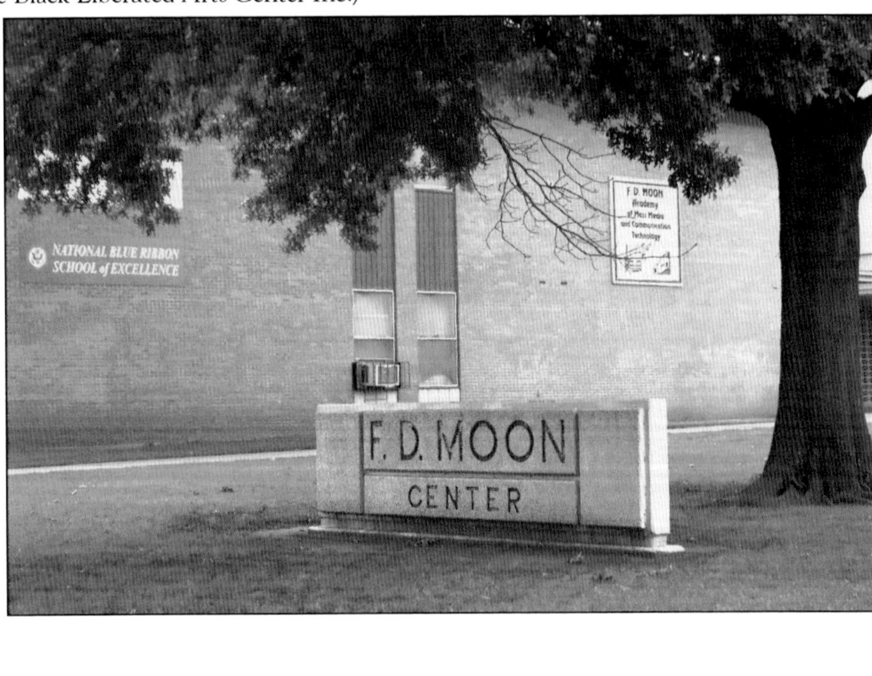

Seven

THE TEACHERS

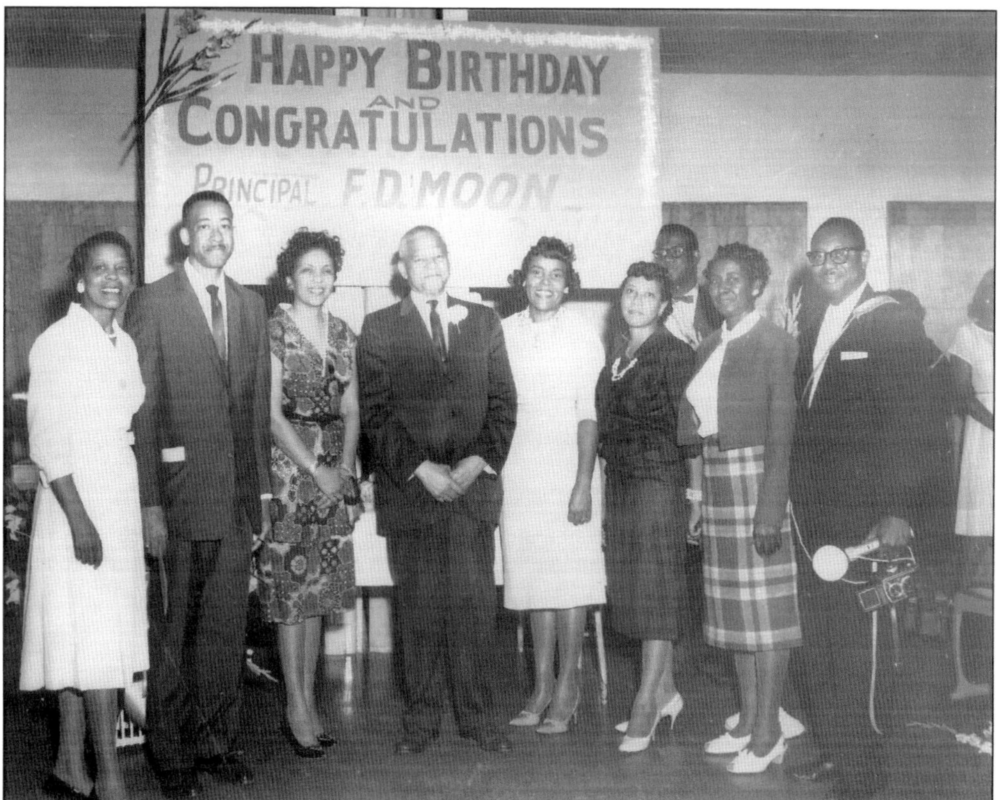

F.D. Moon stands with some of his teachers. From left to right are Zelma R. Love (home economics), L.O. Alexander (tailoring), Augusta Morgan (history and problems in democracy), Moon, Thelma R. Parks (reading instructor), Leavie H. Reid (secretary), Maurice Benefee (upholstery), Jesse J. Moore (home economics), and an unidentified photographer. (Courtesy of Deola Harris.)

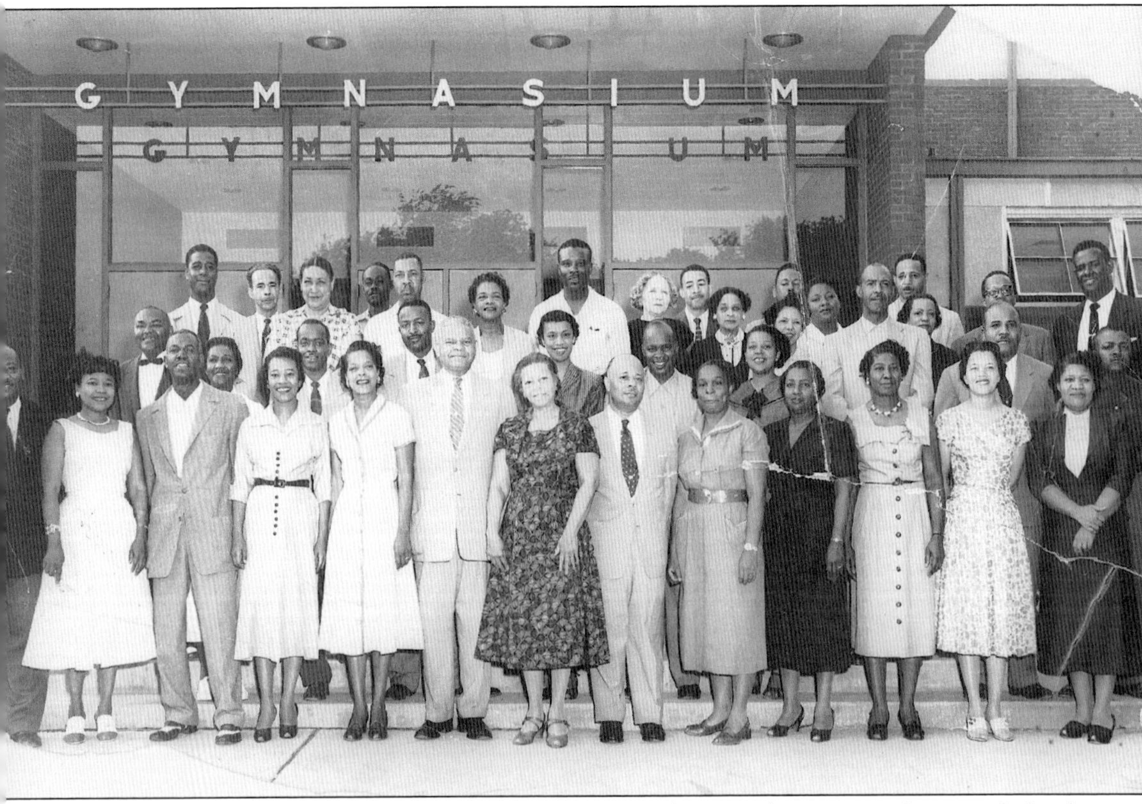

Faculty members during the 1957–1958 school year take an early-morning photograph for the *Douglass Informer* and the annual yearbook. This photograph was taken by Anita Golden, graduating senior of Douglass High School and a photography student of Walter Seward. The faculty stands in front of the gymnasium of the newly built school, located at 900 North Eastern Avenue in Oklahoma City. (Courtesy of Black Liberated Arts Center Inc.)

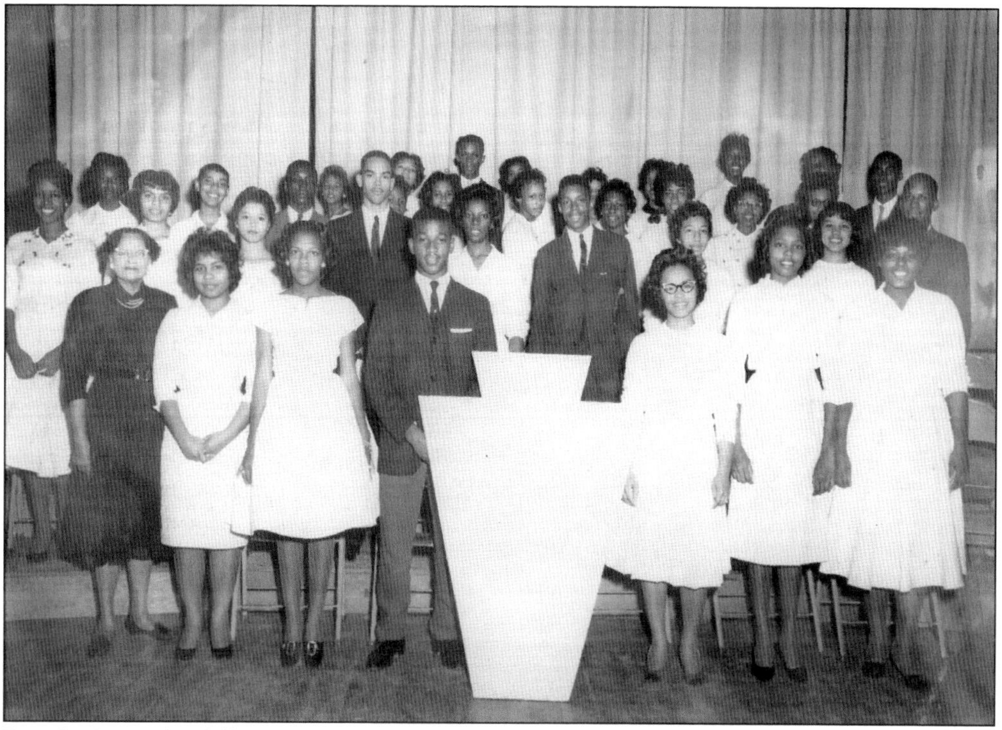

Buzedor B. Ragland (first row, far left), a career English teacher at Douglass High School, stands with the 36 members of 1961 National Honor Society. Not shown are cosponsors Cavannah Clark and J.W. Scott. Beginning in the 10th grade, students worked hard as probationary members to become members of the National Honor Society. Pictured at right is Augusta M. Morgan, a teacher at Douglass who taught English, social science, and history during her educational career. (Both, courtesy of Brenda Seward Johnson, from the Walter Seward Collection.)

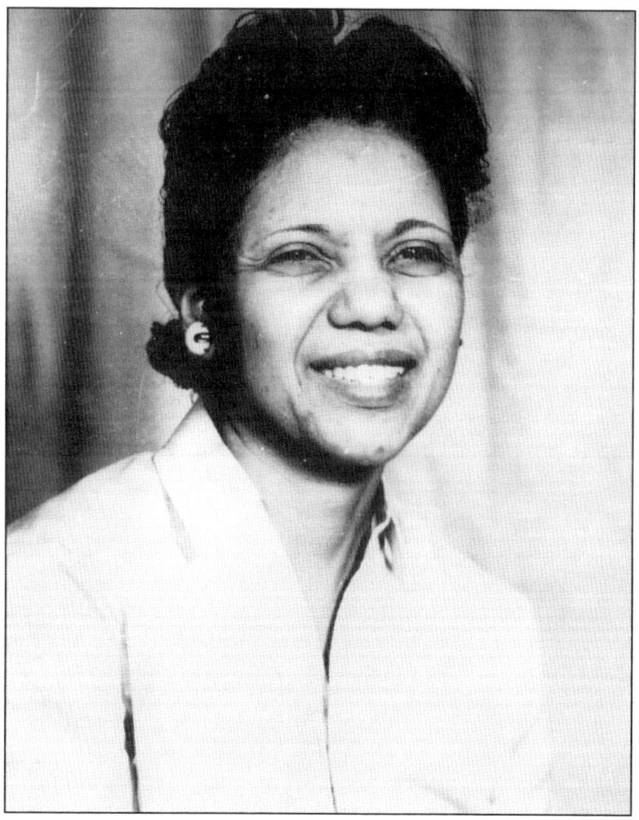

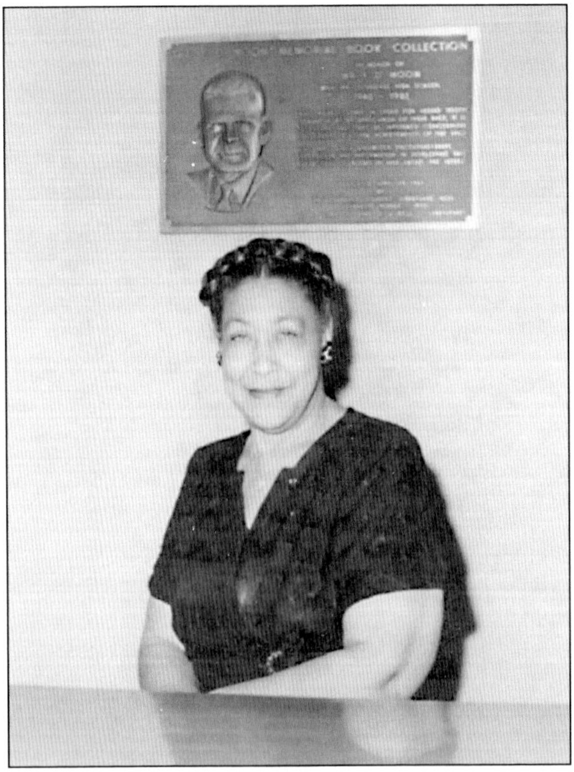

Thelma Boyd Wilson-Tillman, seated under the F.D. Moon Memorial Book Collection plaque, was dean of girls; she replaced Susie A. Haywood. She was an arts instructor and a member of F.D. Moon's and O.M. McDaniels's Administrative Council. Sherman Harris, dean of boys, was also a member of the Administrative Council under both Moon and McDaniels. Harris was one of the football coaches and tennis coach, as well as an instructor of black history, civics, and American history. He was the department head of social studies and commerce. (Left, courtesy of Brenda Seward Johnson, from the Walter Seward Collection; below, courtesy of Deola Harris.)

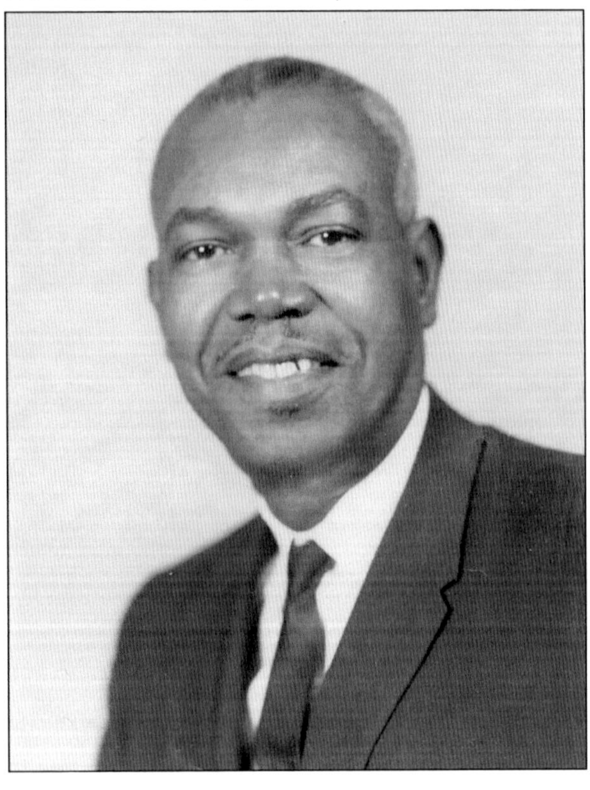

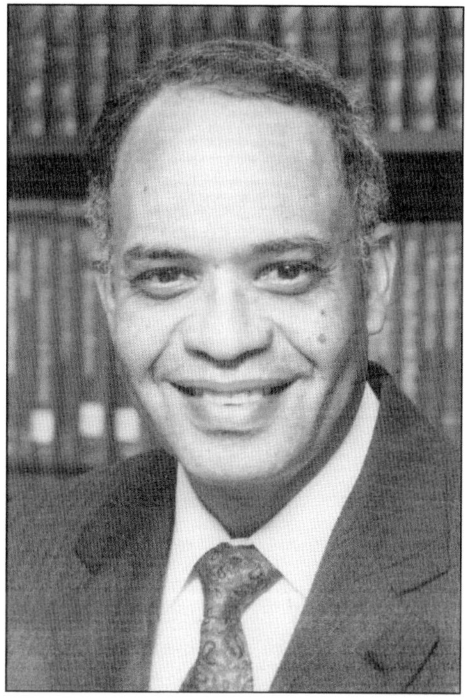

Melvin Todd, a student who briefly became a classroom teacher and counselor at Frederick A. Douglass High School, moved up the Oklahoma education organization chart. He served as principal at Northeast High School and ultimately became Dr. Melvin R. Todd, vice chancellor for academic affairs of the Oklahoma State Regents for High Education. Shown in the photograph below are W.E. Perry, junior high band director, and G.L. Buford, senior high band director. This photograph was taken in one of the music rooms at Douglass High School. (Right, courtesy of Melvin R. Todd; below, courtesy of Brenda Seward Johnson, from the Walter Seward Collection.)

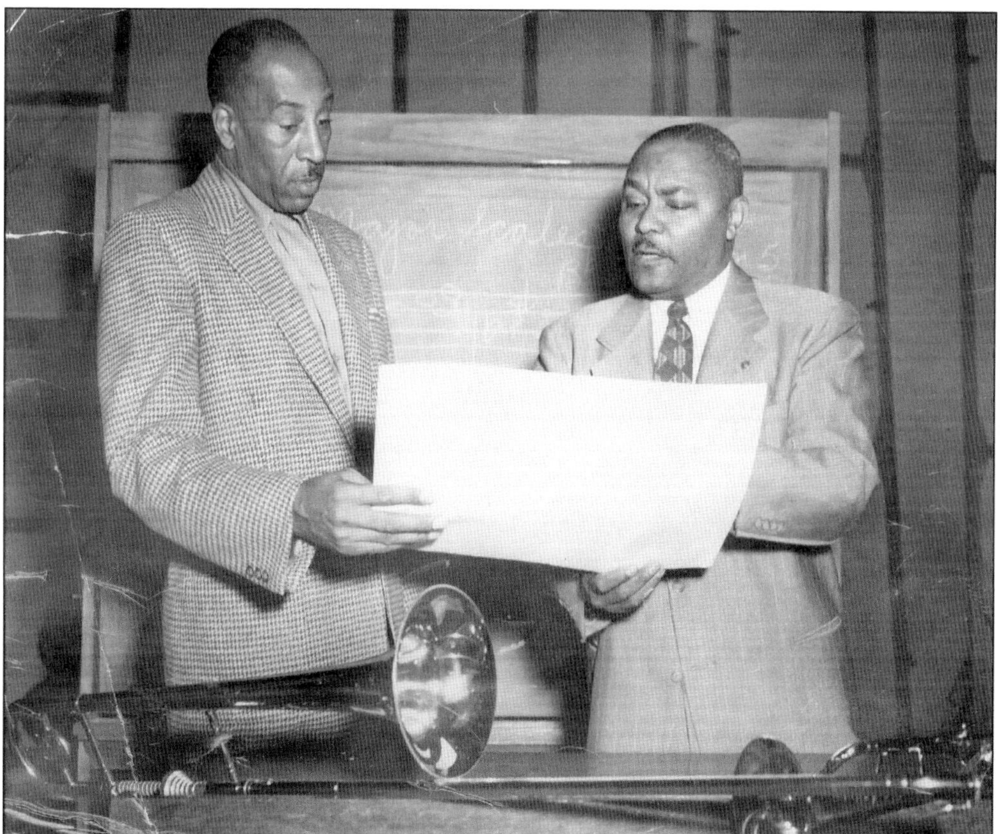

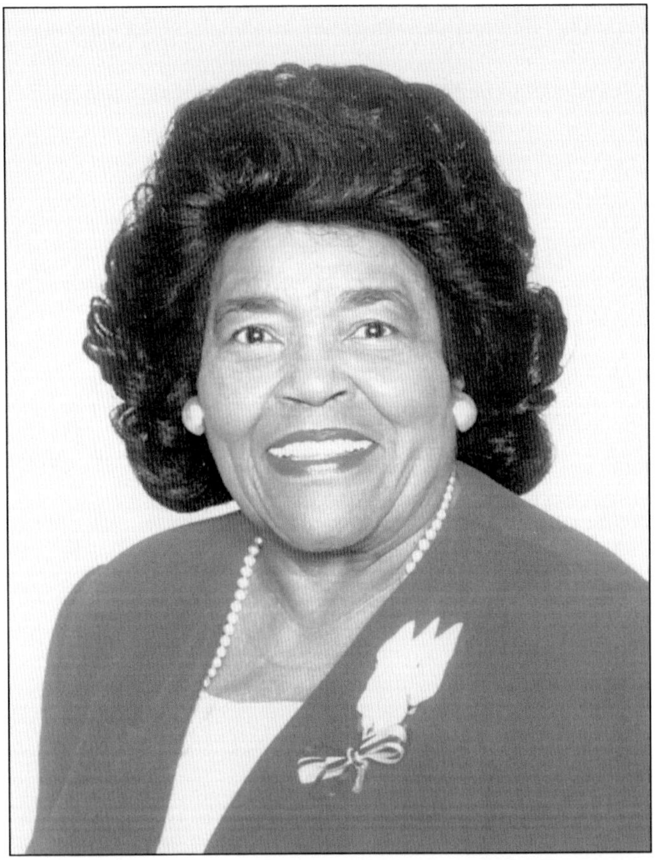

Thelma R. Parks taught for several years at Dunbar and Truman Elementary Schools in Oklahoma City and was the first reading instructor under Principal Moon at Douglass High School. Later, she taught English before becoming chairman of the department. In 1987, she won the District 5 seat on the Oklahoma City Public Schools board. Her community and national achievements and awards are numerous in education and leadership. After her retirement as an educator and education advocate, she was honored with an elementary school bearing her name. (Left, courtesy of Dean's Typesetting Services; below, courtesy of Levi McCullough.)

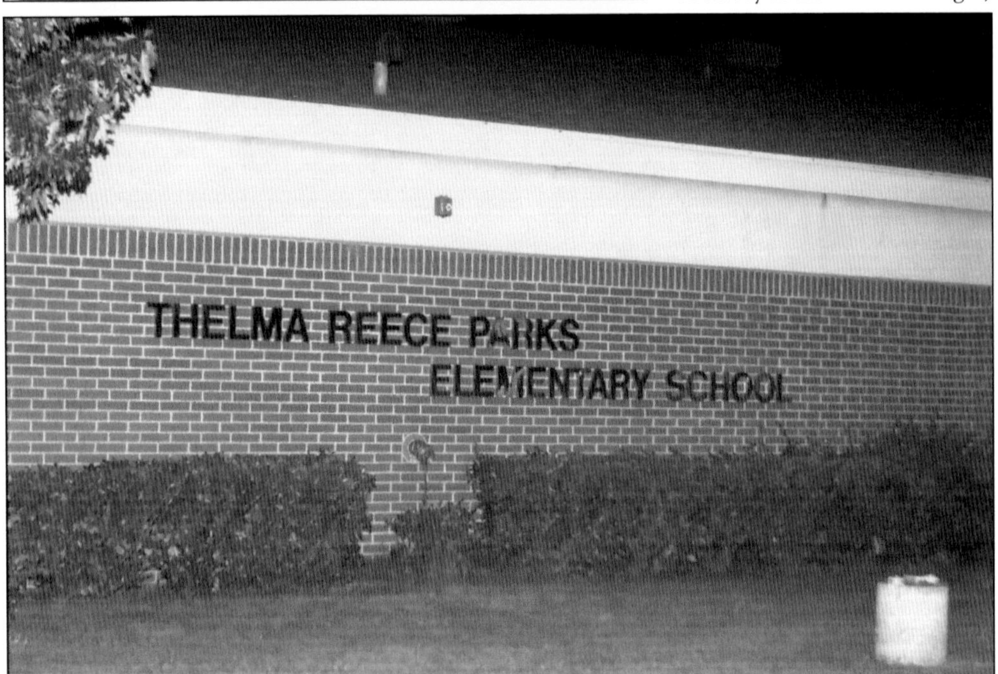

Eight

Succeeding Beyond Limits within Limits

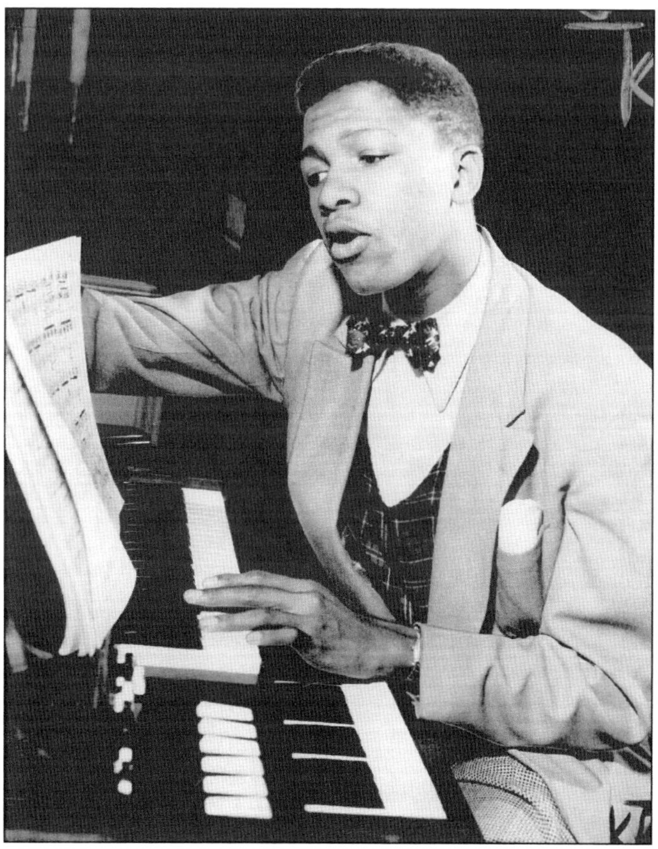

Earl Scarborough, a talented drum major for the Trojan band, placed first in the state's Oratory Interscholastic Meet and won the "I Speak for Democracy" contest sponsored by the Oklahoma City Chamber of Commerce. Born in servants' quarters, he became nationally renowned as a visual artist who started the "Black is Beautiful" movement in America. (Courtesy of Oklahoma Historical Society.)

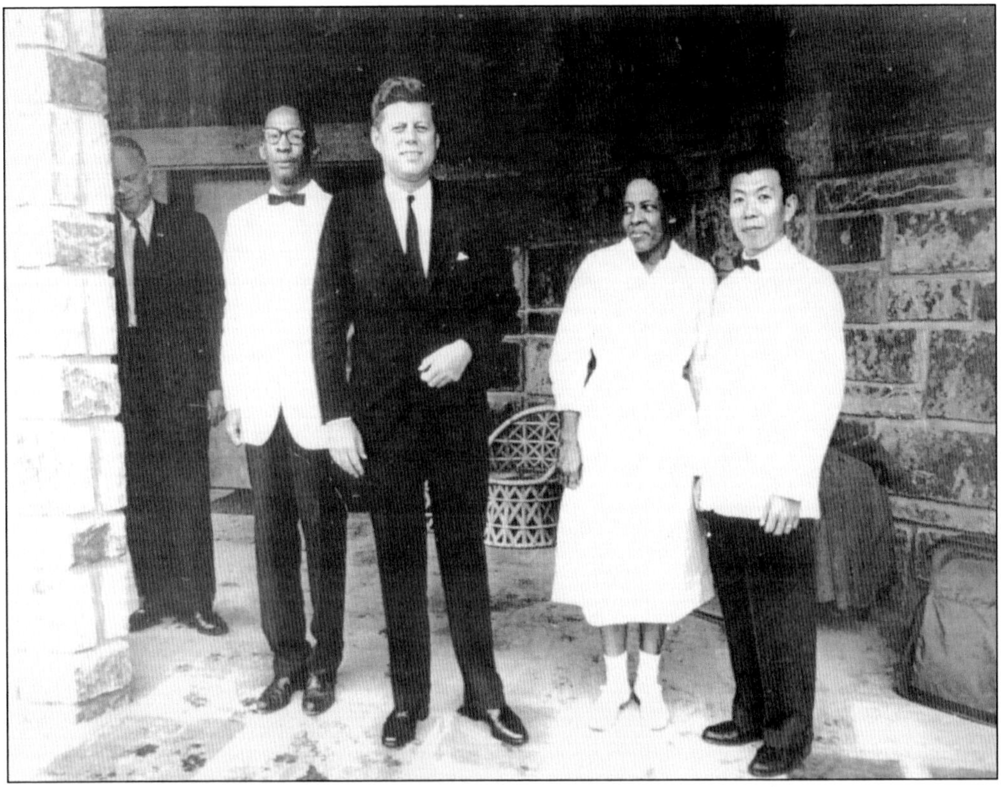

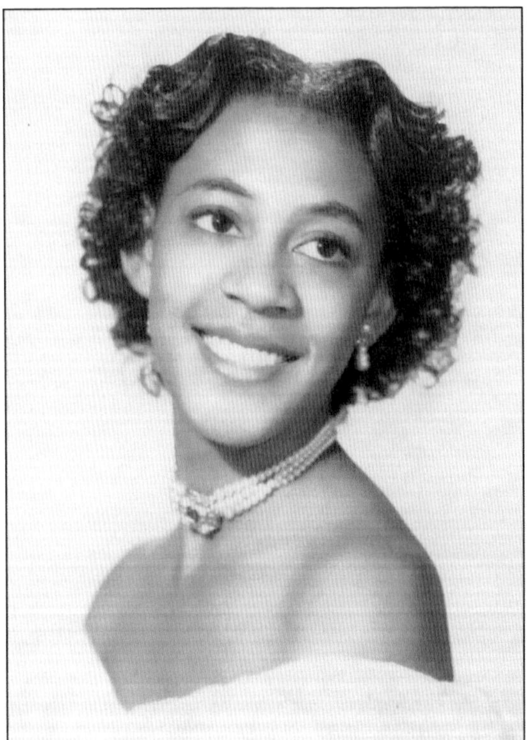

In Oklahoma City, the Brannon family became famous for their upscale restaurant, Alberta's Tea Room, located on the second floor at French Market Mall. Pictured above at the home of Sen. Robert S. Kerr are, from left to right, Kerr (near the column), Roy Lee Brannon (co-owner of Alberta's Tea Room and Douglass graduate), Pres. John F. Kennedy, Alberta Brannon (owner of Alberta's Tea Room), and Bono (Senator Kerr's housekeeper). The photograph at left shows Florence Jones, a Douglass High School graduate who started her restaurant business, Florence's, after graduation. (Above, courtesy of the Alberta Brannon family; left, courtesy of Florence Jones Kemp.)

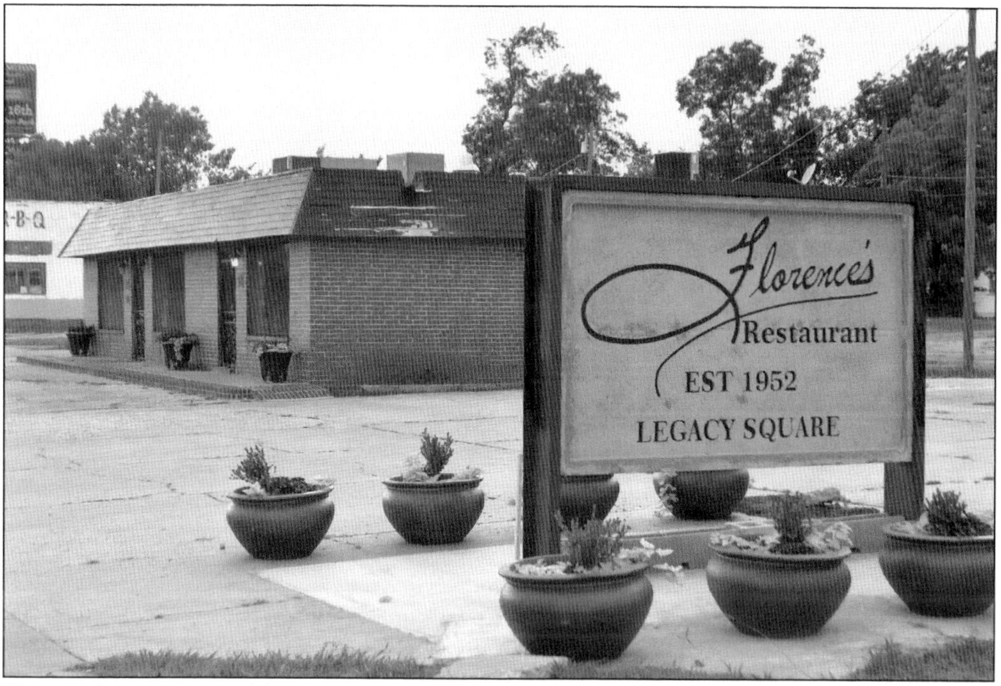

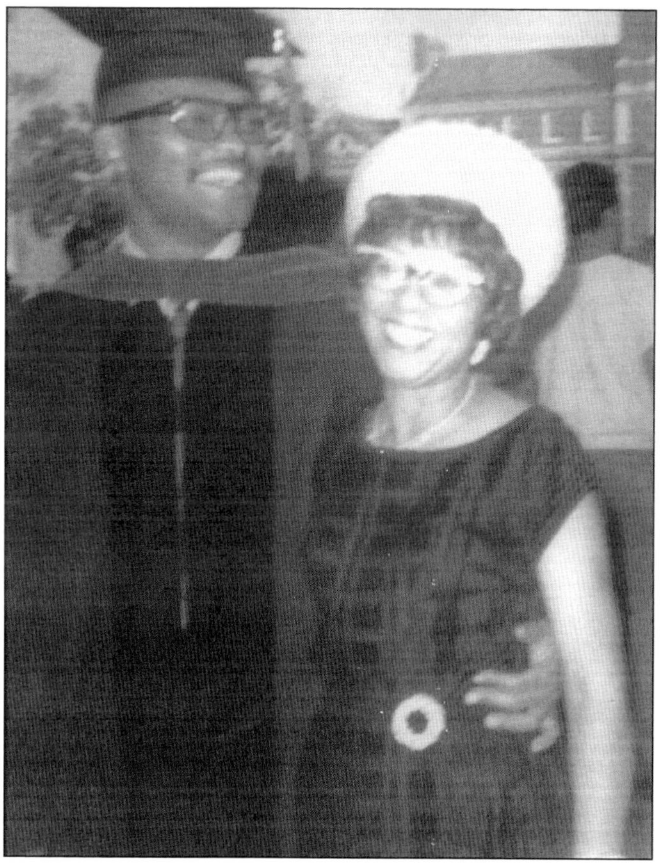

Florence Jones was confident in her talents, skills, and ability when she established her restaurant, Florence's, in 1952. It is located in the heart of the African American community on Northeast Twenty-Third Street. The restaurant, shown above, is an institution in Oklahoma City for lovers of soul food cooking. At right, Douglass graduate Dr. Roger Countee and his mother, Carolyn Countee-Kelly, are a picture of happiness at his graduation from Howard University School of Medicine. Dr. Countee, a board-certified neurosurgeon, earned international recognition for saving the lives of many marginal brain aneurysm patients. (Above, photograph by Levi McCullough, courtesy of Black Liberated Arts Center Inc.; right, courtesy of Jane Countee.)

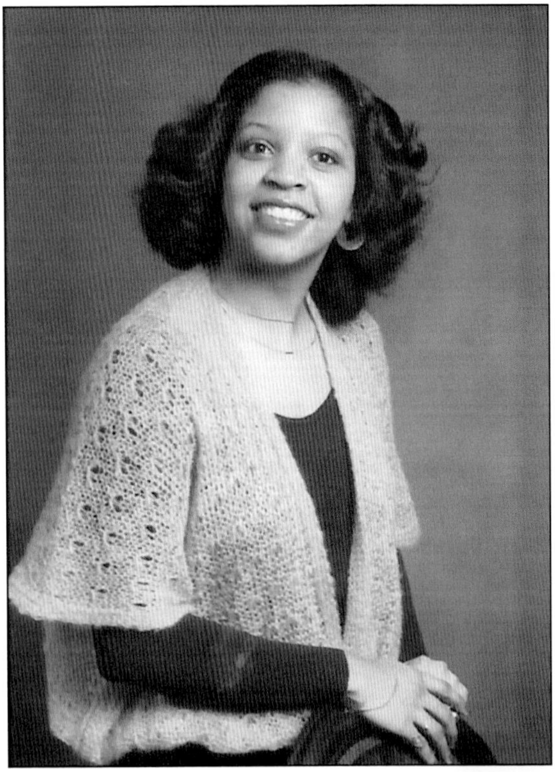

Donna LaVonne Davis (Edwards), a 1970 graduate, was an accomplished musician, trained at Douglass High School under the leadership and guidance of Leroy Hicks, music director, and was a private student of Johnnie M. Kimbro. She was accompanist for the Douglass Concert Choir on the album *Black is Beautiful*. Davis had extraordinary business skills, which launched a long career as executive secretary for Opportunities Industrialization Center. She became executive assistant to the president of United Way of Greater Richmond, Virginia, which made a passionate and sorrowful tribute to her at her funeral service. Donna LaVonne Davis Edwards endured 10 years of trial tests seeking to find a cure for multiple myeloma before succumbing to the disease. (Both, courtesy of the Donna Davis Edwards estate.)

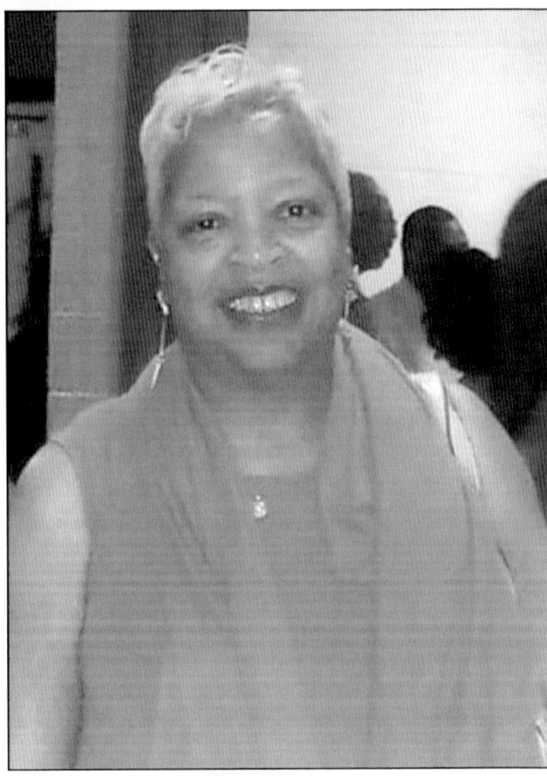

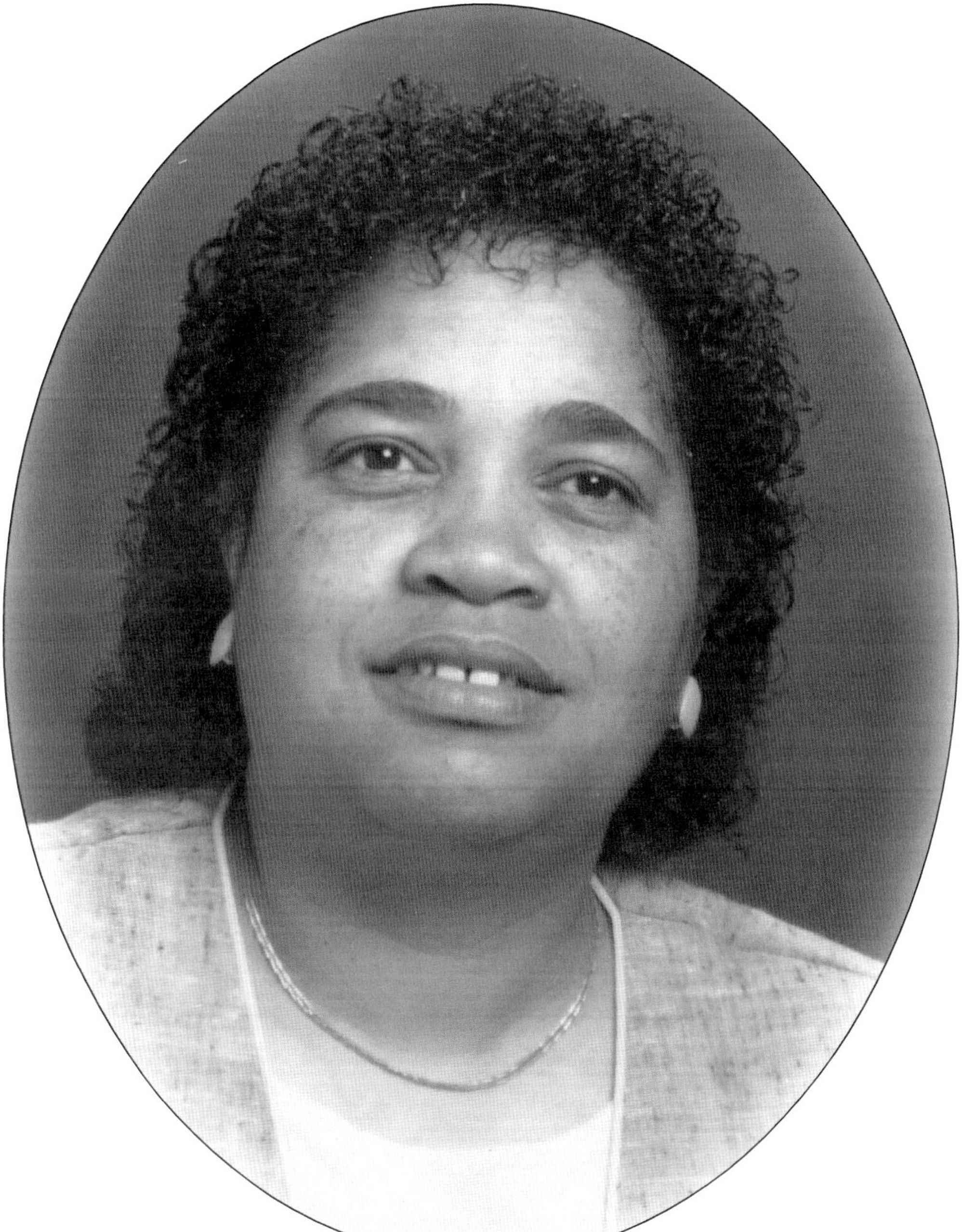

Unknown to many doctors who attempted to diagnose her illness, Carolyn Davis (Blevins) experienced an episodic life of light strokes, mini heart attacks, and, ultimately, loss of speech until the age of 20. Dr. Nazih Zudhi discovered that Davis had been born without the heart's inner wall. He constructed an artificial, disintegrating wall that allowed cells to grow naturally and performed the first open heart surgery of this kind on an African American patient, in Oklahoma City. Carolyn Davis Blevins, mother of six, outlived two husbands. Professionals, scholars, and college graduates make up her family. This Douglass graduate embraced and lived out the values of the Moon model of education despite life's hardships. (Courtesy of Juanita Davis.)

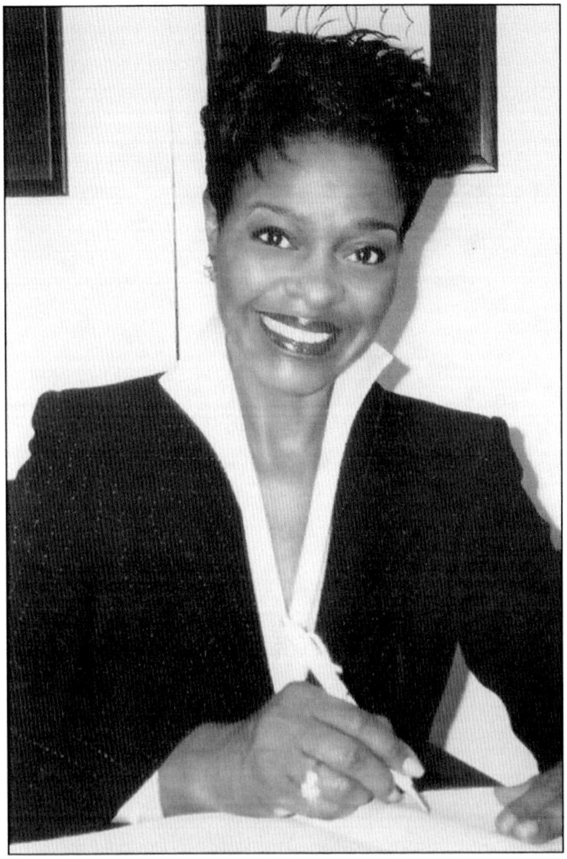

Zora Brown was an internationally recognized, outspoken advocate for breast cancer. The Douglass High School graduate was appointed by Pres. George H.W. Bush to the National Cancer Advisory Board of the National Cancer Institute in 1991. Brown's family carried a cancer gene that claimed many of their lives. Determined to find a cure, she often participated in medical trials. Brown received two special citations from Congress, the final citation given at her death from bilateral breast cancer. In memory of Brown, Oklahoma City named the Oklahoma City Wellness Center's trails the Zora Brown Trails. (Left, courtesy of Joyce Webb; below, courtesy of Levi McCullough.)

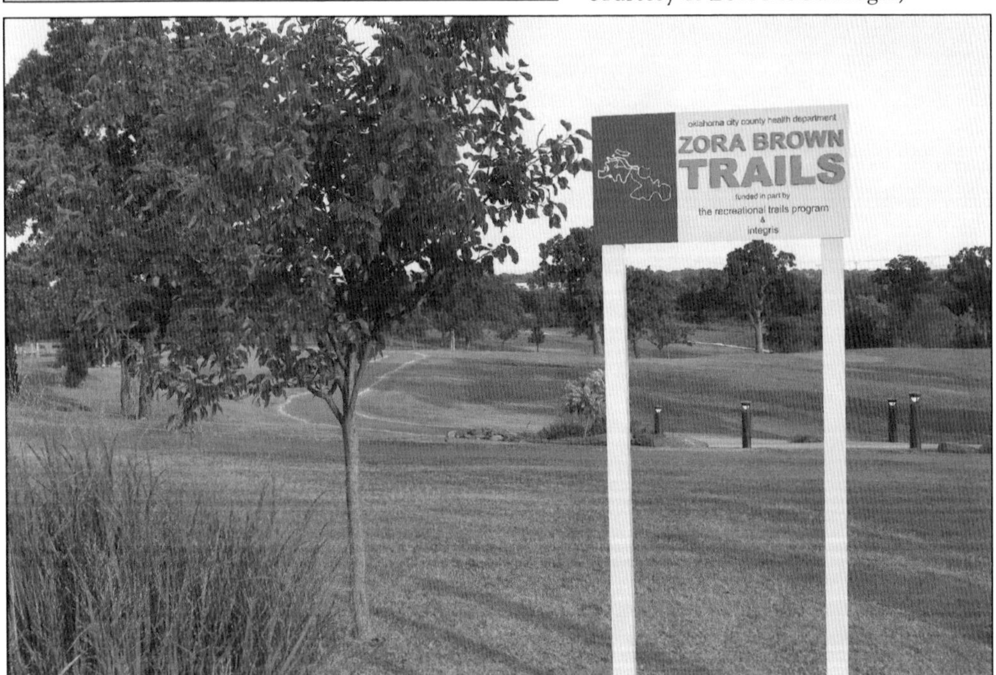

Oklahoma City native Zora Brown (right) graduated from Douglass High School and attended Oklahoma State University, majoring in business administration. She went on to do important work in health research. She opened doors, blazed trails, and advocated for breast cancer victims. In the photograph below, Maurice Spears (left) and his brother Louie B. Spears receive the Charlie Christian Jazz Music Award from Black Liberated Arts Center Inc. The Douglass graduates moved to California and earned reputations as excellent musicians, bandleaders, and music composers. Maurice composed music across genres for many Emmy Award winners. (Right, Courtesy Helen Webb; below, courtesy of the Black Liberated Arts Center Inc.)

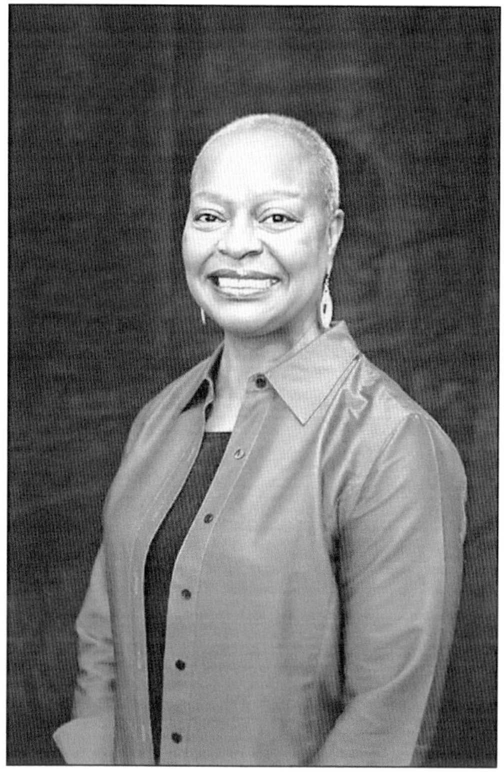

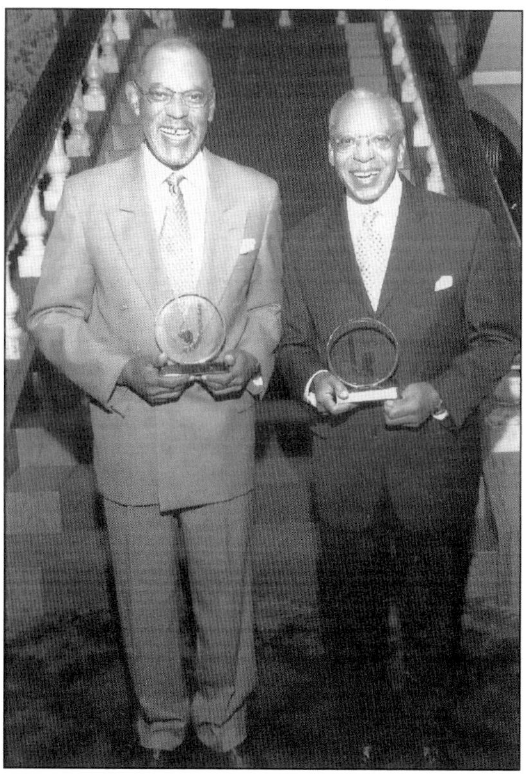

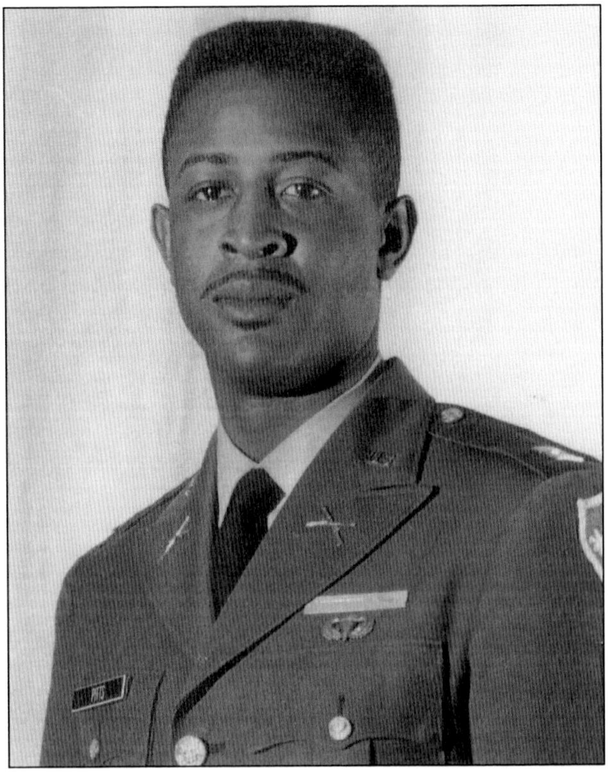

Douglass graduate Riley Leroy Pitts became a captain in the US Army after graduating from Wichita State University. Following graduation, he was assigned to lead a battalion in Vietnam. The photograph below was the last taken of him on the final day of his tour in Vietnam. He was killed after, bravely falling on a grenade to save his comrades. Pitts was the first African American to receive a Congressional Medal of Honor. He left two children, Mark and Stacie, and a wife, Eula. (Both, courtesy of Eula Pitts.)

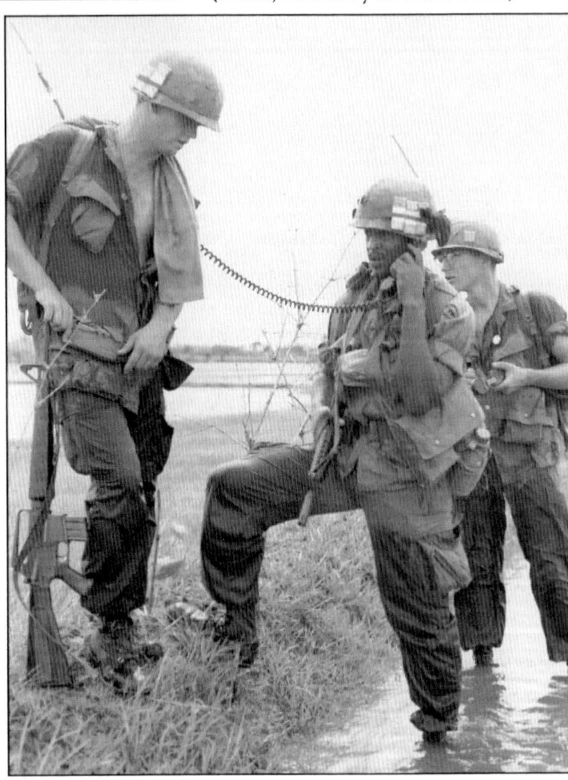

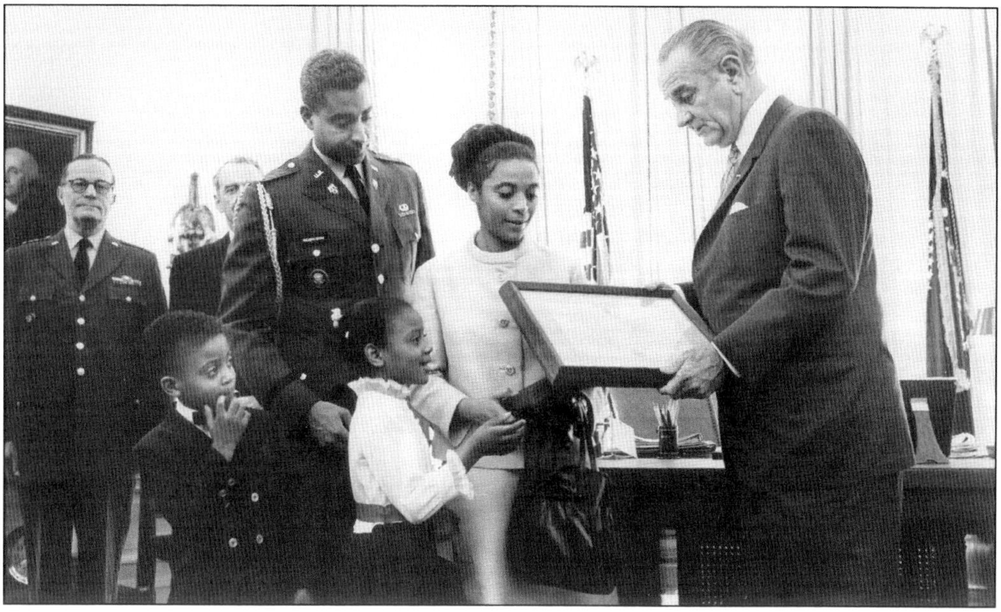

Mark and Stacie Pitts look on as their mother, Eula Pitts, receives the citation that accompanied the Medal of Honor plaque. It was given posthumously to her husband, Riley Leroy Pitts, from Pres. Lyndon B. Johnson on October 22, 1967. Captain Pitts also received the Silver Star for gallantry in action at the White House the same day. The next month, the Purple Heart was awarded to him. (Both, courtesy of Eula Pitts.)

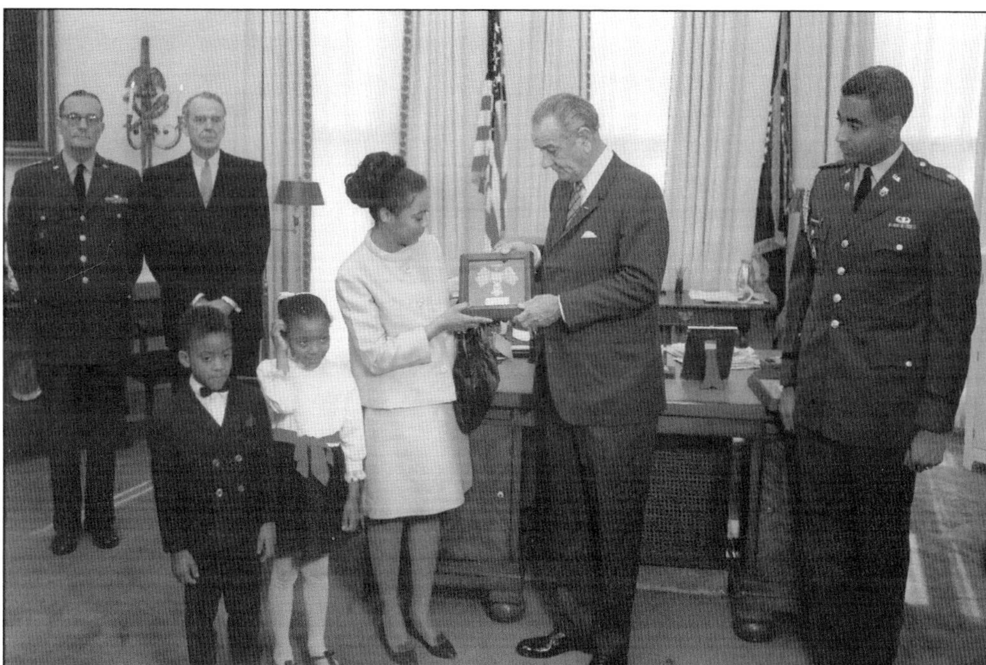

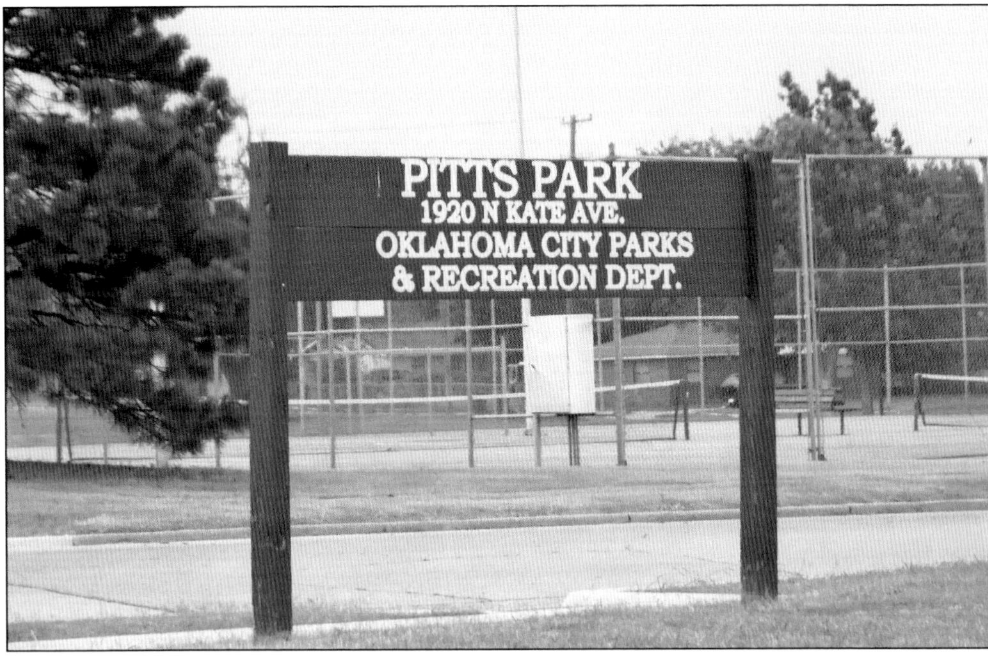

For 50 years, in Germany and across the world, buildings, parks, centers, roads, certificates, scholarships, and awards were named in Riley Leroy Pitts's honor. In Oklahoma City, a park and recreation center in northeast Oklahoma bears his name. The University of Wichita named a building after him as well. Below, his wife, Eula, is greeted by Pres. Barack Obama at the White House, where she received appreciation as a member of Sons and Daughters in Touch, a national organization that celebrates Father's Day at the White House for fallen heroes. (Both, courtesy of Eula Pitts.)

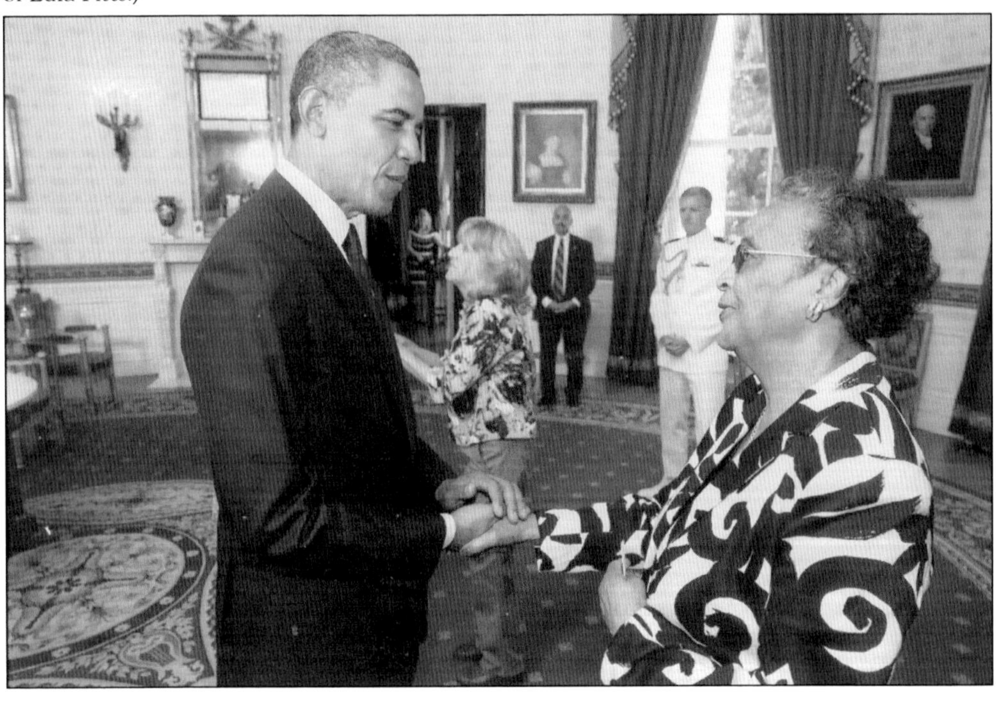

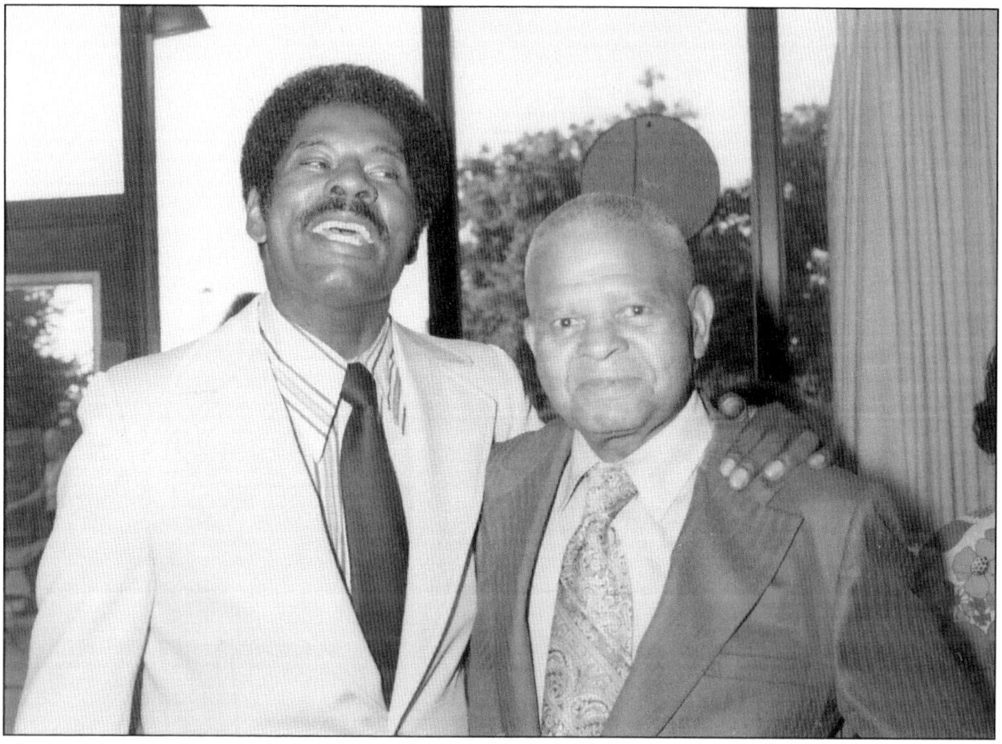

Carl Holmes dedicated his life to fire and life-safety initiatives. He founded the Carl Holmes Executive Development Institute, whose purpose is to build management skills for firefighters. The institute has trained more than 5,000 firefighters across America, Africa, Canada, and the Caribbean. The Oklahoma City native attended Frederick A. Douglass High School and was one of the first black firemen hired by the Oklahoma City Fire Department. Holmes rose to become fire chief. Above, F.D. Moon, his principal, congratulates Holmes on his promotion. The photograph below shows graduates of the Carl Holmes Executive Development Institute. (Above, courtesy of Helen Gray; below, courtesy of Carl Holmes.)

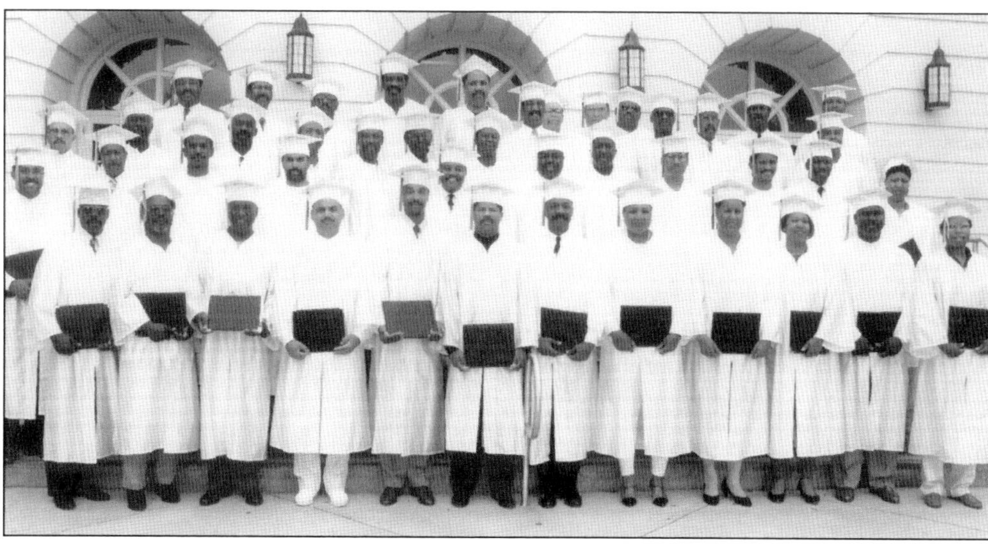

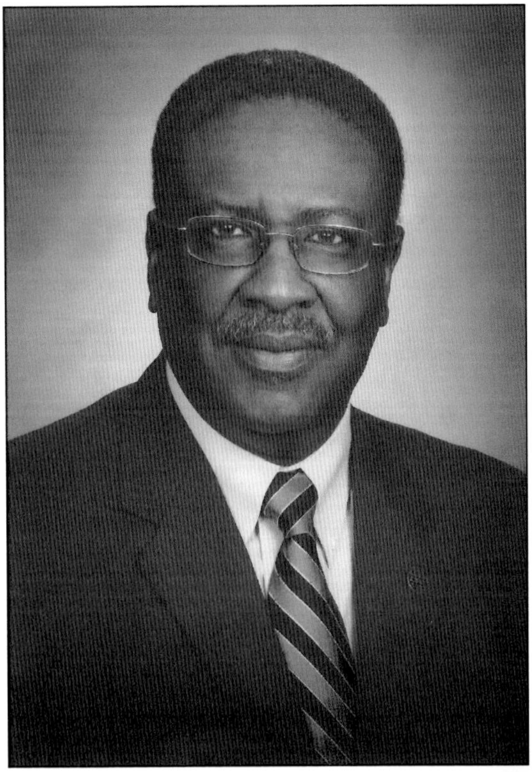

Dr. Donnie Nero (left) graduated from Dunjee High School in 1967. He received a bachelor of science degree in education in 1971, a master of science degree in educational administration, and a doctor of education degree in occupational and adult education from Oklahoma State University. After 38 years in education, he became president of Connors State College, the first black to become president of a predominately white school. Dr. Frank Wilson (below), a graduate of Douglass High School, matriculated with his twin sister, Frances, to Fisk University. He attended medical school at Howard University and received specialty training at the University of Missouri at Kansas City. He returned to Oklahoma City after serving military duty to become the first black board-certified OB-GYN doctor in the city. (Left, courtesy of Donnie Nero; below, courtesy of Black Liberated Arts Center Inc.)

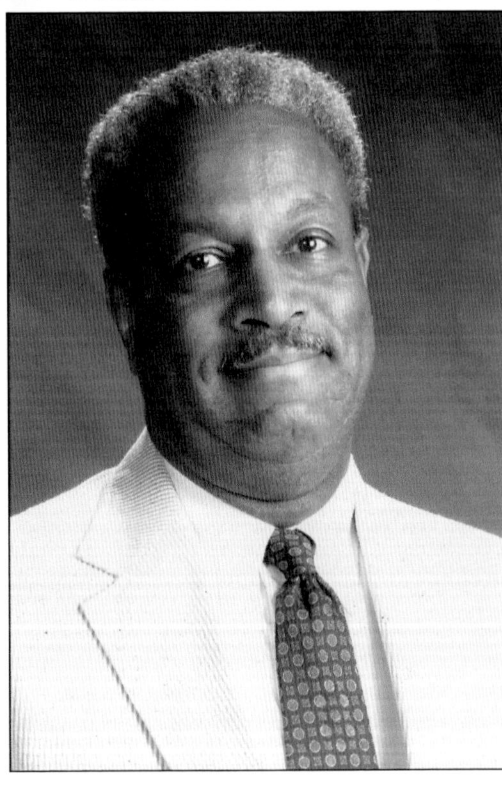

Nine

THE GLORY YEARS

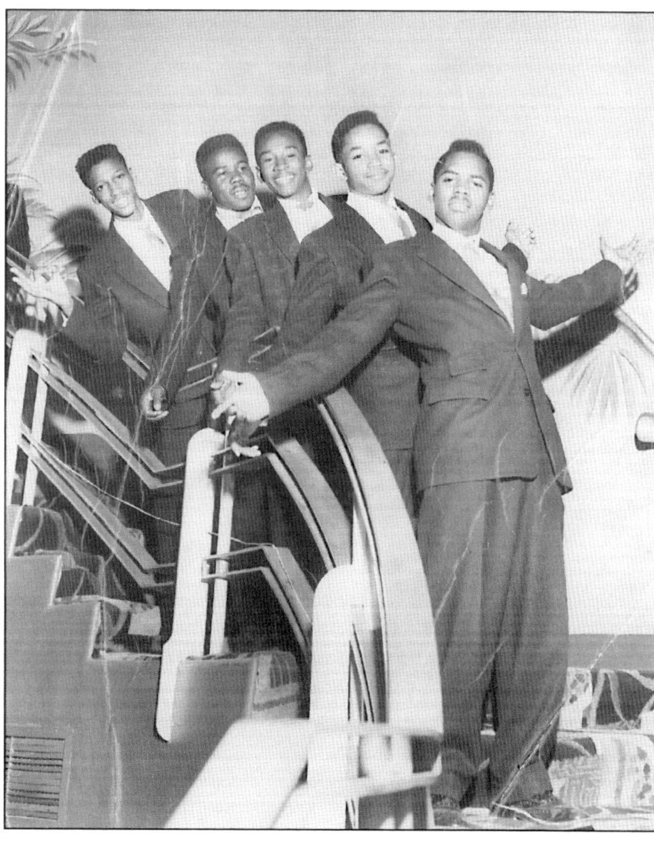

One of the hottest musical groups to graduate from Douglass High School in the mid-1950s was The Dukes. These school friends moved to Las Vegas to establish a singing and recording career. From left to right are Billie Armstead, Richard Williams, Everett Edwards, Willie Moon, and Donald Nero. (Courtesy of Black Liberated Arts Center Inc.)

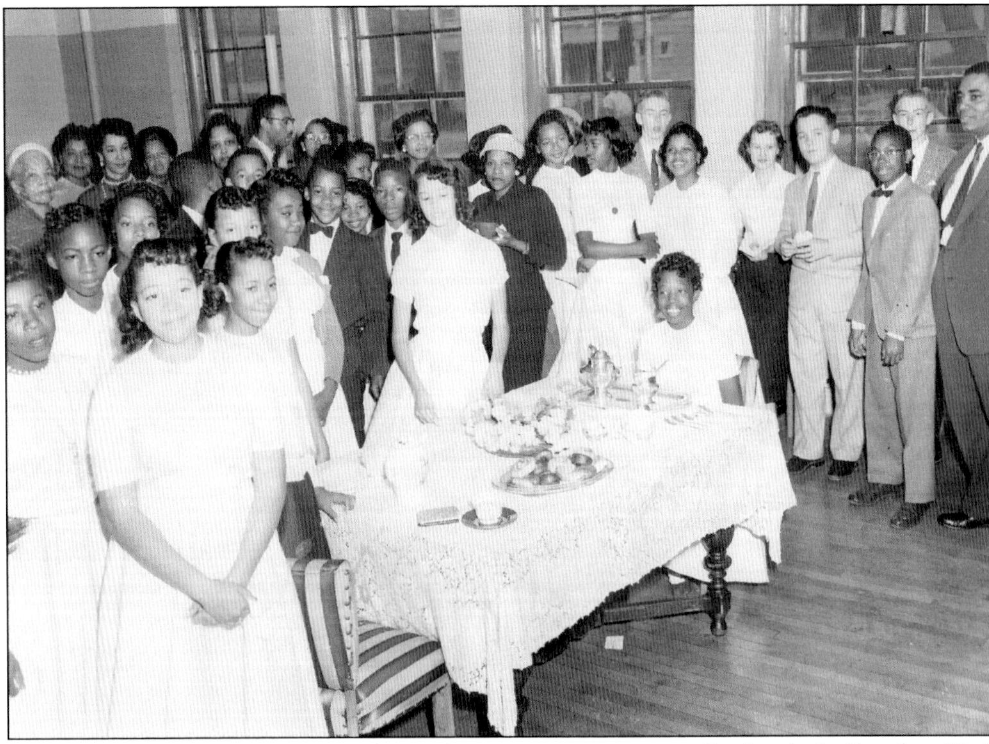

Etiquette, manners, tea parties, and sweethearts were en vogue at Frederick A. Douglass High School on premise or off. Above, James Jenkins (dean of boys), standing at far right, looks over the tea party given at McFarland YWCA as students, parents. and others pose for a picture. The photograph below shows the social debut of the National Sub Debs Club, of Douglass High School, on the school auditorium stage as F.D. Moon, far right, and an unidentified lady are seated in front of club members. (Both, courtesy of Brenda Seward Johnson, from the Walter Seward Collection.)

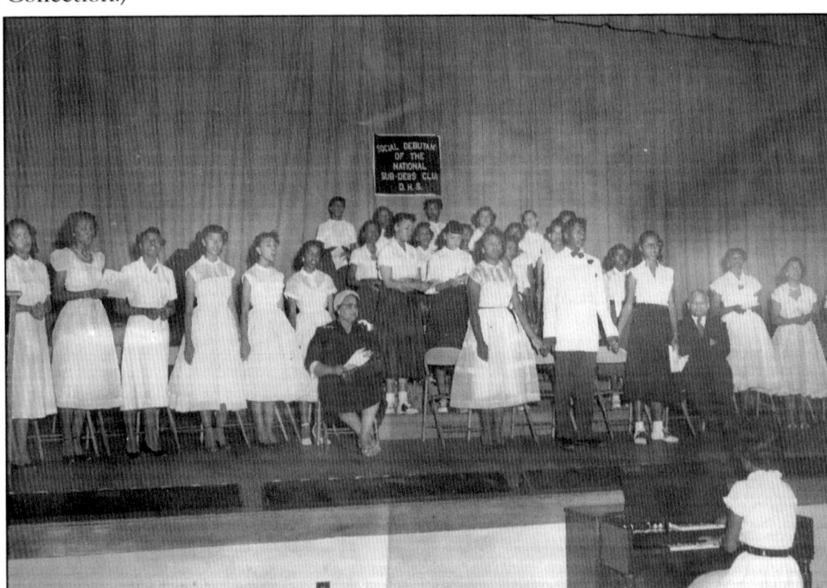

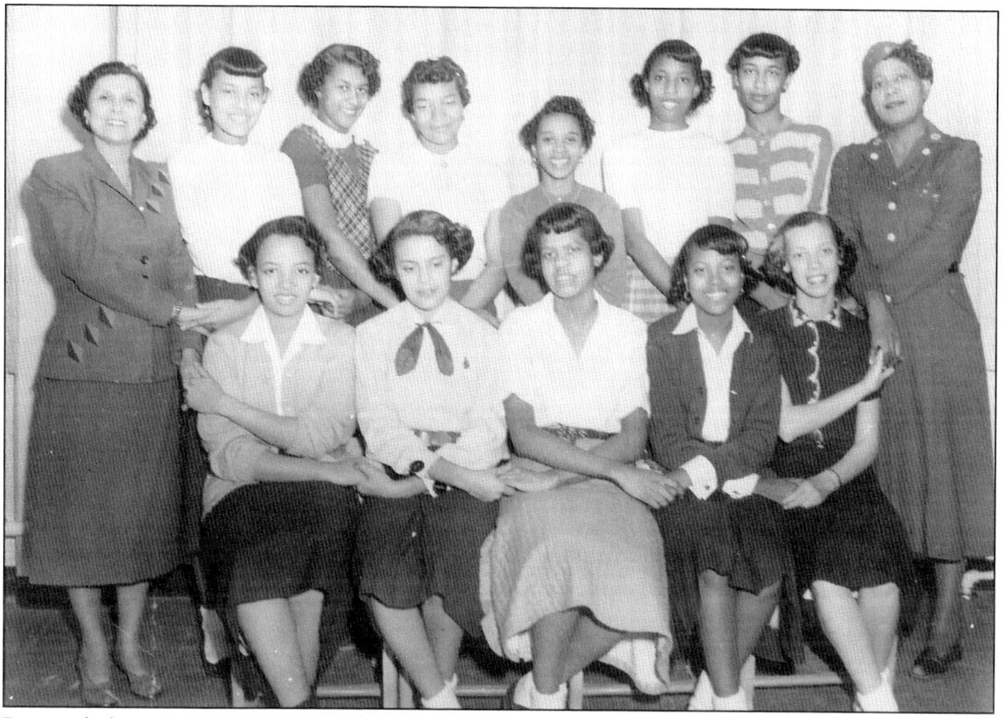

Pictured above are uniformed Girl Scout leaders Sadie Boyd (standing left) and Leoshia Moon (standing right), wife of Principal Moon, with Douglass High School's Santa Maria Mariner Girl Scouts. Both leaders were parents of members. The image below captures the Douglass High School Student Council with its sponsors, Augusta Morgan (history instructor; second row, far left, in the dark suit) and Dorothy Burnett (business instructor; second row, far right). (Both, courtesy of Brenda Seward Johnson, from the Walter Seward Collection.)

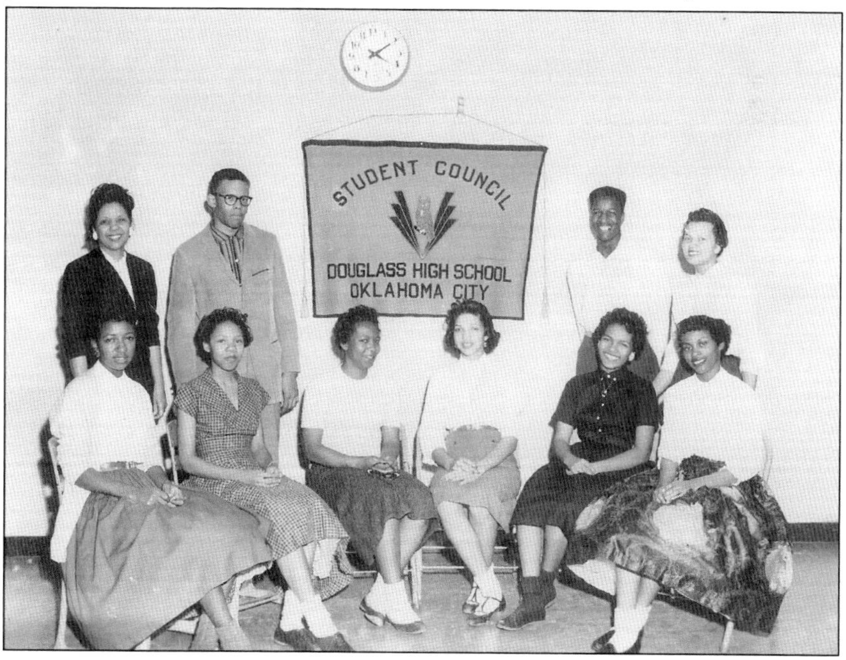

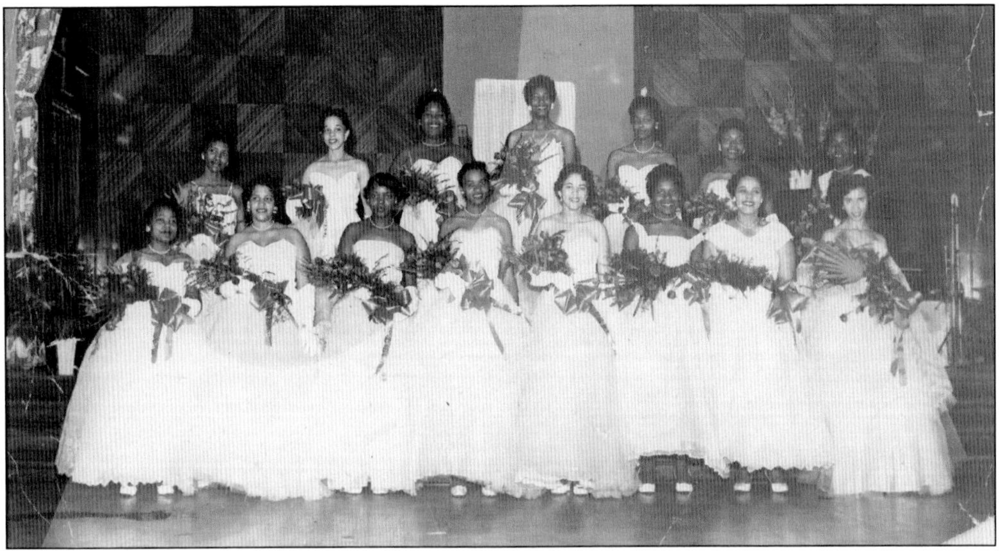

The above photograph shows the 1957 Hi-Y Sweethearts. Hi-Y ladies dressed alike and carried floral bouquets given to them by their dates before heading to the dance floor at the ball. The annual tradition was sponsored by the YMCA. Another annual celebration was the Miss Homecoming queen. A special assembly program is planned and presented by the New Homemakers of America. This program kicks off a number of student activities associated with the event. Douglass High School students and teachers look forward to it. (Both, courtesy of Brenda Seward Johnson, from the Walter Seward Collection.)

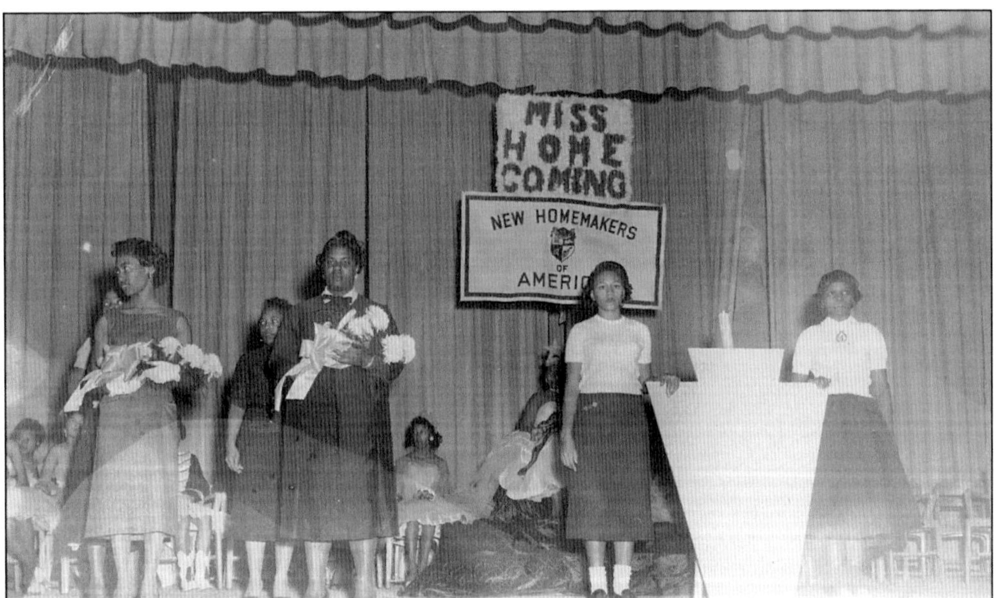

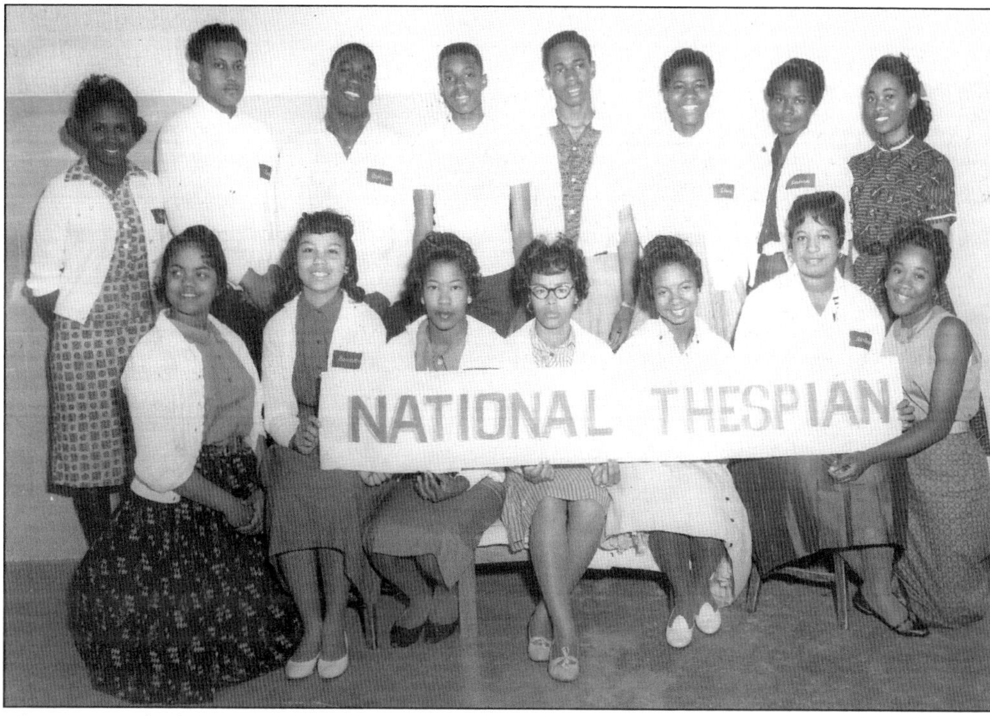

The National Thespian Club (above), sponsored by the Department of Fine Arts, presented one or two plays each year. Most were drama students under G.D. Waterford or Consuelo V. Tompkins. Waterford taught English literature, and Tompkins taught debate and public speaking. There were also foreign language clubs. Spanish Club members (below) present a program during assembly on the auditorium stage. (Both, courtesy of Brenda Seward Johnson, from the Walter Seward Collection.)

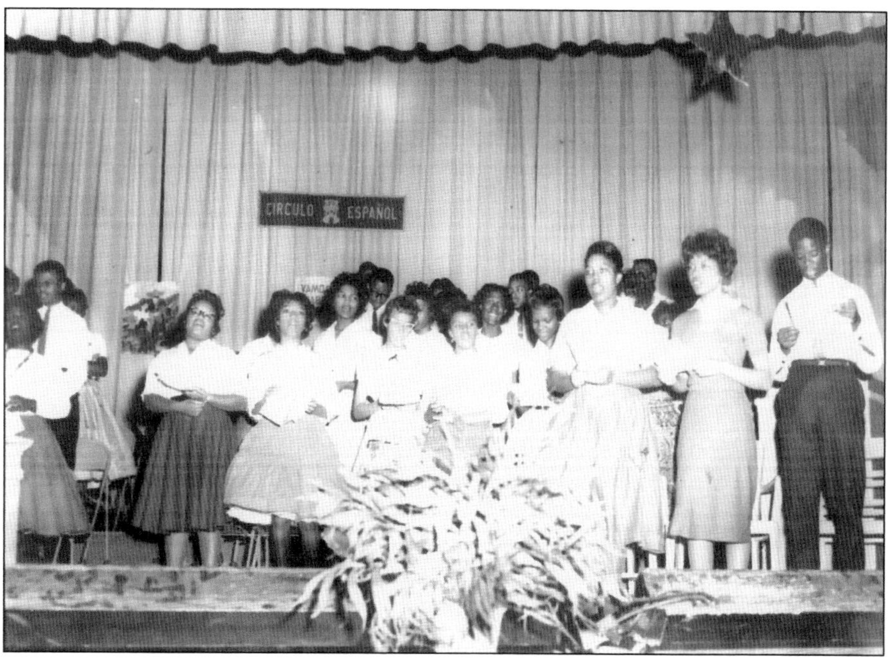

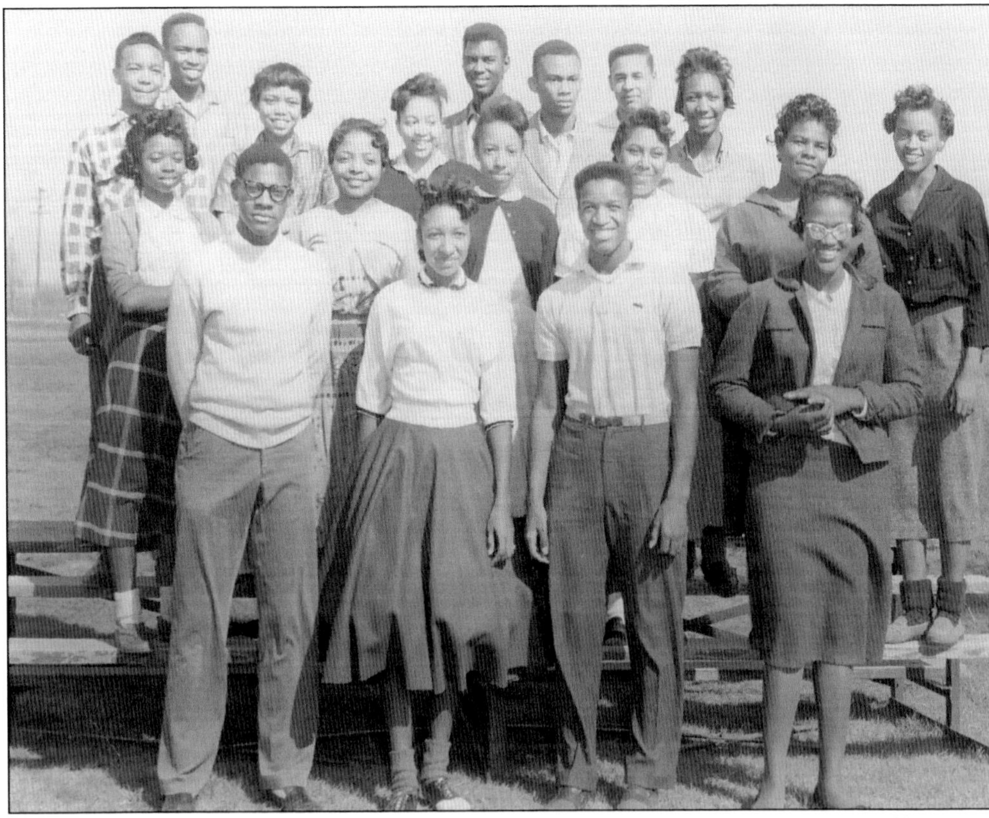

Each year, the *Trojan World* staff, under the leadership of one or two teacher sponsors, would organize to start working on the yearbook. It required a great deal of coordination between departments, clubs, organizations, administrative staff, and the photography class to set deadlines and schedules to ensure that the book would arrive on time. The above photograph shows the 1958–1959 yearbook staff. Below, the 1958 members of the Honor Society sit for a photograph to be included in the yearbook. (Both, courtesy of Brenda Seward Johnson, from the Walter Seward Collection.)

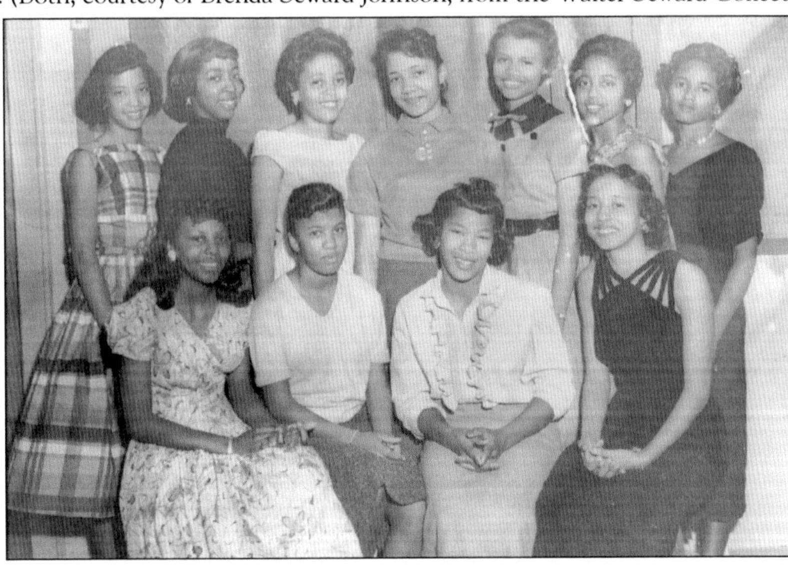

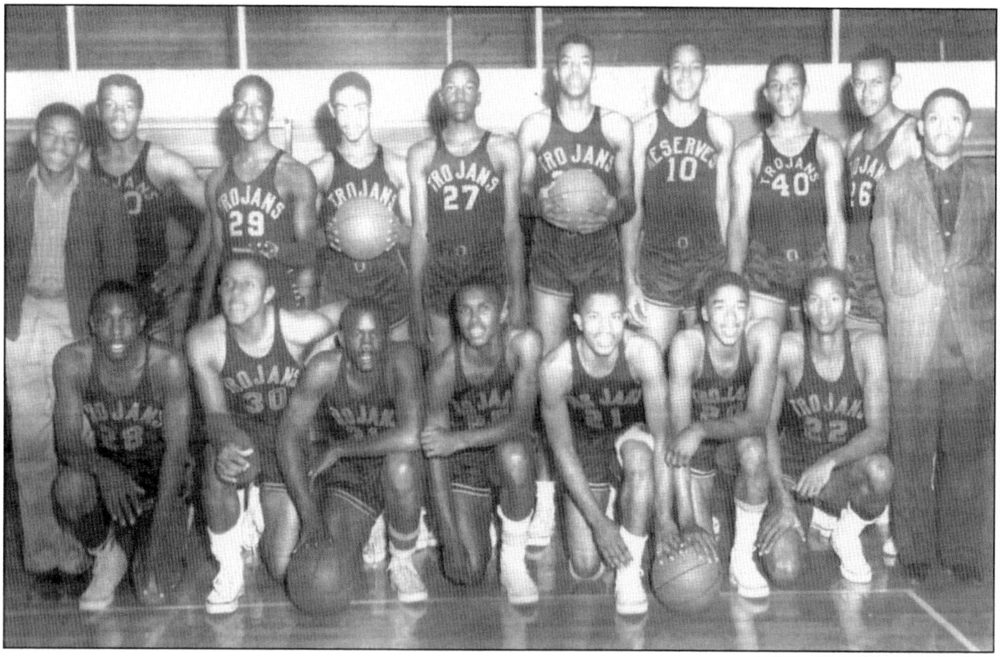

Members of the 1959 basketball team, under the leadership of Coach Lawrence Cudjoe (standing, far right in suit), took second place in the state conference. Cudjoe played with the Harlem Globetrotters. Anthony Watson, a future Olympian who ran track in Rome for the University of Oklahoma, stands between numbers 27 and 10. Watson was inducted into the Oklahoma City Public Schools Foundation's Wall of Fame. The 1956–1957 Lettermen's Club of Douglass High School is shown below. (Both, courtesy of Brenda Seward Johnson, from the Walter Seward Collection.)

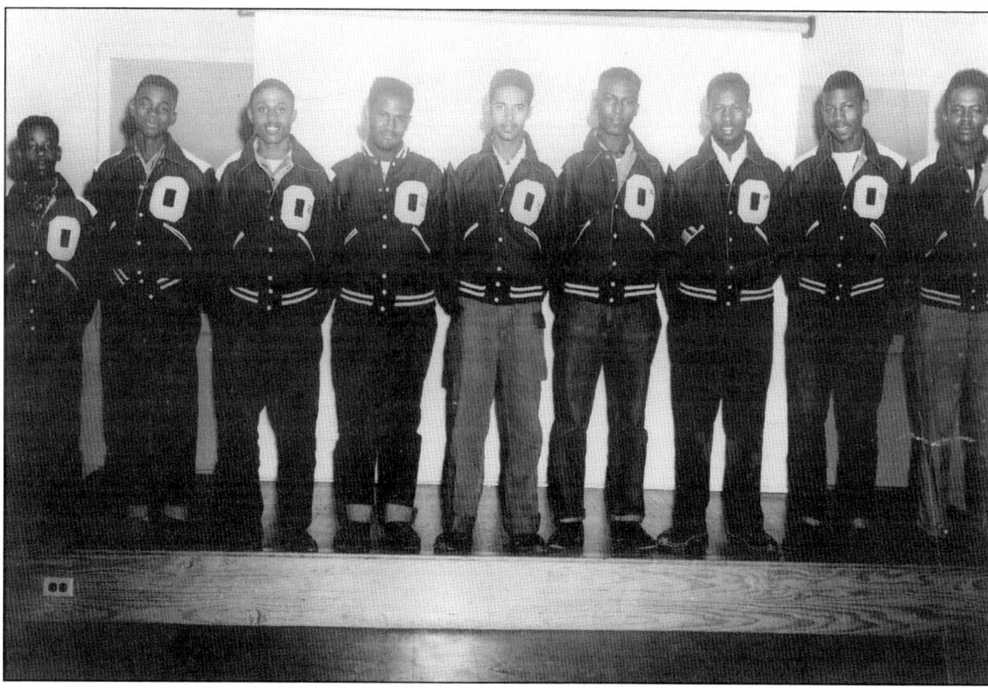

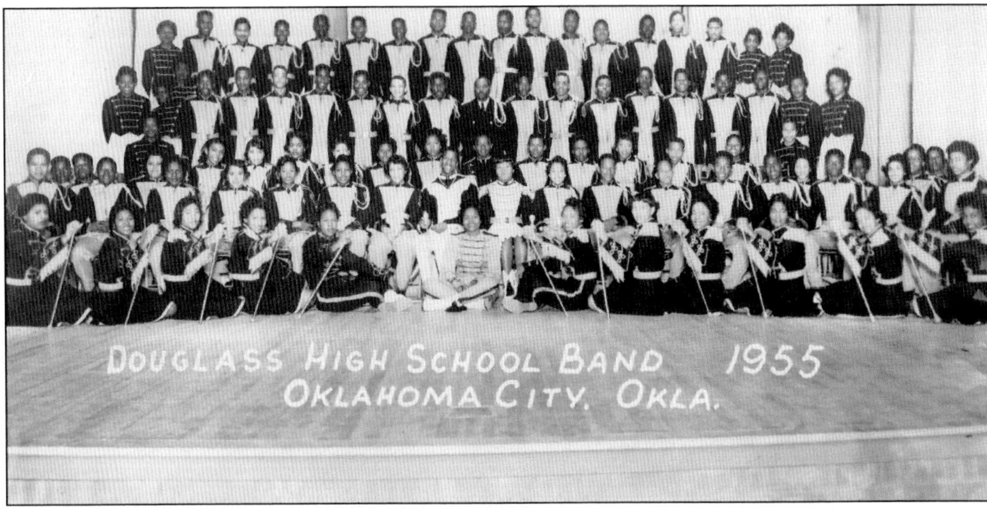

The 1955 Douglass High School Marching Band was the best of the best bands during the glory years of Douglass High School "family" history. The band was under the direction of G.L. Buford, who enjoyed a long career at Douglass. During that era, William Johnson became principal of the developing Moon Junior High School, with the supervision of F.D. Moon under the Oklahoma City Separate School system. Below, Johnson (left) stands with the track team and coaches. (Both, courtesy of Brenda Seward Johnson, from the Walter Seward Collection.)

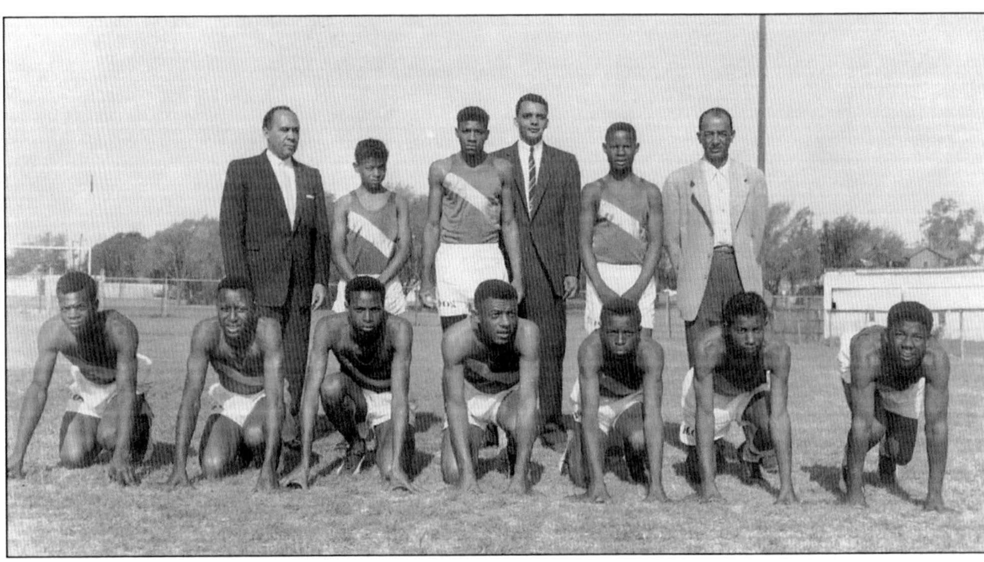

Ten

The Graduates

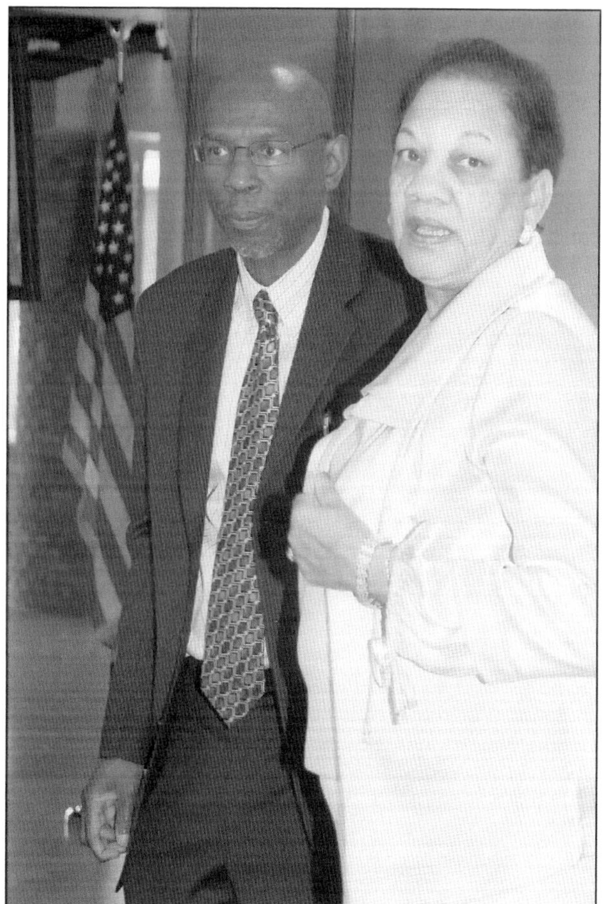

Anita Golden Arnold, Douglass High School graduate, accompanies Geoffrey Canada (appointed by First Lady Michelle Obama to serve as her education ambassador in America) into an educational forum in Oklahoma City. Canada had just been honored by the State of Oklahoma for his work with the Harlem Children's Zone. His education model boasted a 100 percent college acceptance rate of his students. (Courtesy of the Black Liberated Arts Center Inc.)

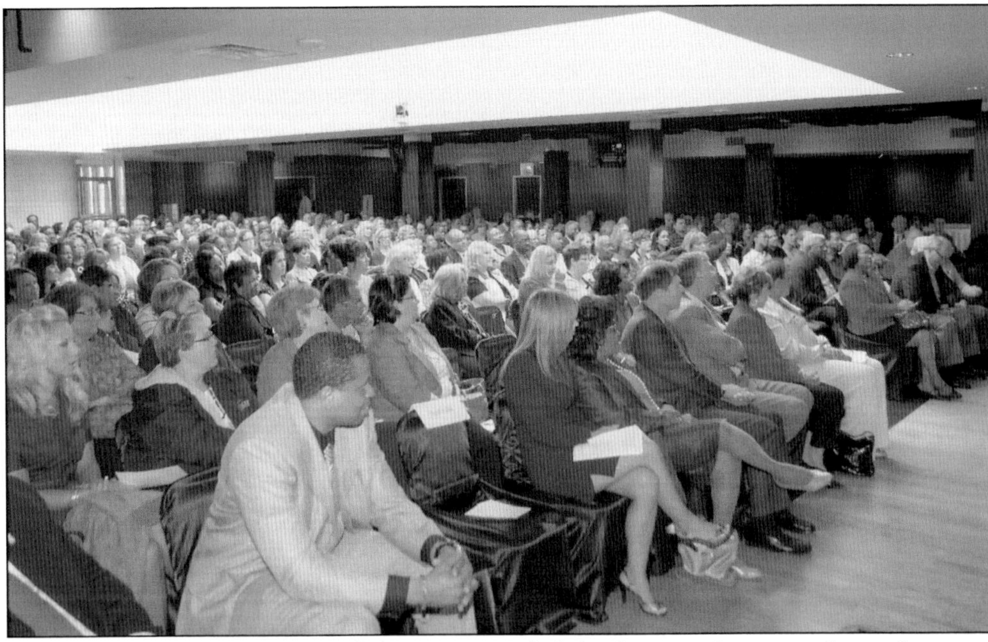

Leaders from Oklahoma City and the state attended the forum with principals, teachers, and administrators to understand Geoffrey Canada's efforts, failures, and successes as the founder of one of the most successful education systems in America. The photograph below shows Douglass graduate Shirley Bruce-Darrell, who was appointed by Judge Luther Bohanan to lead the desegregation plan in Oklahoma City. Bruce-Darrell served on the Oklahoma City Public Schools board and was the first black county commissioner in Oklahoma. She graduated from Hampton University and earned a master's degree from Oklahoma City University. (Above, courtesy of Black Liberated Arts Center Inc.; below, courtesy of Dean's Typesetting Service.)

Angela Monson (right), valedictorian of her class at Douglass, received her undergraduate degree from Oklahoma City University and earned a master of science in public administration from the University of Oklahoma. Monson served as Oklahoma state representative and state senator from 1990 to 2005. Her advocacy was health care, education, and criminal justice. Monson serves her community and has national and international influence in the health field through the Oklahoma Health Science Center. Wallace Johnson (below) was a graduate of Douglass High School. He attended the University of Oklahoma (OU) on a full football scholarship and graduated with honors. Johnson had the highest grade point average of anyone in sports at OU. He retired from a distinguished Army career, with service in Vietnam as a lieutenant colonel, and later taught at George Mason University in Washington, DC. He was inducted into the Oklahoma City Public Schools Foundation's Wall of Fame and is a consistent financial supporter of the organization. (Right, courtesy of Dean's Typesetting Service; below, courtesy of Black Liberated Arts Center Inc.)

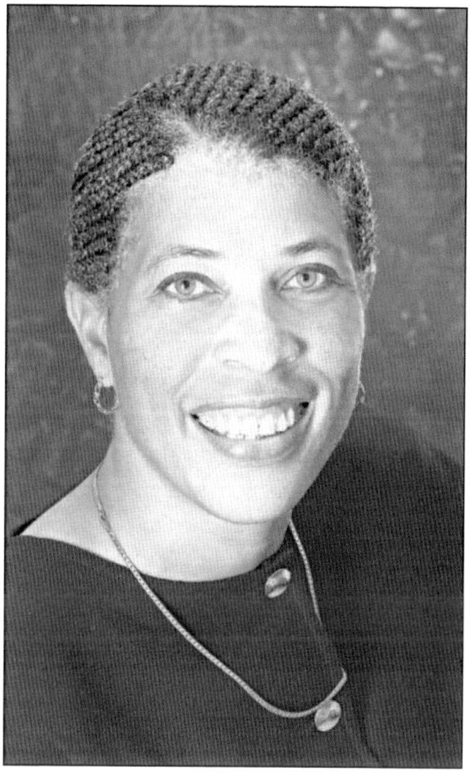

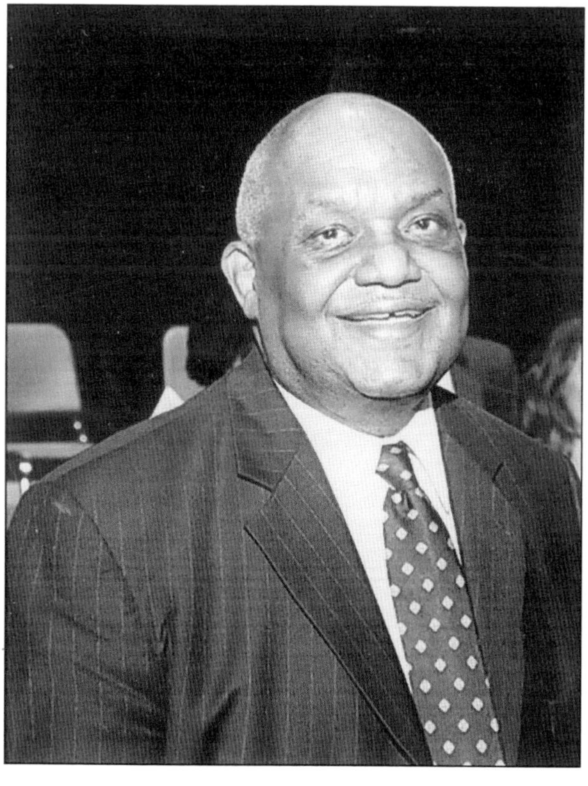

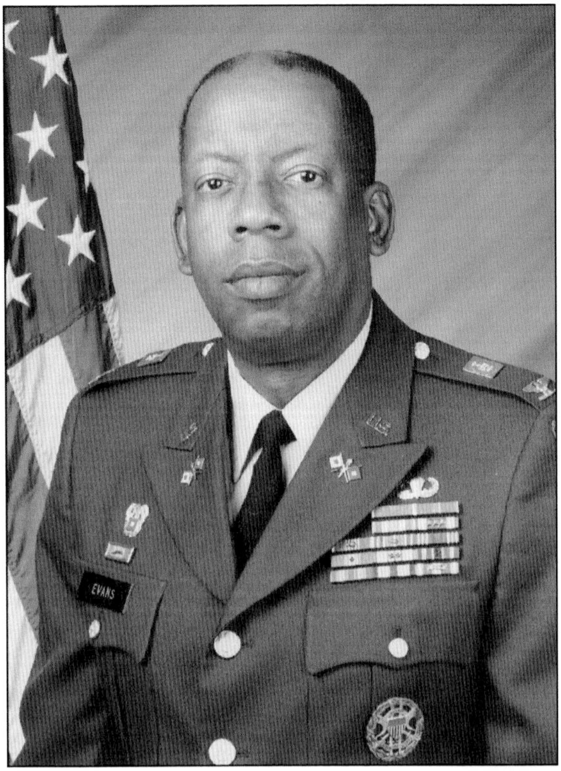

Stanley Evans graduated from Douglass High School in 1964. He earned a bachelor's degree in business administration at the University of Central Oklahoma, a master's degree in business administration at the University of Texas, and his law degree at OU. His professional military education includes graduation from the Army Command and General Staff College at Fort Leavenworth, Kansas, and the Army War College at Carlisle, Pennsylvania. Colonel Evans is a Vietnam War veteran who received numerous military honors and awards. He has served on many boards and committees in support of his community. Evans assumed the position of assistant dean for students at the University of Oklahoma College of Law in 2003 immediately after his law school graduation. He is the first African American to be appointed to a dean position at any law school in Oklahoma. (Both, courtesy of Stanley Evans.)

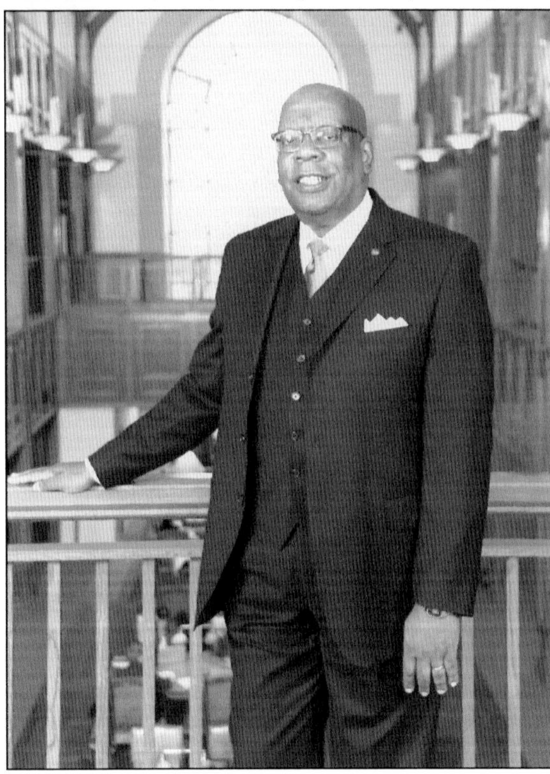

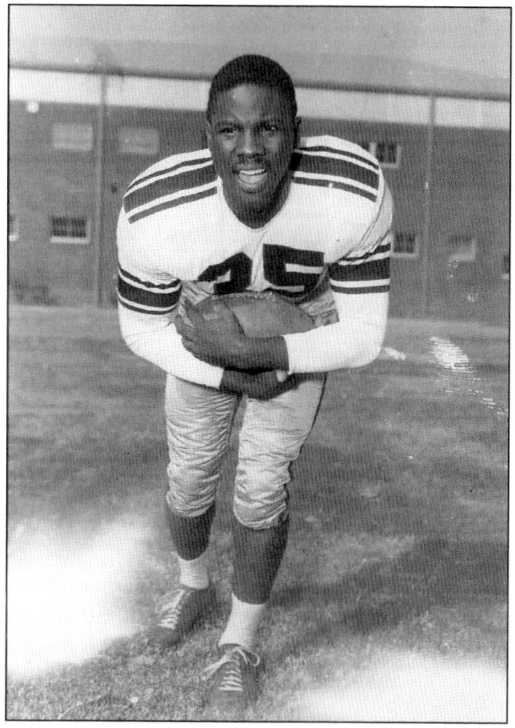

Prentice Gautt (right) graduated from Douglass High School and became a running back for OU in 1956. His senior year, he was the first black to play in the all-state game, earning MVP honors. Gautt was the first black football player at OU. He became a two-time All–Big Eight player and the 1959 Orange Bowl MVP, and was named to the Academic All-American team and later played professionally for the Cleveland Browns and the St. Louis Cardinals. He coached football at the University of Missouri and earned a PhD in psychology before starting a career in athletics administration. He died in 2005. Willard Pitts (below) was a drum major for the Douglass High School Marching Band. After graduation, he attended Lincoln University and became its drum major. (Right, courtesy of Bonita Edwards; below, courtesy of Eula Pitts.)

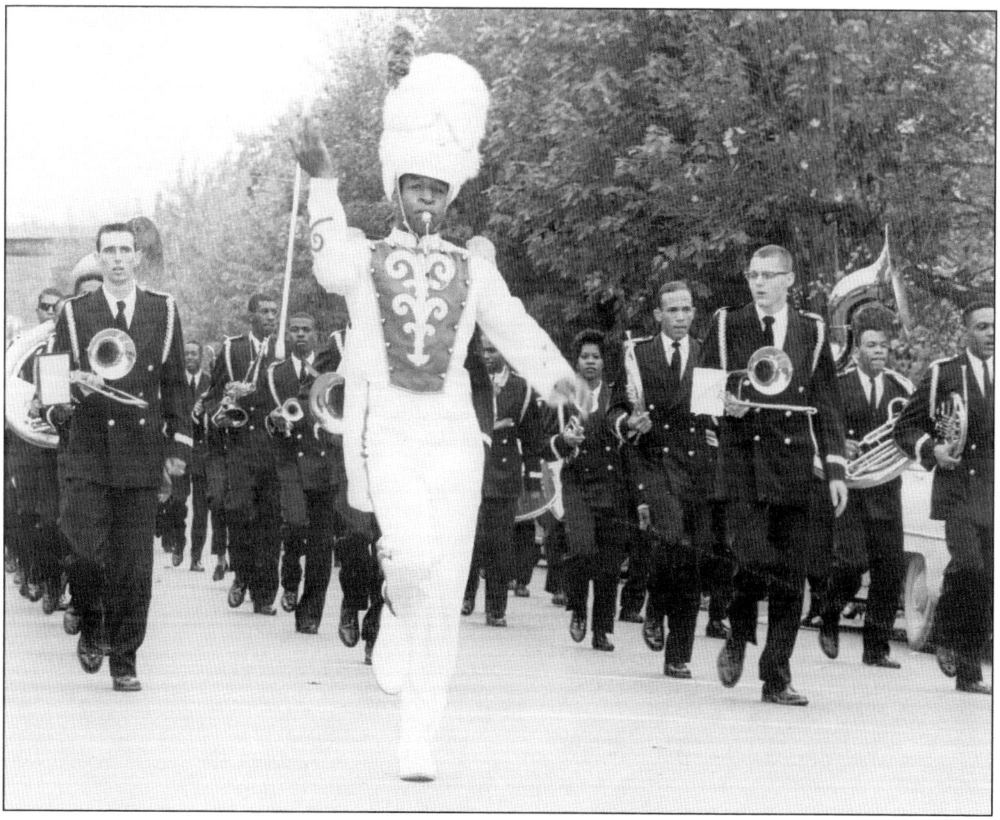

Willard Pitts (left) received his bachelor of arts in journalism from Lincoln University, a master of education in English at the University of Central Oklahoma, and completed all course work toward a doctorate at OU prior to his death. He taught at Douglass High School and Langston University, producing award-winning yearbooks. Pitts served on education and journalism boards and committees around the world. He took hundreds of students abroad to study. Lucy Thurmond Livingston (below), a Douglass graduate, earned her bachelor's degree in elementary education from Hampton University and a master's degree in special education from Central State University in Oklahoma. She received a certificate in school administration from Texas Women's University and taught elementary school in Missouri and Texas, earning wide recognition for working with special education children. She is a nationally recognized inventor. (Left, courtesy of Eula Pitts; below, courtesy of Lucy Thurmond Livingston.)

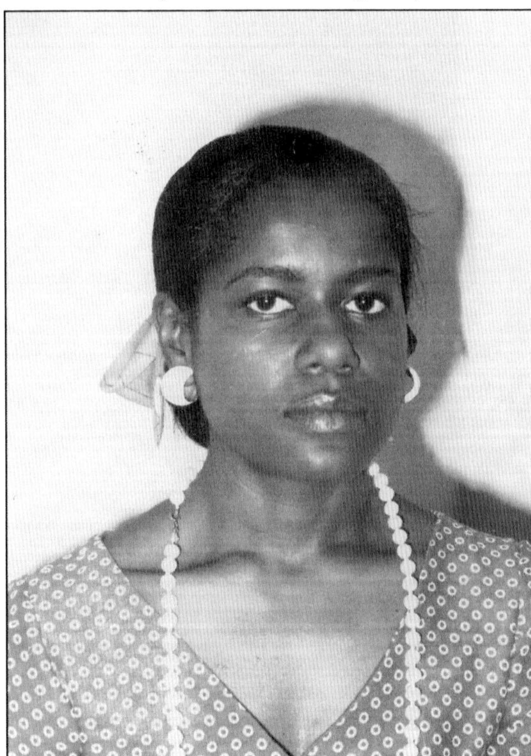

At right, Timothy D. DeGuisti greets Sherriel Bluitt Waldrop at a reception at Douglass High School honoring him for his induction into the Oklahoma City Public Schools Foundation's Wall of Fame. Both are Douglass High School graduates. DeGuisti is a federal judge on the US District Court for the Western District of Oklahoma, and Waldrop is a retired banker. DeGuisti received all of his degrees from the University of Oklahoma. Dr. Ruth Colbert Barnes (below) has a bachelor of science in behavioral science/ biochemistry, a master of education in educational psychology, and a doctorate in applied research. Barnes is CEO of the Colbert Group/R.J. Colbert Enterprises Inc. She is a community research investigator on the OU Health Science Center Research Team, an appointee to the president's task force on women's issues, and an author. (Right, courtesy of Black Liberated Arts Center Inc.; below, courtesy of Ruth Barnes.)

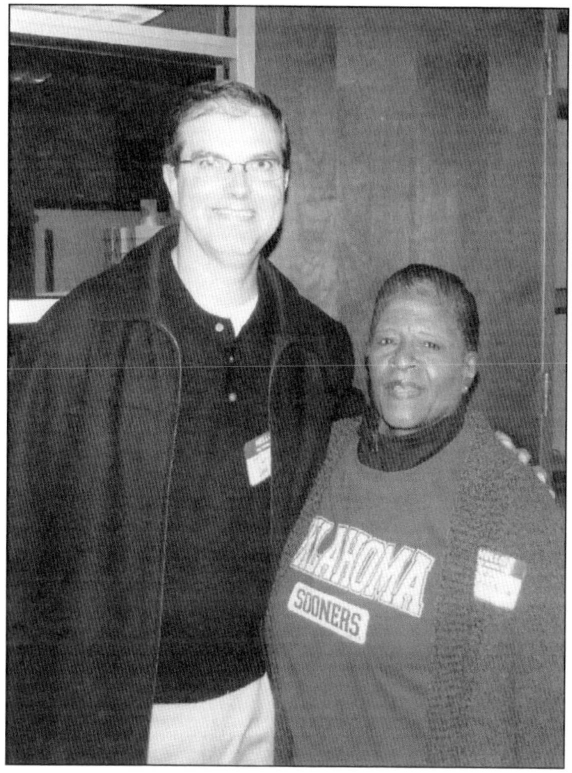

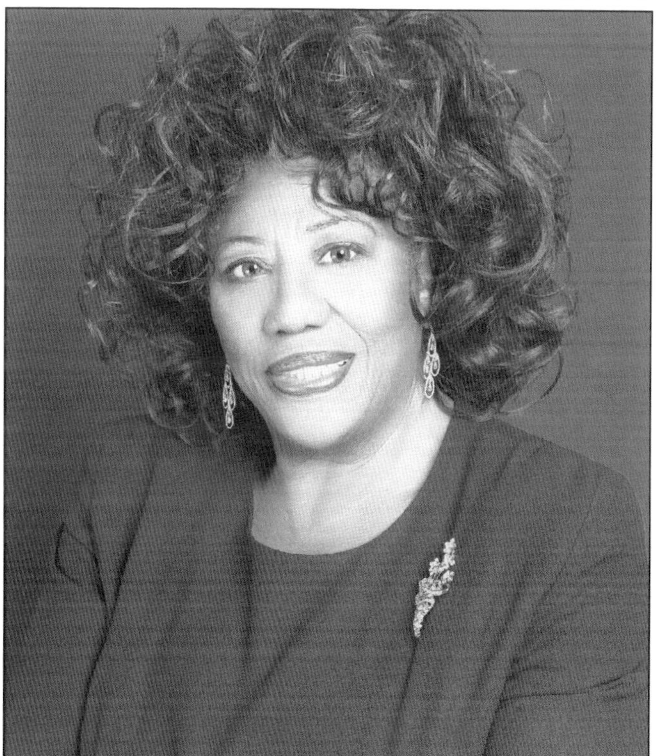

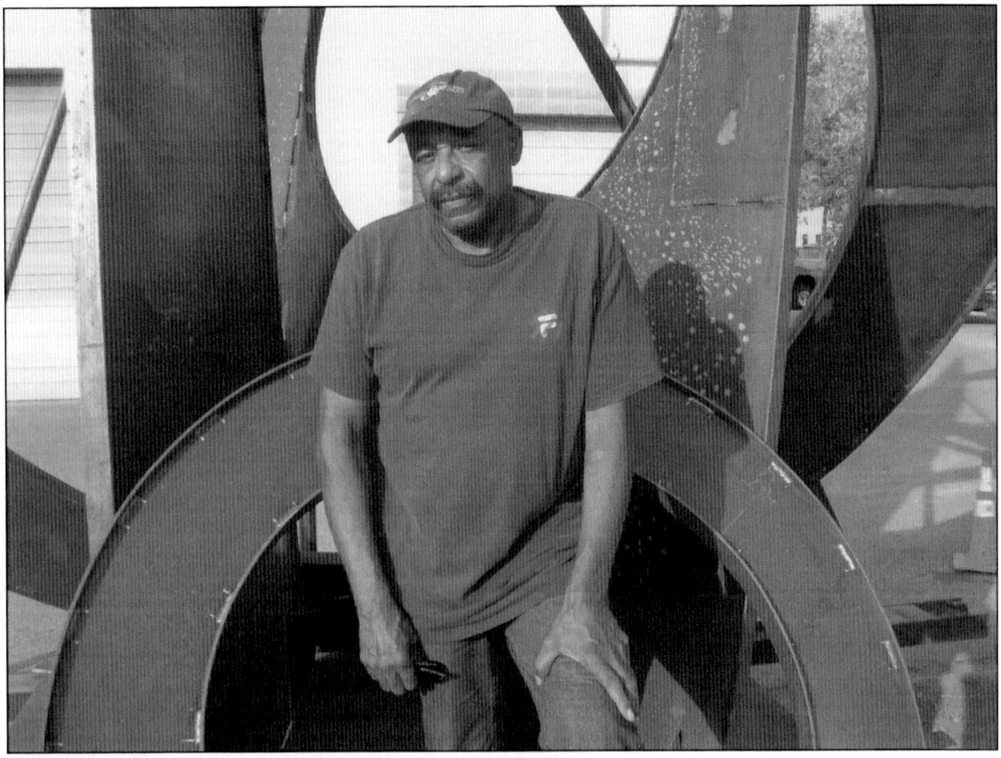

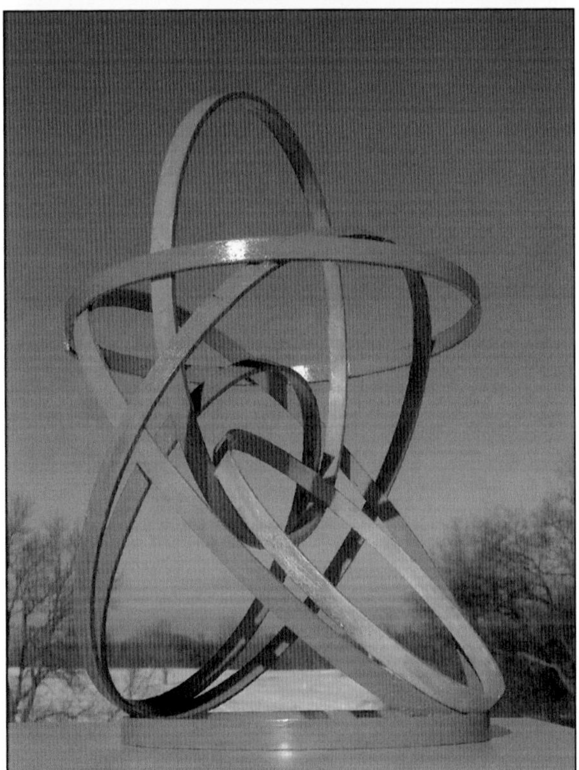

Melvin R. Smith (above) is a well-known artist in the Midwest and Southwest. The native Oklahoman was an art student of Margaret Dabney at Douglass High School. His paintings are mostly about people and places in Oklahoma City. He received a bachelor's degree in journalism from the University of Minnesota and became a certified tennis instructor. His sculptures and collages are exhibited and collected by institutions, including the Oklahoma State Arts Collection at the Capitol in Oklahoma. His sculpture *The Warrior*, shown at left, is exhibited at the University of Minnesota. (Both, courtesy of Melvin R. Smith.)

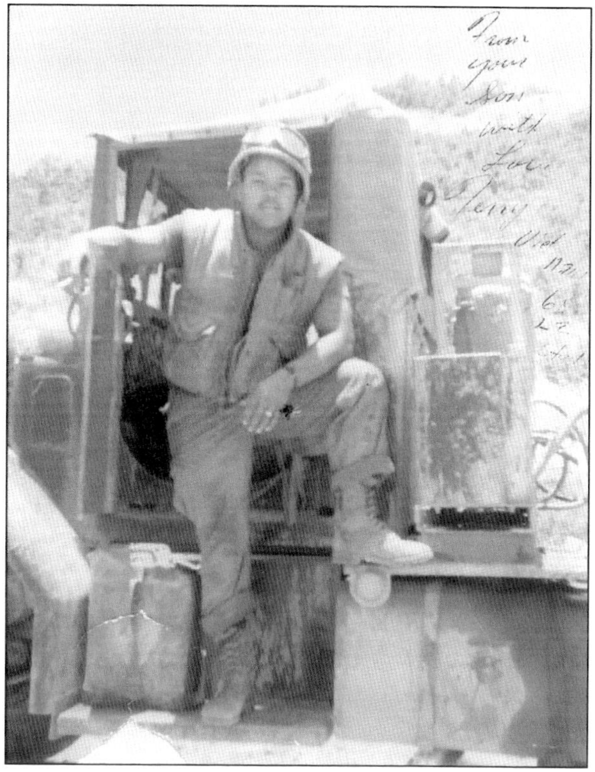

Terry Lee Davis was cocaptain of the 1965 and 1966 Trojan football teams. He matriculated to Oklahoma State University, where he received a draft notice from the military. Davis enlisted in the US Marine Corps for four years and was sent to Vietnam for a 13-month tour of duty. He was wounded in the Tet Offensive at Khe Sahn fire base and received the Purple Heart for meritorious valor, the Vietnamese Cross of Gallantry, the Unit Naval Citation, and a host of other medals and honors. He returned to Oklahoma City and joined the US Postal Service, working his way up to manager of distribution operations. Davis earned his bachelor of business administration from the University of Central Oklahoma. (Both, courtesy of Terry Davis.)

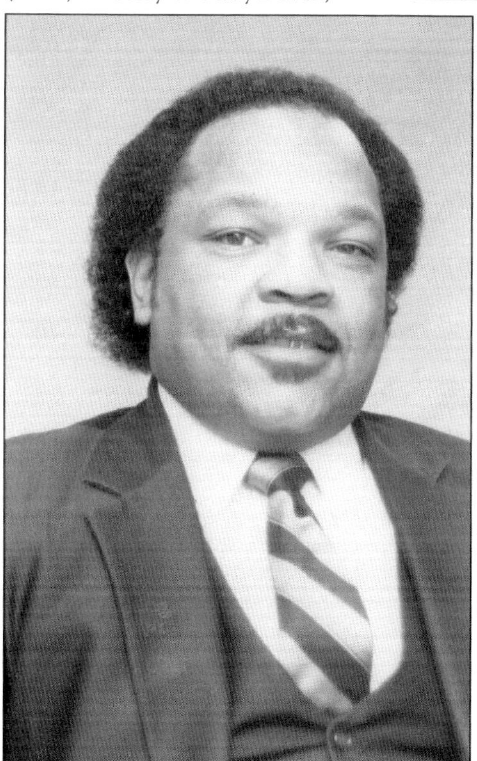

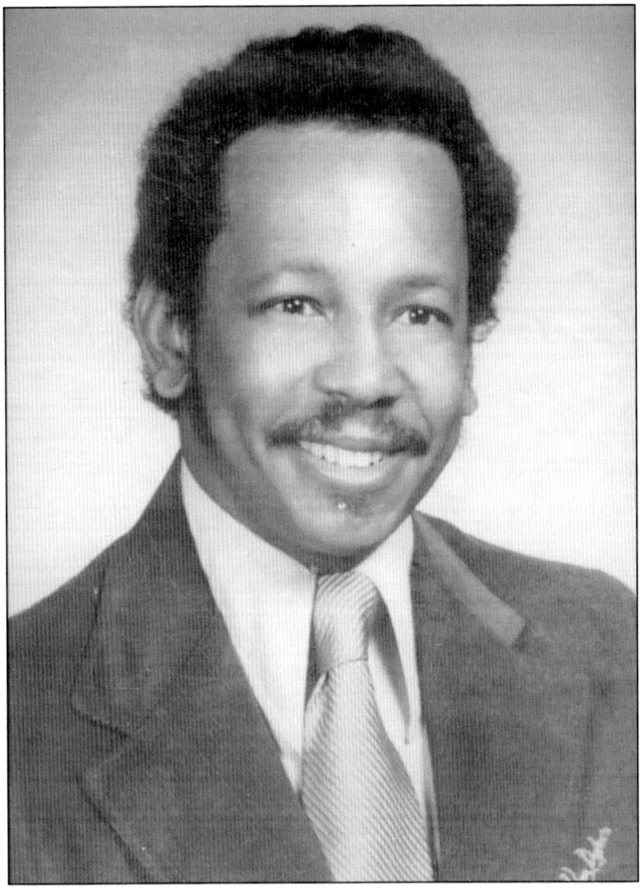

Joe Littlepage graduated from Douglass High School in 1960. He graduated with honors from Hampton University with a bachelor of science degree. Littlepage served a tour of duty in Vietnam with the US Army. 1st Lieutenant Littlepage was awarded a Bronze Star for meritorious achievement in ground operations against hostile forces and was honorably discharged in 1970. He received his pilot's license in 1973 and purchased a plane with Dr. Charles Biscoe and Levert Graham. He was also a partner in one of the early black-owned soda bottling companies, the Pop Factory. He enjoyed a long and distinguished career with the Gillette Company, Papermate Division, as a regional sales manager. He received numerous commendations and awards from the company. He died on October 26, 2002. (Both, courtesy of Edwina Littlepage.)

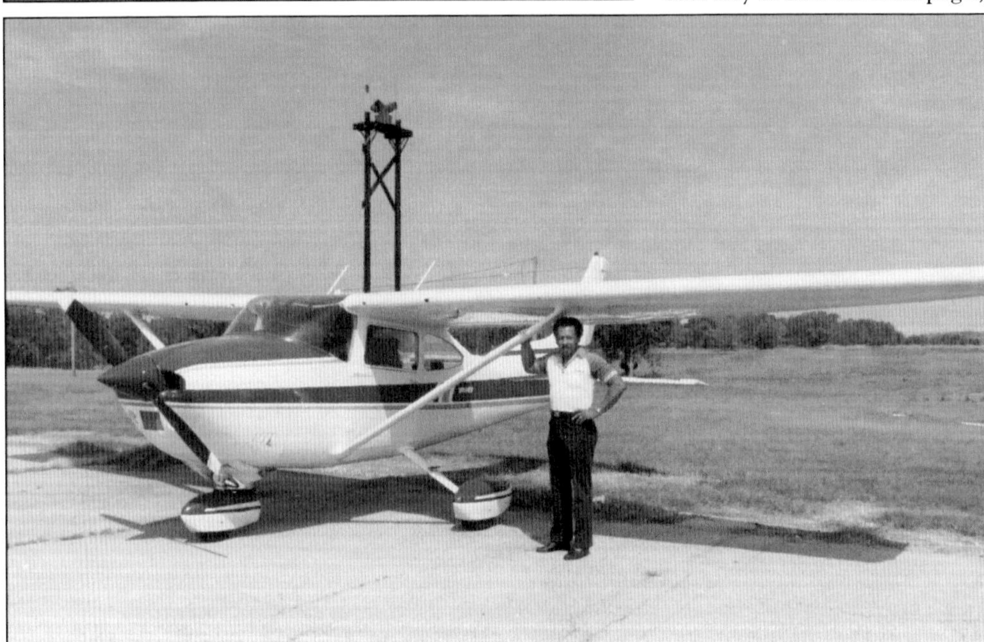

Anita Golden Arnold (right) holds degrees from Oklahoma State University and Memphis State University, and did graduate work at the University of Oklahoma. Arnold served at the highest levels of management in AT&T and the US Postal Service for more than 30 years. She is a real estate broker and executive director of Black Liberated Arts Center Inc. Joyce Jackson (below) is founder and publisher of *SHADES of Oklahoma* magazine, a publication designed to expand media representation and enhance the knowledge of Oklahoma's African American community. She is also the founder of Women of Color Expo. Jackson is a former Peabody Award–winning broadcast journalist, producer, and talk show host for KOCO-TV in Oklahoma City. She worked 15 years as a public information officer for the Oklahoma Department of Corrections. Both are Douglass graduates. (Right, courtesy of Anita Arnold; below, courtesy of Joyce Jackson.)

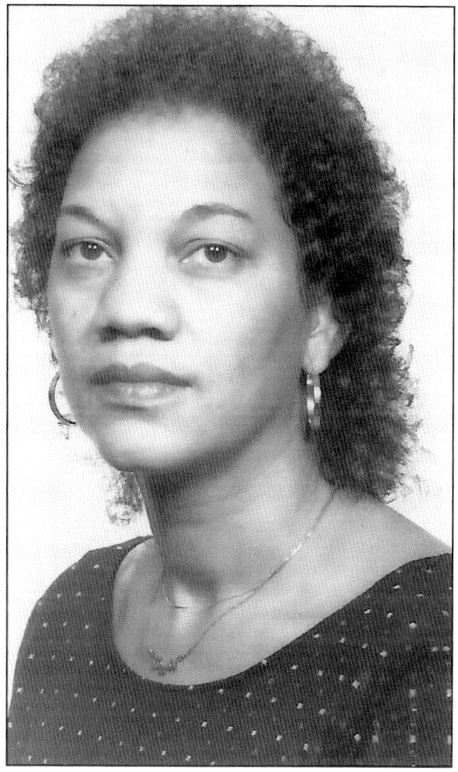

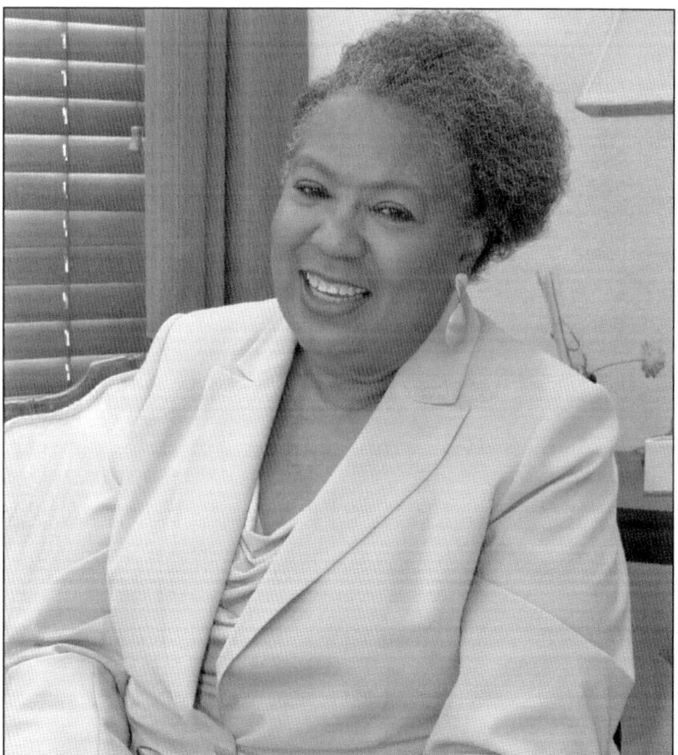

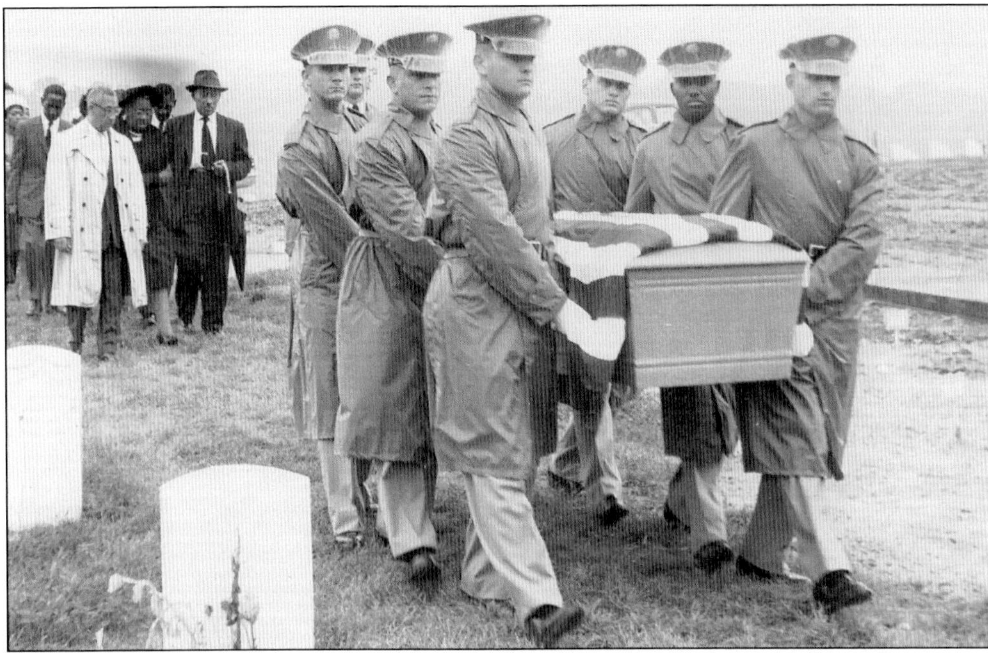

Everything about Cleo Hearn seems to be about cowboys, but it is not. He graduated from Douglass High School in 1957 and went to Oklahoma State University on a rodeo scholarship. In 1962, he was selected to become a member of the Casket Bearing Team Presidential Honor Guard at Arlington National Cemetery, during the John F. Kennedy Administration. He is shown on duty in both photographs at Arlington. In the photograph above, he is in the middle of the two officers to the right carrying the casket. (Both, courtesy of Cleo Hearn.)

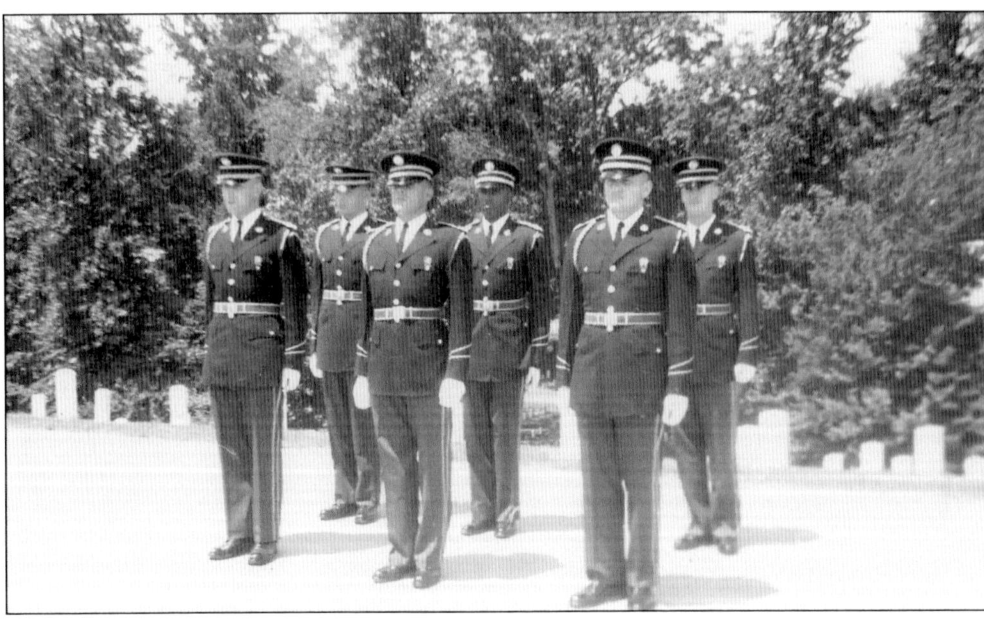

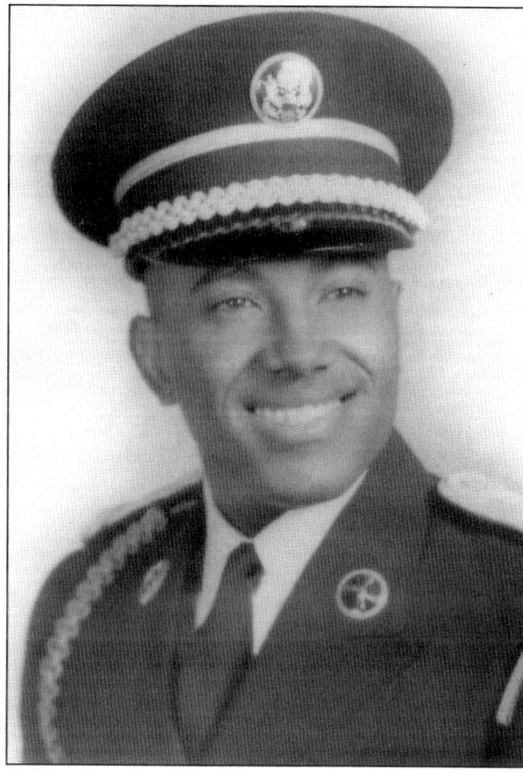

Cleo Hearn is pictured here in the 1970s during his calf-roping days. He began his career as a professional cowboy in 1959 and was the first to win calf roping in the National Stock Show event in 1970. He is known as "Mr. Black Rodeo" in local, national, and international cowboy circles. He put on his first rodeo in Harlem for 10,000 children and began producing rodeos in Texas in 1985. He is the founder of Cowboys of Color Rodeo, based in Lancaster, Texas, the largest multicultural rodeo tour in the world, highlighting the contributions of African, Indian, Hispanic, European, and Asian cowboys. (Both, courtesy of Cleo Hearn.)

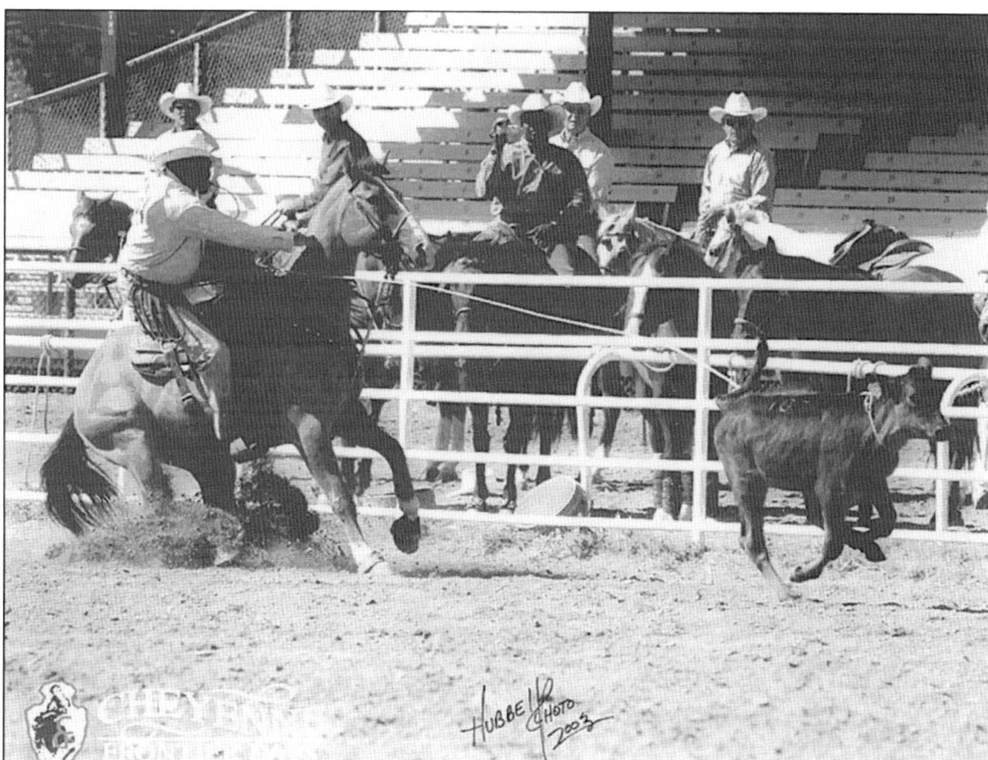

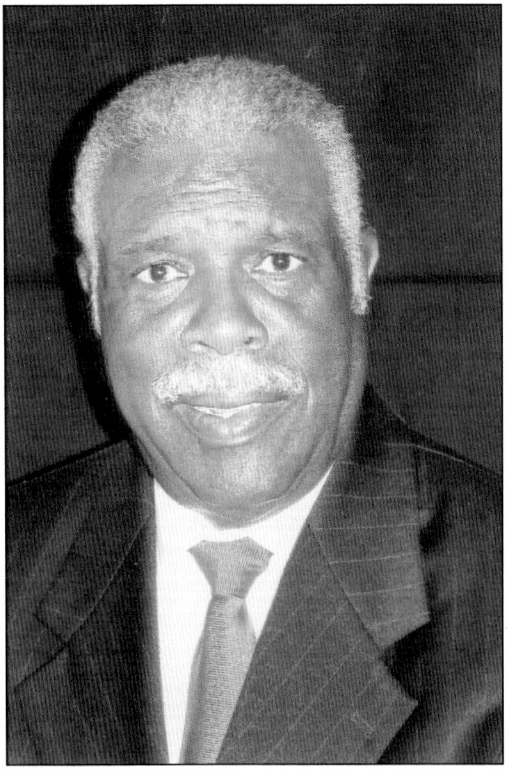

Horace Stevenson's background is business administration. He started out as head waiter at the Oklahoma City Sportsman's Club and Jack Sussy's restaurant in 1958. Today, he is a member of the country club. Stevenson is a McDonald's franchise owner. By 2010, he owned 10 McDonald's in Oklahoma City and Tulsa and was named Businessman of the Year three times by the McDonald's corporation. Horace founded the Little Giant Golf Tournament, the charitable arm of his business, which attracts golfers from across America. Below, he is seen at the golf course. A generous donor to several charities, he is a passionate supporter of public schools and his alma mater, Douglass High School (class of 1957), in their efforts to improve the community. He is a member of the Oklahoma City Public Schools Foundation's Wall of Fame. (Both, courtesy of Horace Stevenson.)

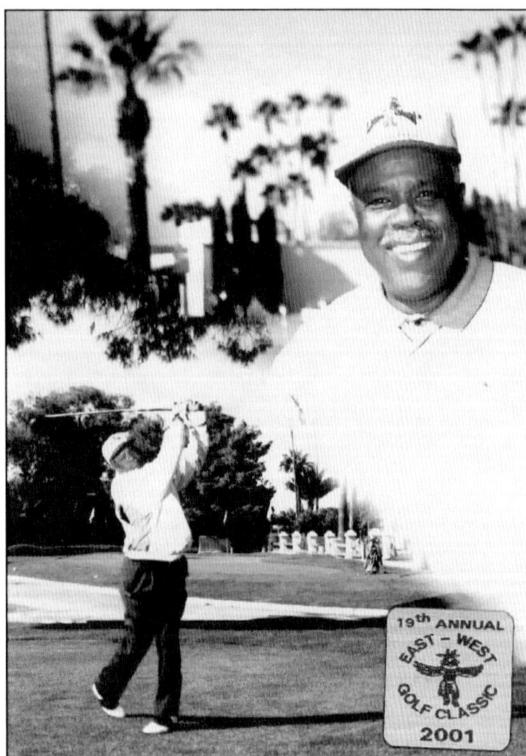

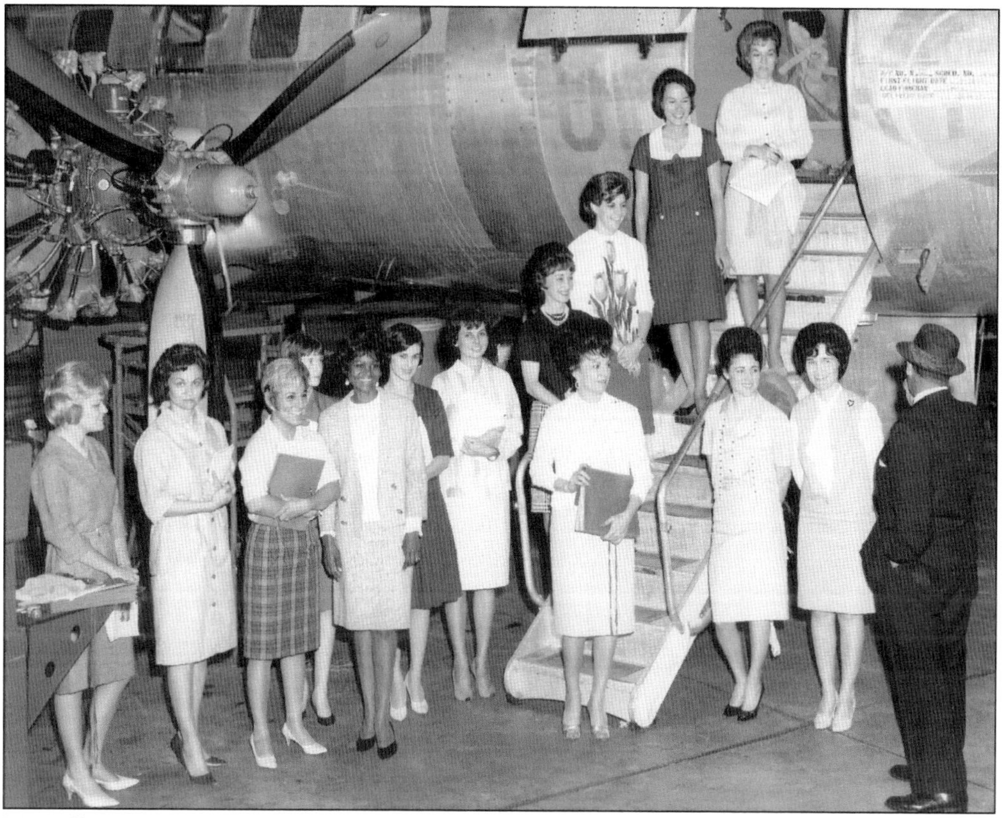

Marvella Newsome Holmes is shown above with trainees on the steps of a plane at the Federal Aviation Administration in Oklahoma City, where she was a training specialist for faculty development and certification. She stands fifth from left. Below, from left to right, Marvella Holmes, Carl Holmes (Marvella's husband), F.D. Moon (principal of Douglass High School), City Councilman Goree James, and Katie James (Goree's wife) celebrate Carl Holmes's promotion to fire chief. (Above, courtesy of Marvella Holmes; below, courtesy of Helen Gray.)

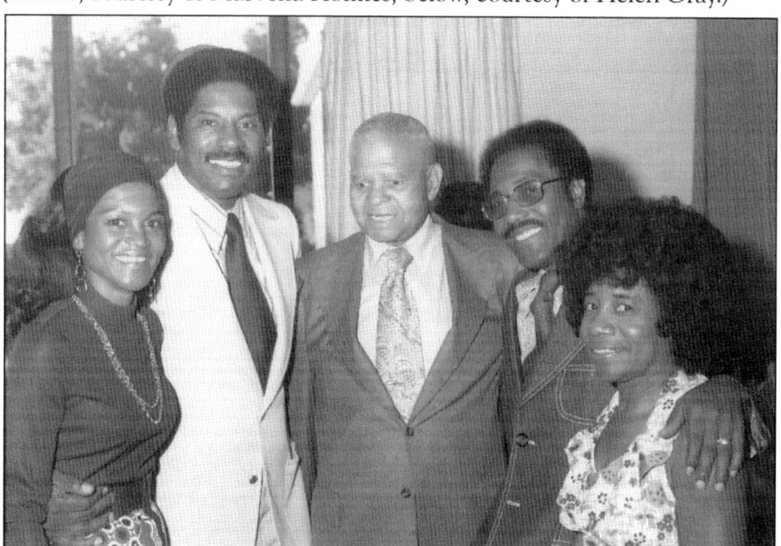

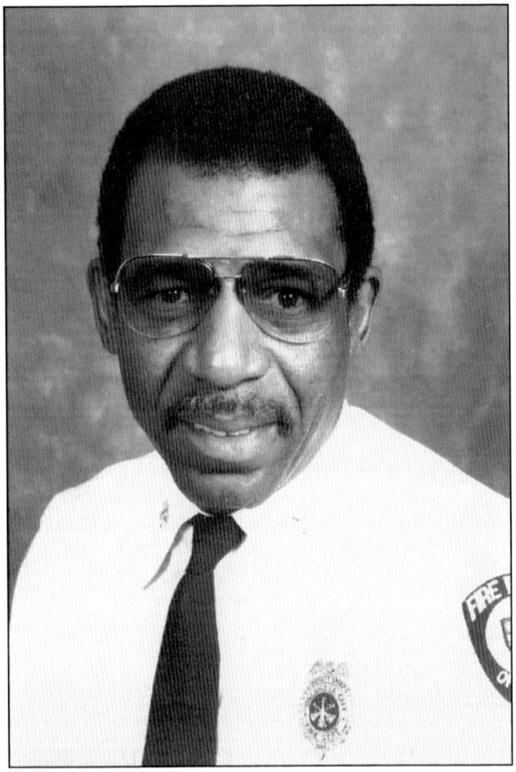

Sherman Carthen (left) was as passionate about the Oklahoma City Fire Department as he was about his neighborhood association and Douglass High School. He advanced through the ranks from firefighter to major and was the first African American to hold a position as a training officer. He is credited with establishing a Public Education Division, whose purpose was to reduce fire deaths in Oklahoma City. He founded, organized, and served as the first president of the Oklahoma City Firefighters Organization and worked closely with Chief Carl Holmes to train women as firefighters. The photograph below shows women firefighters attending the Carl Holmes Executive Institute. (Both, courtesy of Sherman Carthen estate.)

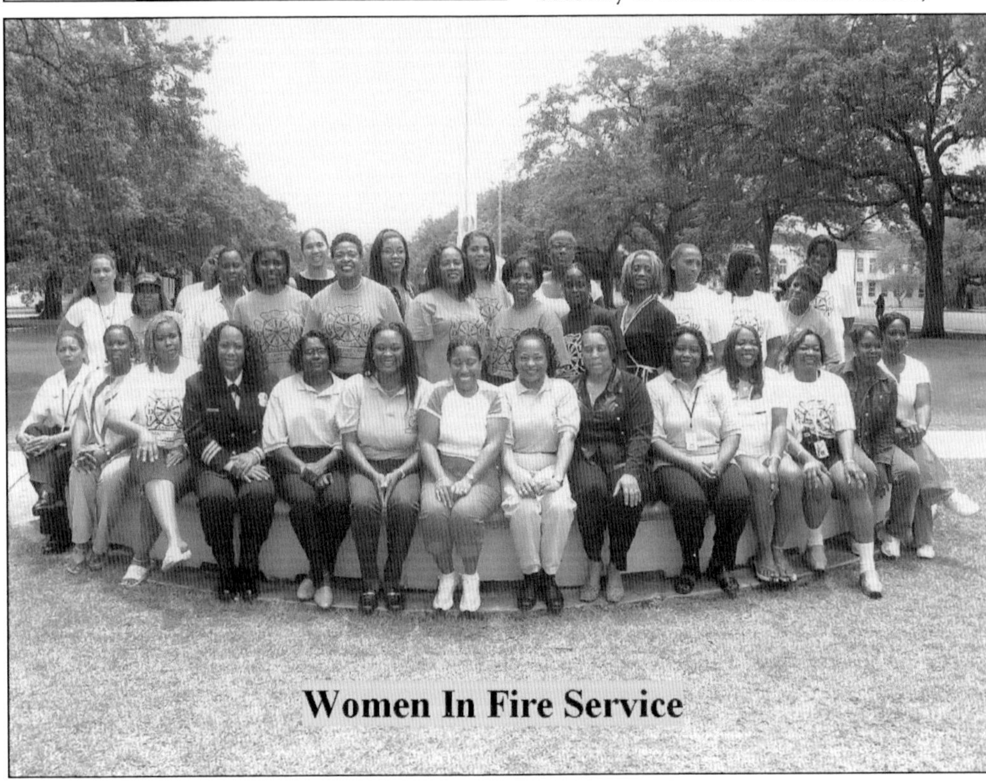

Juanita Vivette Harris (right) attended college at Lincoln University, the University of Oregon, and the University of Oklahoma. She was the first African American female employed by Grayson's Shop of California and later as accountant and assistant to the sales manager at Hirsch Weiss Company. She was employed at Tinker Air Force Base for 17 years. She retired from the US Treasury Department, Internal Revenue, and also the Oklahoma Corporation Commission. She was a fashion model and narrator. Freddye Harper Williams, below, worked at Tinker Air Force Base for 30 years. She served five years on the Oklahoma City Public Schools Board of Education and 10 years as Oklahoma state representative for District 99. Both were valedictorians in the Douglass High School class of 1933. (Both, courtesy of Dean's Typesetting Service.)

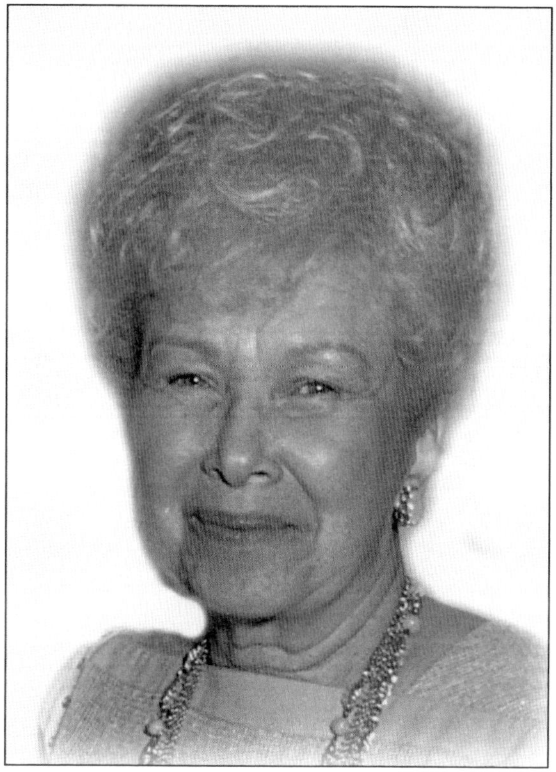

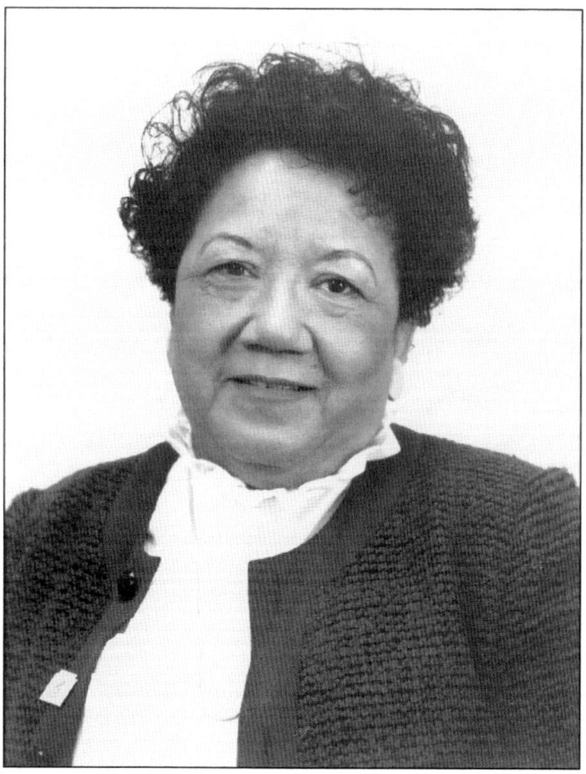

Dr. Donda C. West (left) graduated from Douglass High School in 1967. West participated in the 1958 sit-in demonstrations under the leadership of author Clara Luper. She earned a bachelor's degree in English at Virginia Union University, a master's degree at Atlanta University, and a doctorate in English education from Auburn University. She taught at Morris Brown College and was chairman of the English department. After working at Chicago State University for 24 years, she retired to become general manager for her son, singer Kanye West. Chester Thompson (below) was also a graduate of Douglass High School and began his music career in Oklahoma City but experienced extraordinary success in California as a musician and composer with Tower of Power for 10 years and later with Carlos Santana for 26 years. Here, Thompson is shown receiving the Charlie Christian Jazz Music Award. From left to right are Brenda Davis, Chester Thompson, and Mary Pointer. (Left, courtesy of Dean's Typesetting Service; below, courtesy of Black Liberated Arts Center Inc.)

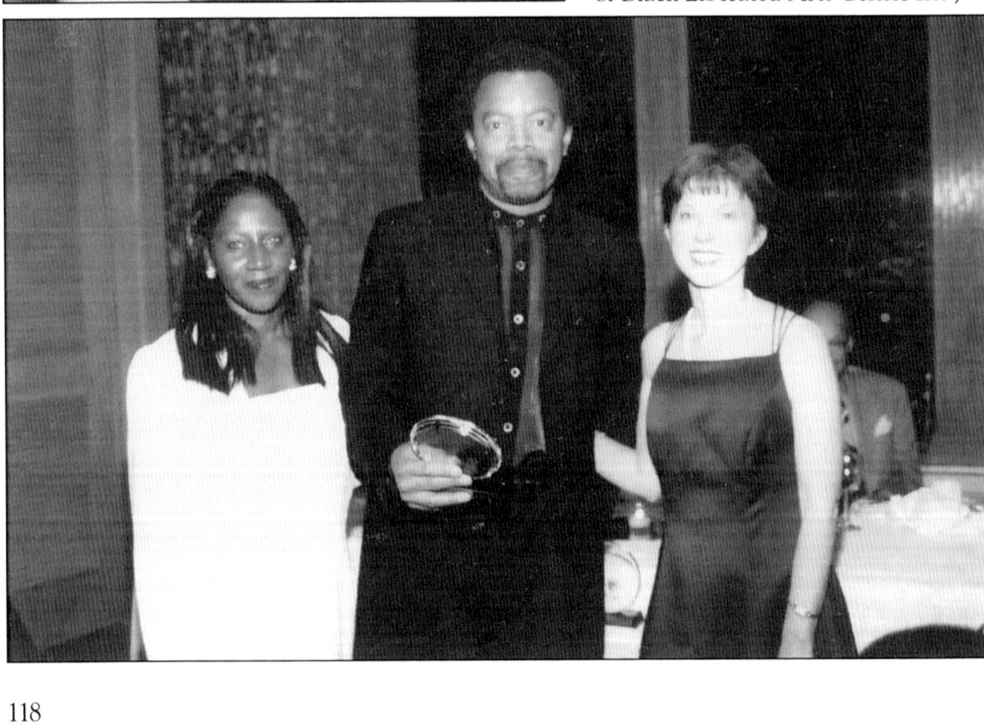

Leonard D. Benton (right) is a 1957 graduate of Douglass High School who earned a bachelor's degree in education and two master's degrees from Grambling State University. He was president of the Urban League of Oklahoma City and served as regional director for the National Urban League. Benton served the Urban League for more than 30 years. He was one of the founders of the Southwest Urban Foundation, a minority-established community foundation. Dr. Lee E. Cooper Jr. (below), a Douglass High School graduate, is pastor of Oklahoma City's Prospect Baptist Church, well known for emphasizing education for all, especially young people. Fine arts and the educational academy are two of more than two dozen ministries. He is a member of the board of directors of the Southwest Urban Foundation. (Both, courtesy of Dean's Typesetting Service.)

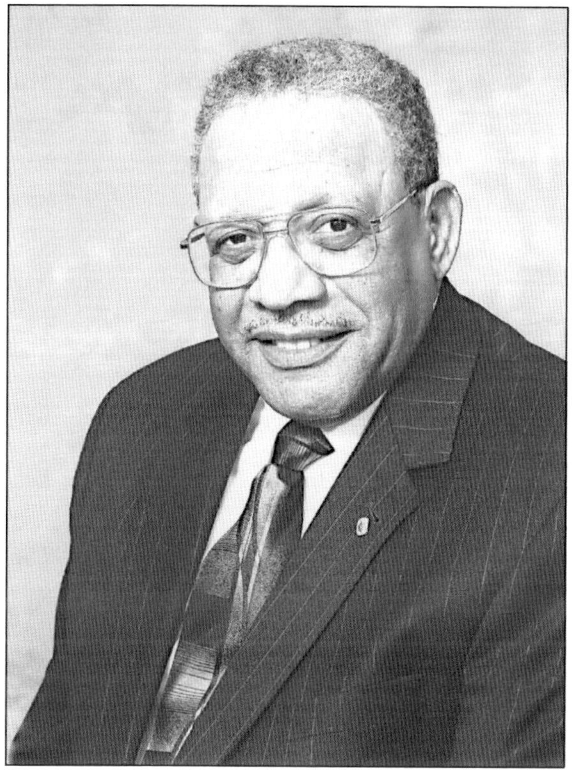

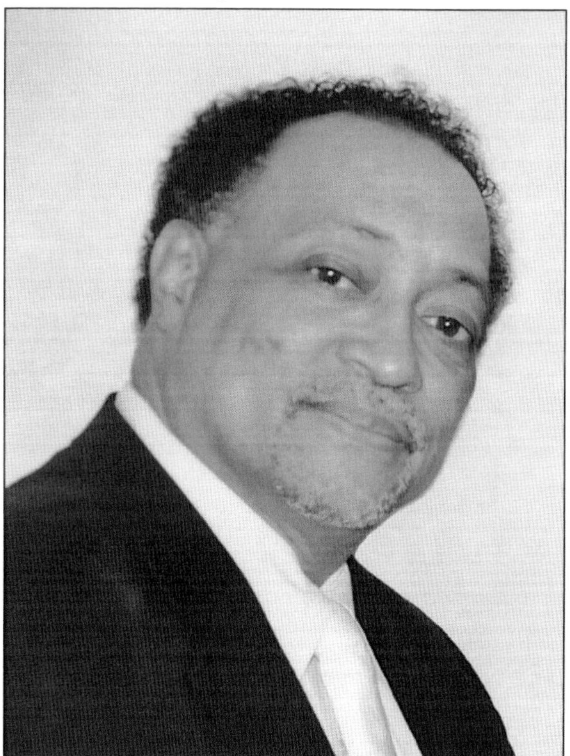

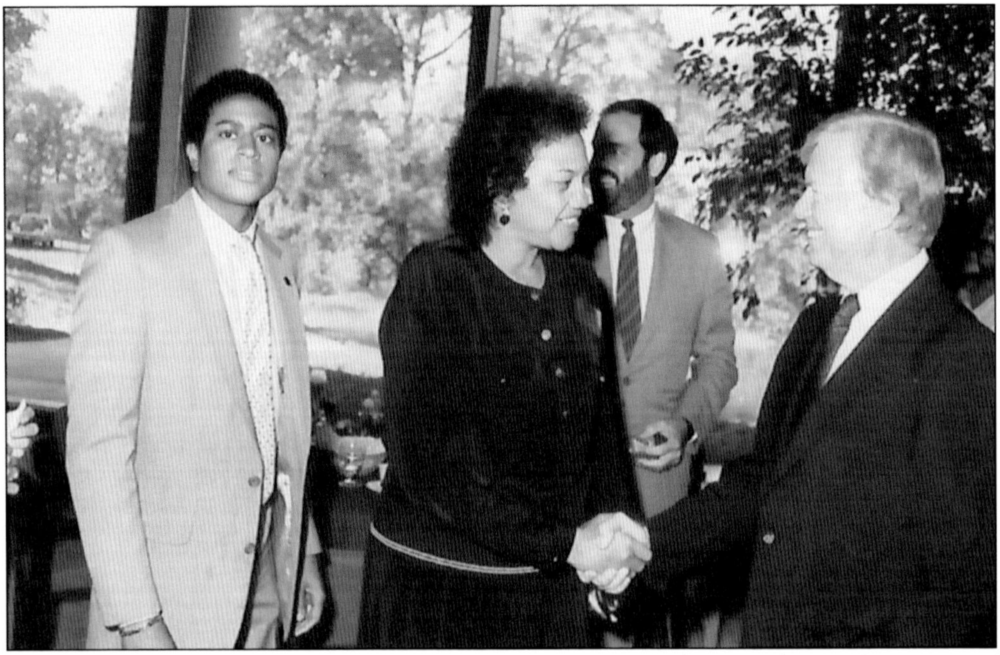

Anita Golden Arnold (above) received a four-year appointment to the Site Selection Committee of the Democratic National Committee for the 1988 Democratic Convention in Atlanta. She traveled around the country meeting officials at the highest levels of government. Arnold is the only person from the state of Oklahoma to serve on that committee. Here, Arnold is greeted by Pres. Jimmy Carter as Ron Magnus, special assistant to the president, looks on. Below, from left to right, Lt. Colonel Wallace Johnson visits with broadcasting mogul Russell Perry as Ranola Perry (Russell's wife) looks on. Perry Publishing and Broadcasting owns 14 radio stations in Oklahoma, Arkansas, and Georgia. All graduated from Douglass High School. (Above, courtesy of Anita Arnold; below, courtesy of Marland Johnson.)

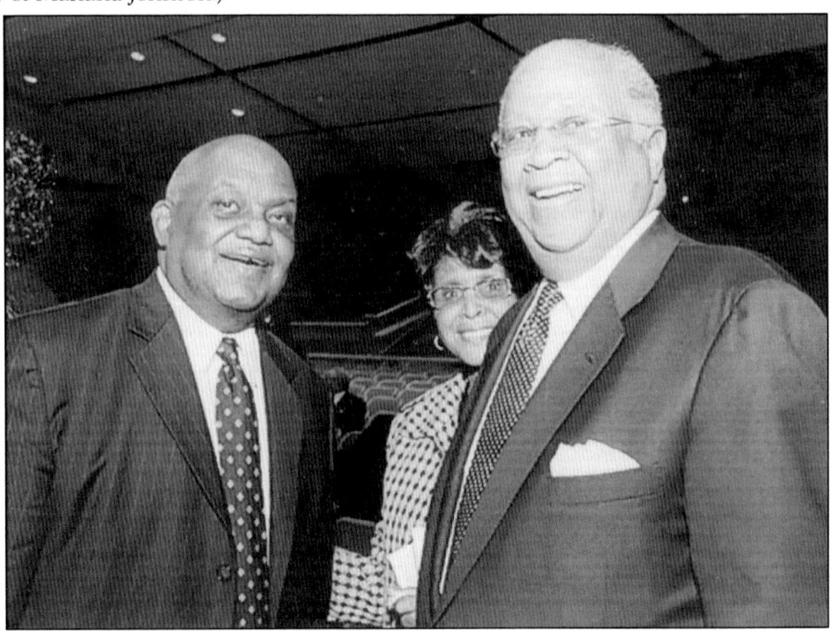

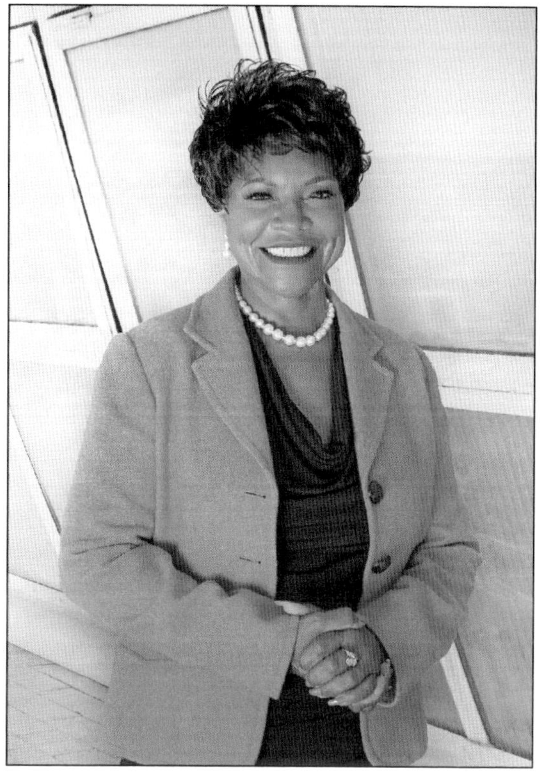

Sen. Constance Johnson (right) is a 1970 Douglass High School graduate. She served 12 years as an Oklahoma state senator and became the first African American woman nominated for a major statewide office in 2014 when she won the Democratic primary run-off in the US Senate special election in Oklahoma. She is running for governor of Oklahoma. She has a bachelor's degree in French and a master of science in education from the University of Pennsylvania. Rev. Larry Foster (below) is pastor of Progressive Baptist Church in Oklahoma City, and Douglass High School is his alma mater. He hosted fundraisers for many years to raise scholarship money for students at Douglass. (Right, courtesy of Sen. Constance Johnson; below, courtesy of Dean's Typesetting Service.)

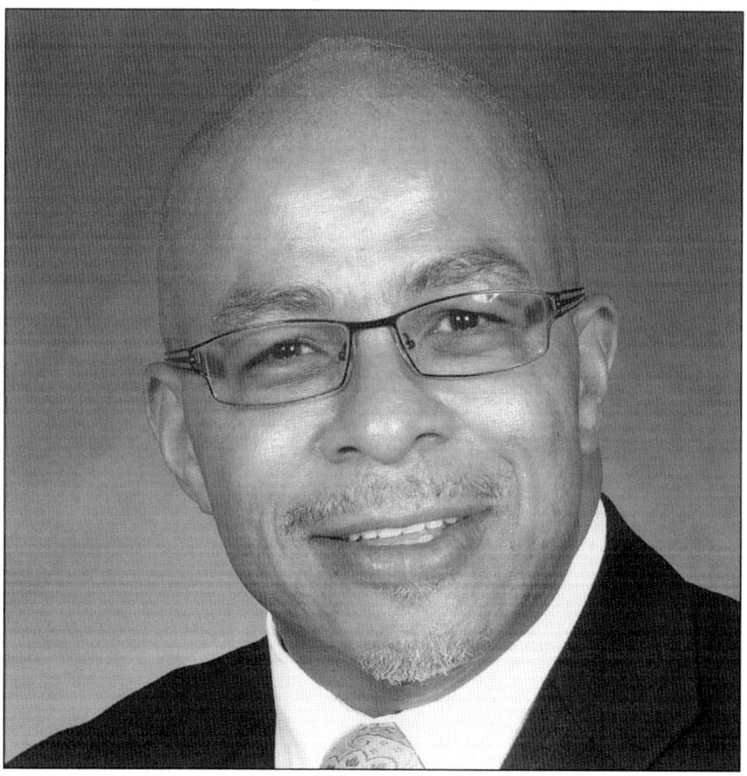

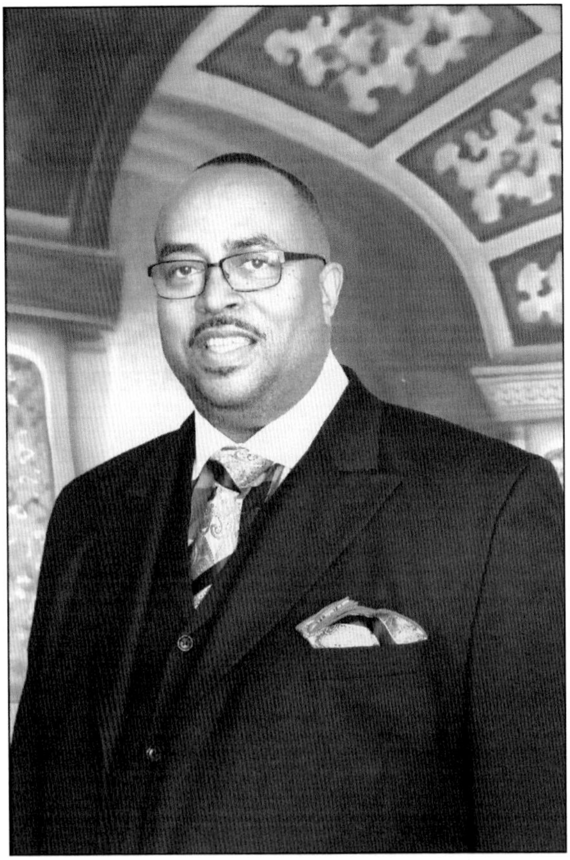

Pastor E. Jennings Tyson is senior pastor of New Hope Baptist Church, a church known for notable mission work in the community. The church was built in 1929 and enjoyed the leadership of seven ministers since then. Tyson maintained and expanded the facility, while enhancing features that preserve the original structure. His ministry of service and outreach extends beyond the Oklahoma borders, and he is known as an orator of stature. He graduated from Douglass High School. (Both photographs by Levi McCullough, courtesy of Dean's Typesetting Service.)

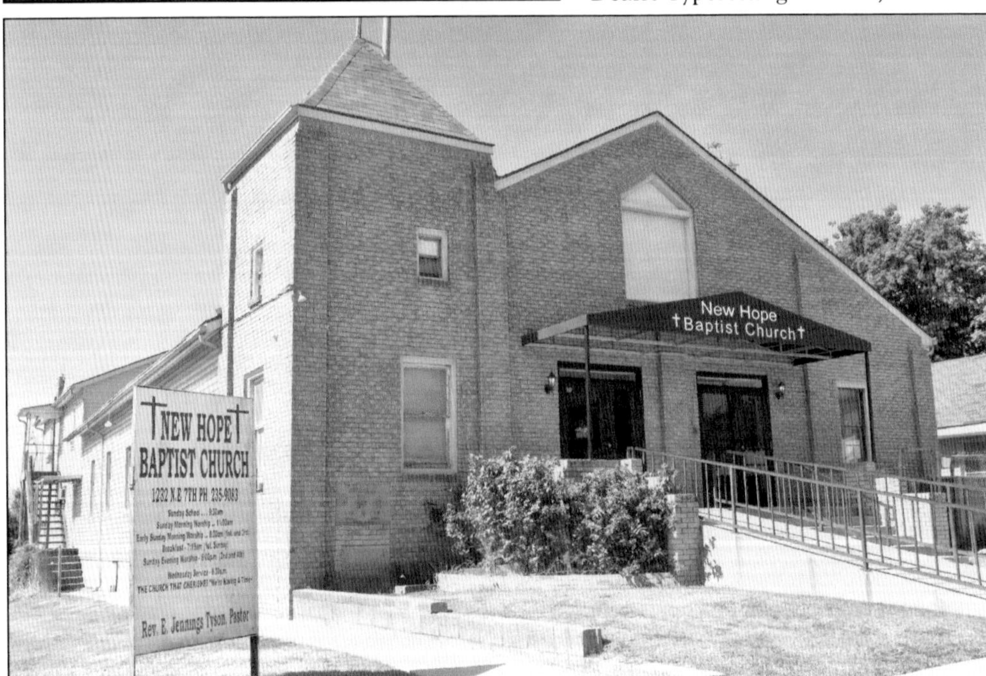

The wedding photograph of Delores Dement and Larry Anderson is shown below. From left to right are Andy Dement Jr. (brother of bride), Andy Dement Sr. (father of bride), Helen Dement (bride's mother), the bride and groom, Barbara Kirkpatrick Coley, and an unidentified minister. Andy Dement Sr. was the well-respected head custodian at Douglass High School. All of the Dement children are Douglass graduates. Andy Dement Jr. taught at Douglass High School and received a Fulbright scholarship that landed him in Turkey, where he began a career as an educational counselor in Istanbul, and later Morocco and Japan. He returned to Oklahoma and became deputy superintendent of the Oklahoma Metro Technology Center. Melvin Combs (right) graduated from Douglass High School and became a pharmacist first and later an attorney. He is a member of the Oklahoma Bar Association and a recipient of the Oklahoma Bar Association Trail Blazer Award for making a profound impact on the legal profession by paving the way for more African American law students to pass the bar exam. (Right, courtesy of Melvin Combs; below, courtesy of Delores Plunkett.)

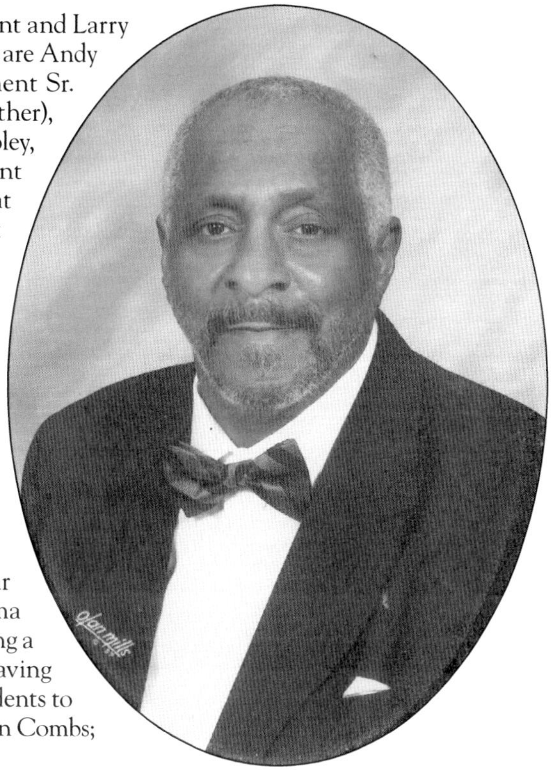

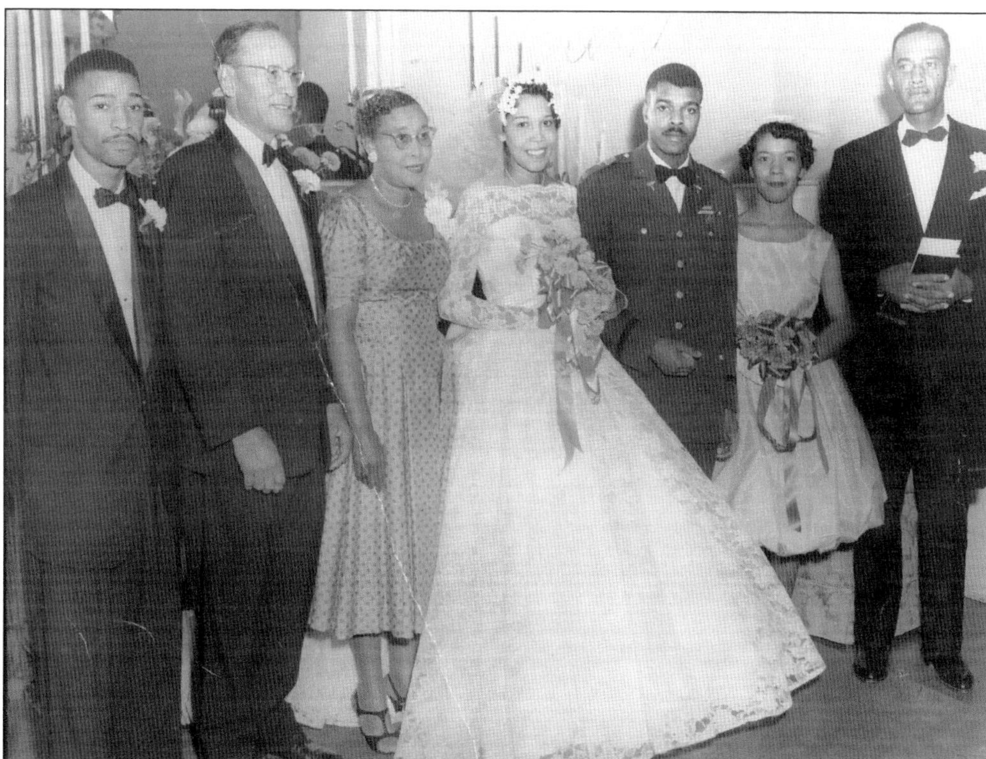

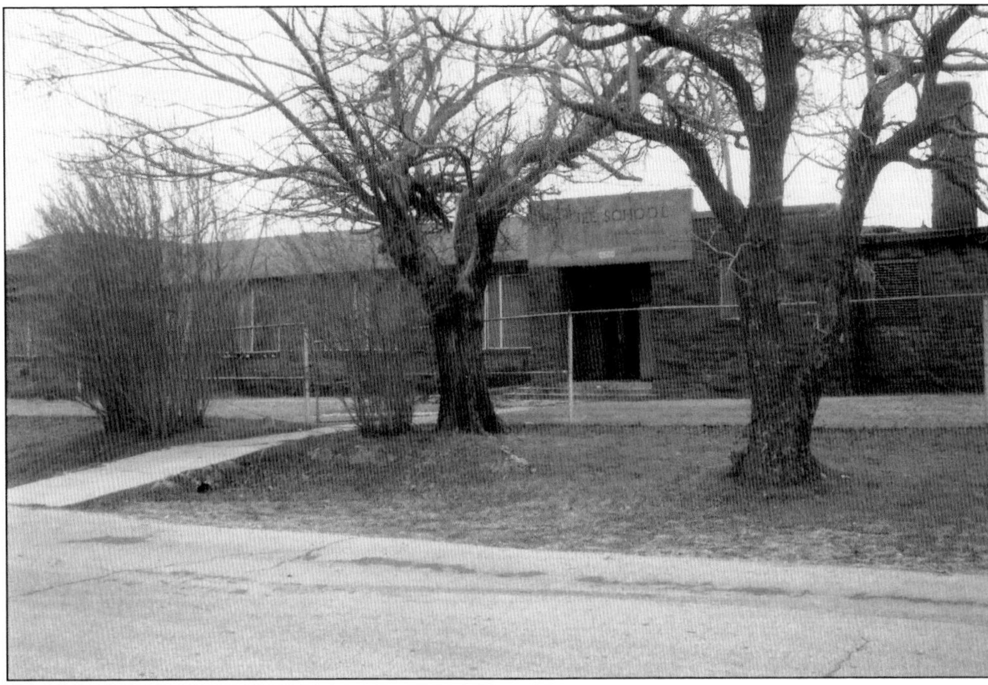

Dunjee High School had graduations and graduates until it closed. Oklahoma's integration plan shifted Dunjee students to the Star Spencer School in 1972. All hopes of reopening it were dashed when a fire severely damaged the building. The above photograph shows the front of the building. Below is the vocational trades building. (Both, courtesy of the Dunjee Alumni Association.)

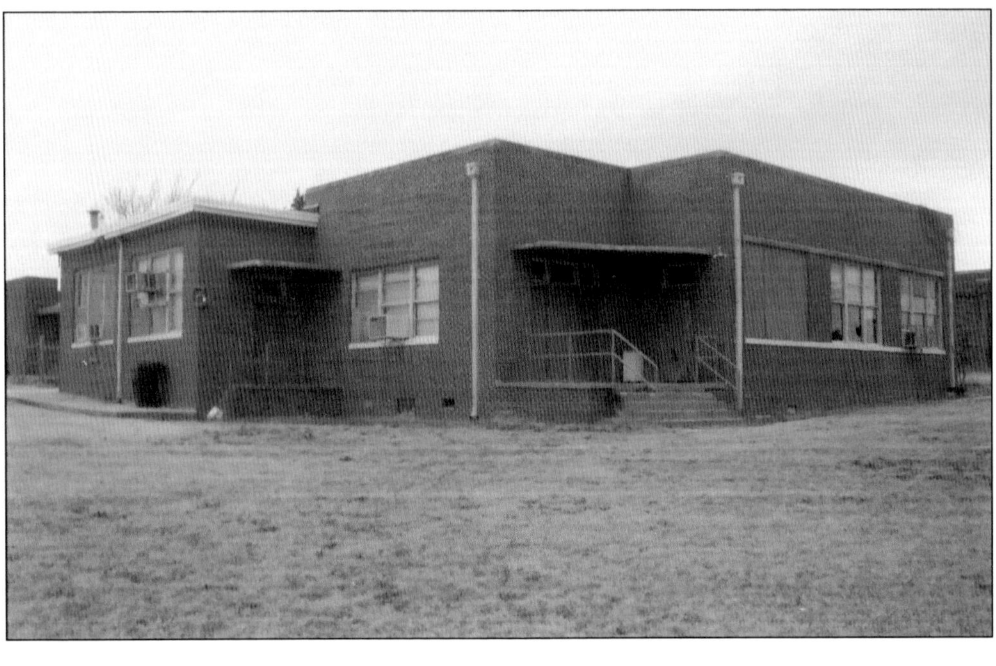

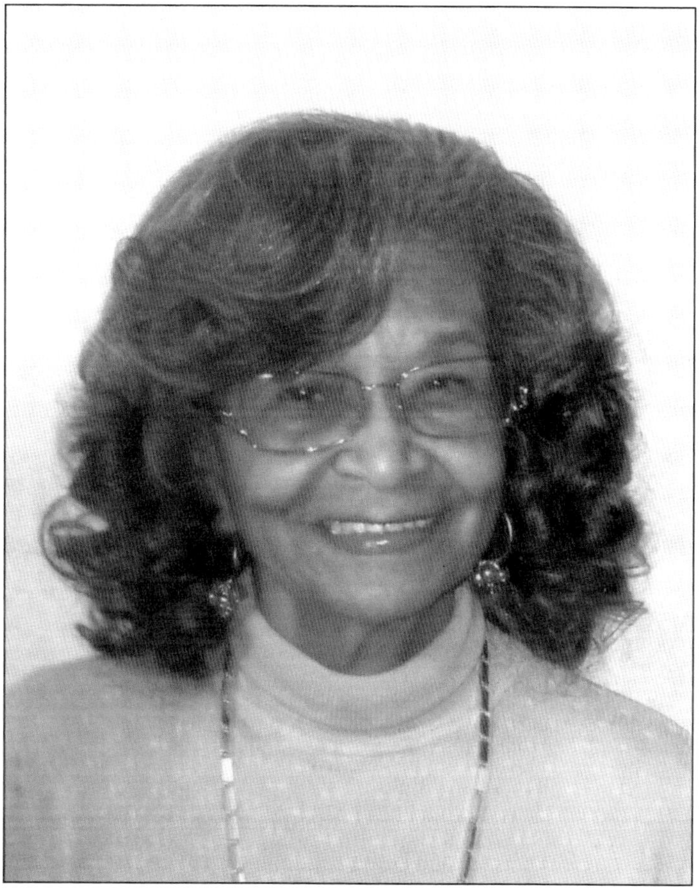

Bettye Wells Wedgeworth graduated from Dunjee High School as valedictorian. At Dunjee, she played the tenor saxophone and was part of the debate team. She graduated magna cum laude from Langston University and received her master's degree from the University of Oklahoma. Wedgeworth became a public schools teacher and an author of note in Oklahoma City, writing about buildings, streets, and public facilities that were named for African Americans in the area. Some of her teachers are in the faculty picture below taken at Dunjee. (Both, courtesy of Bettye Wedgeworth.)

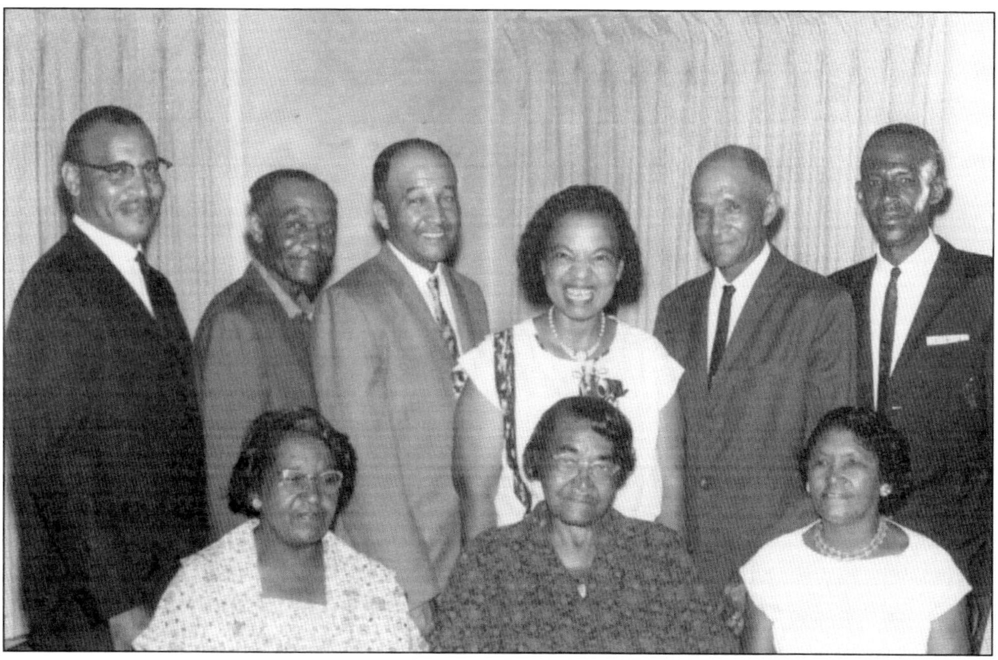

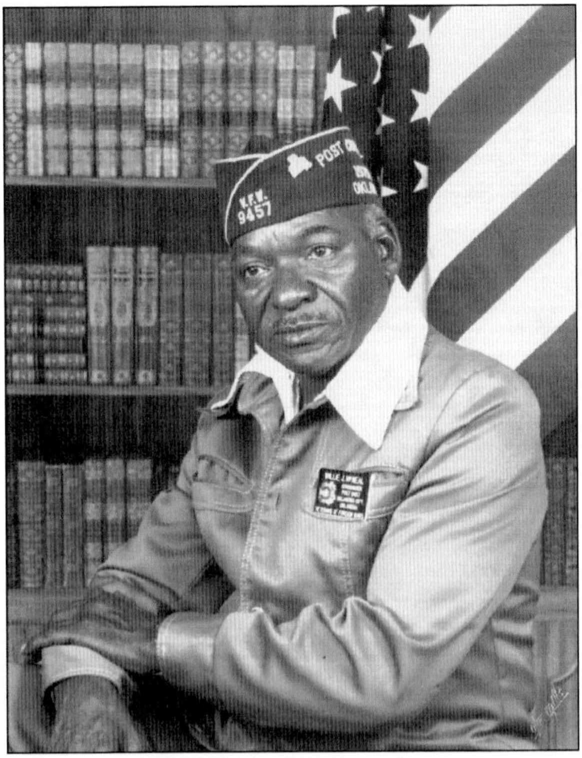

Willie J. McNeal Sr., a World War II veteran, and his family attended Frederick A. Douglass High School. With the "Douglass Family" (an F.D. Moon reference to faculty, staff, students, and the community), reunions are commonplace. At the family reunion below, McNeals remembered Douglass, their alma mater. From left to right are (first row) Rita McNeal Freeney, Brenda McNeal Lewis, Irene McNeal (wife of Willie), Wanda McNeal Cudjo, Sheila McNeal Dangerfield, and Marcia McNeal Jones; (second row) Willie J. McNeal Jr., J. McNeal, and Walter I. McNeal. (Both, courtesy of Rita McNeal Freeny.)

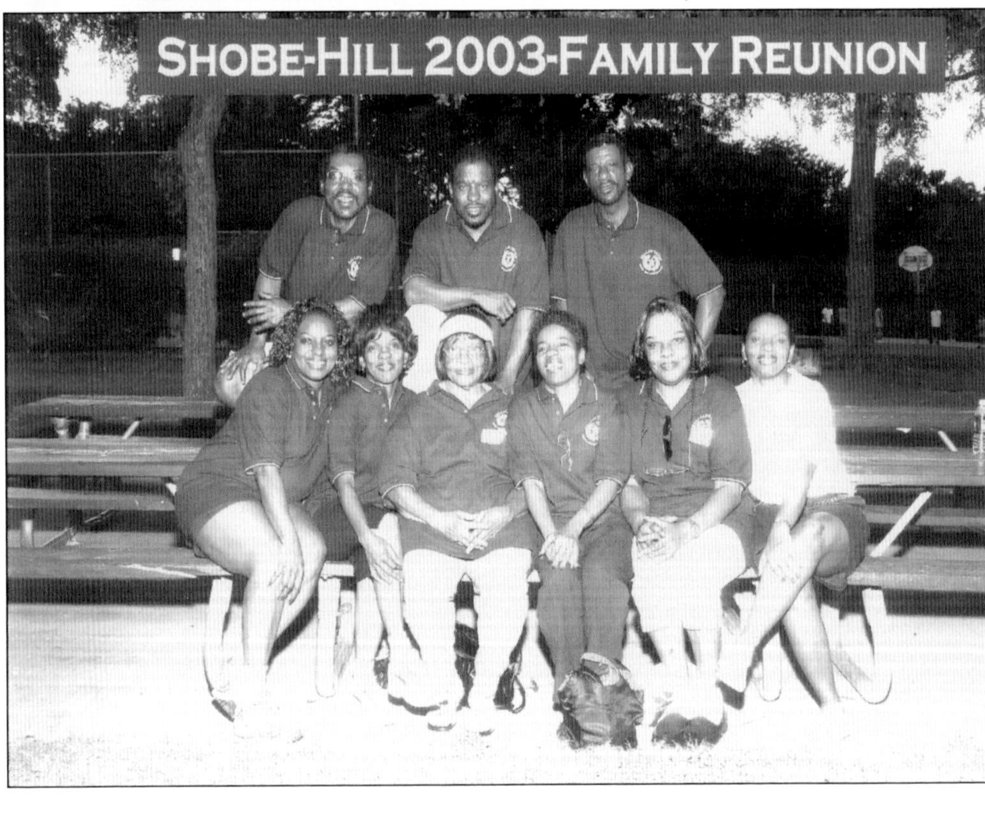

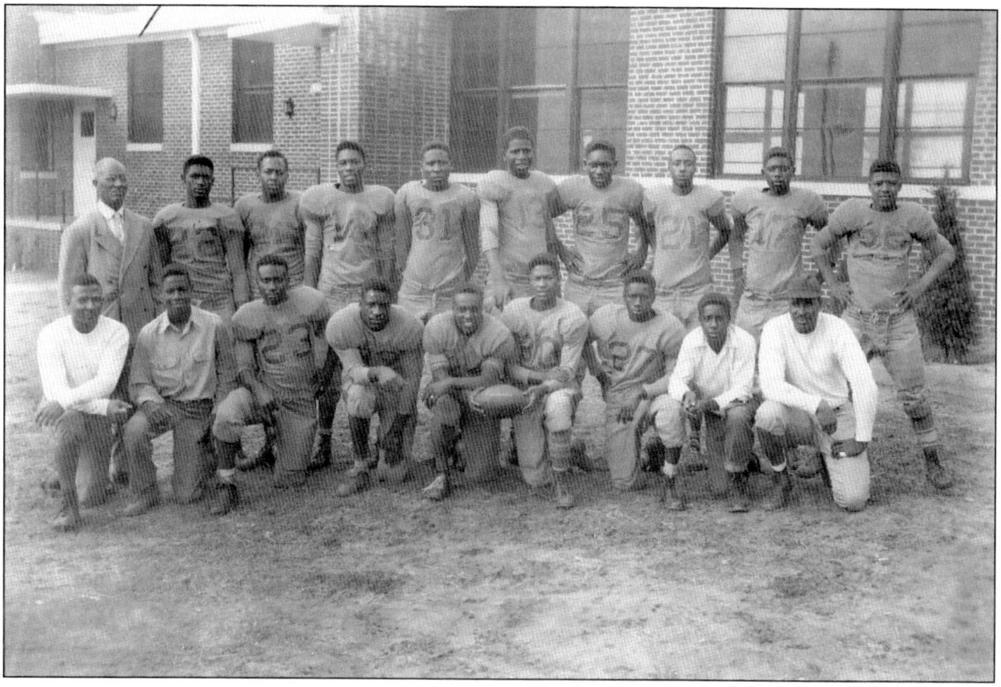

Teams, reunions, and more united Frederick A. Douglass and Roscoe Dunjee High Schools. Dunjee's Tigers football team is shown with its coaches, O.E. Rice (first row, left) and Curley Sloss (first row, right). Sloss would eventually become an instructor at Douglass High School. The photograph below was taken at the Douglass High School class of 1958 reunion. The late Henry Hawkins, class member (first row, sixth from left in a dark suit), wrote one of the most comprehensive histories of Douglass High School. He was the first African American journalist hired by the *Daily Oklahoman*. (Above, courtesy of Bettye Wells Wedgeworth; below, courtesy of Bonita Forrest Edwards.)

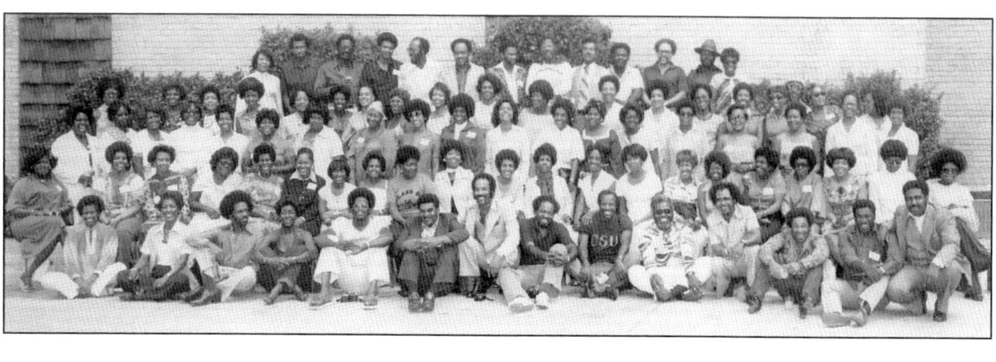

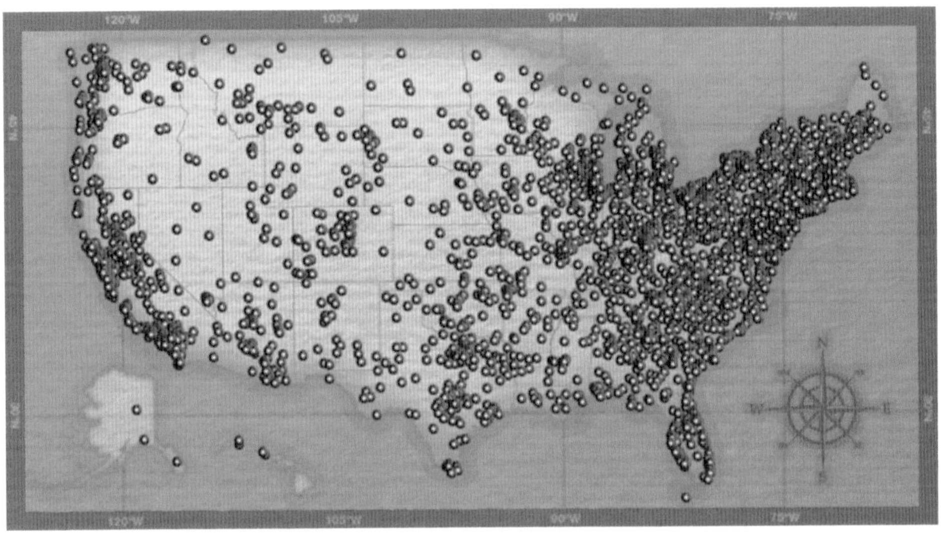